DAEMONIC FIGURES

"Étude de Chloé." From *Jean-Léon Gérôme, 1824–1904: Peintre, sculpteur, et graveur*. Published by the City of Vesoul, © 1981. Reproduced by courtesy of the publisher.

DAEMONIC FIGURES

Shakespeare and the Question of Conscience

NED LUKACHER

Cornell University Press

ITHACA AND LONDON

First published 1994 by Cornell University Press.

Library of Congress Cataloging-in-Publication Data

Lukacher, Ned, 1950–
    Daemonic figures : Shakespeare and the question of conscience /
Ned Lukacher.
      p. cm.
    Includes bibliographical references and index.
    ISBN 0-8014-3052-6 (alk. paper). — ISBN 0-8014-8223-2 (pbk. :
alk. paper)
     1. Shakespeare, William, 1564-1616—Criticism and interpretation.
2. Conscience in literature. I. Title.
PR3069.C56L84 1994
822.3'3—dc20   94-20850

Printed in the United States of America

∞The paper in this book meets the minimum requirements of the American National Standard for Information Sciences—Permanence of Paper for Printed Library Materials, ANSI Z39.48–1984.

Nous sommes à l'intérieur du soleil.
                                    —FRANCIS PONGE

A sun—a shadow of a magnitude.
                                    —JOHN KEATS

CONTENTS

ACKNOWLEDGMENTS

This work was aided at its inception by a fellowship for independent study and research from the National Endowment for the Humanities. Subsequent support from the Humanities Institute of the University of Illinois at Chicago and a sabbatical leave from the University of Illinois at Chicago were also very helpful. A three-year University Scholar's grant from the University of Illinois at Chicago helped bring the project to completion.

I benefited from the responses of the various audiences before whom I presented portions of the manuscript over recent years. I thank the following people for inviting me to read this work at various stages of its formation: Marco Dorfsman and the students and faculty of the Comparative Literature Department at the University of Wisconsin, Madison; Joan Copjec and the participants in the Buffalo Symposium in Literature and Psychoanalysis in May 1991; Ellen Carol Jones and Geraldine Friedman at Purdue University; Tilottama Rajan and the Centre for the Study of Theory and Criticism at the University of Western Ontario; and Peggy Kamuf and the other organizers of the conference on the work of Jacques Derrida that was held at the Centre Culturel, Cerisy-la-Salle, France, in July 1992.

Portions of my discussion in Chapter 1 of Freud's *Moses and Monotheism* and his theory of drives, or *Trieblehre,* appear in my essay "The Ring of Being: Nietzsche, Freud, and the History of Conscience," in *Intersections: Nineteenth-Century Philosophy and Contemporary Theory,* ed. Tilottama Rajan and David L. Clark (Albany: State University of New York Press, 1994). Portions of my discussion of the sources of *Hamlet* in Chapter 3 appear in my essay "L'oreille de Pyrrhus: La césure de l'identification dans *Hamlet,*" in *Le passage des frontières: Autour du travail de Jacques Derrida,* ed. Marie-Louise Mallet (Paris: Galilée, 1994). Portions of my discussion in Chapter 4 of Freud's responses to *Macbeth* appear in my essay "Chiasmatic Reading, Aporetic History: Freud's *Macbeth,*" in *Reading Freud's Reading,* ed. Sander Gilman, Jutta Birmele, Jay Geller, and Valerie D. Greenberg (New York: New York University Press, 1994). These discussions have all been substantially revised for inclusion in *Daemonic Figures.*

In the effort to think and write about a notion of conscience that lies beyond debt and calculation, I have nevertheless felt increasingly indebted to friends and colleagues without whom these arguments and readings would never have attained their present form. I thank here, in no particular order, Philip Stewart, the late Joel Fineman, John Edward Hardy, Jacques Derrida, Gene Ruoff, Andrzej Warminski, Jay A. Levine, A. Leigh DeNeff, Bernhard Kendler, J. Hillis Miller, Monique David-Ménard, David Spurr, Maryline Lukacher, Josué Harari, Donald G. Marshall, Jay Geller, Herman Rapaport, Gerald Graff, Clark Hulse, Paul Berlanga, John Cullars, Michael Lieb, Kenneth McLintock, and Richard Macksey.

N.L.

Evanston, Illinois

DAEMONIC FIGURES

The Daemon's Ghostly Secret:
Shakespeare, Heidegger, Freud

Our state to be disjoint and out of frame. . . .
The time is out of joint.
> —*Hamlet*

Let the frame of things disjoint.
> —*Macbeth*

The decision to calculate is not of the order of the calculable, and must not be.
> —JACQUES DERRIDA, "Force of Law"

Daemonic Figures is an attempt to tell two closely linked stories: the first concerns Shakespeare's place in the history of conscience; the second focuses specifically on Shakespeare's relation to, and his effect on, the interpretations of conscience by Heidegger and Freud. Rather than hope to recount the immense and perhaps inexhaustible history of conscience and the interpretations of moral law leading up to Shakespeare and those that follow in his wake, I have chosen to emphasize only certain scenes in that history and certain moments in texts such as Plato's *Republic*, the Pauline Epistles, Kant's *Critique of Practical Reason*, Hegel's *Phenomenology of Spirit*, and many of the writings of Freud and Heidegger. I argue that Shakespeare plays a daemonic and uncanny role in this history insofar as he questions both the Christian ontotheological interpretation of conscience, which regards it as the residue of a divine spiritual fire, and the classical interpretation of the *daimon*, which regards it as a principle of natural law, an indwelling presence that watches over the soul but is neither of divine origin nor of human making. Shakespeare unsettles both interpretations while nevertheless insisting on the necessity of posing the question of conscience again and again.

Daemonic Disjunctions

The uncanny world of the ancient Greek *daimonion* and the *daimones* lies between the human and the divine world, which is to say between the world of human consciousness and that which, unseen and uncomprehended, underlies the forms and expressions of consciousness and sustains its very existence. The daemon is the cipher, the name, and the figure for the incontrovertible ghostliness, the familiar strangeness, that dwells between the perceptions and reflections of consciousness and the enigmatic ground of Being itself. The daemon as guardian of the soul, the silent inner voice, the figure of the language of moral judgment, describes a fundamental relation of language to self-consciousness which exceeds the very limits of the self-relation.

The topology of the daemon lies somewhere between our experience and our reflection on it, between the way we feel about our actions and our sense of how we might have acted, between (to use a familiar Kantian distinction) our "pathological" existence and our existence as moral beings, our sensible existence and our supersensible being. Conscience is a figure for the difference between the way things appear and the way they might actually be, between the being of what is or has been and what might be, what *ought* to be. Through the silent speech of conscience, the realm of moral values seems to put pressure, to exert its force, upon the frailty of merely existent being. It is from within this silent speech, within this most intimate and yet intangible experience of the force of the categorical imperative of conscience, that the daemon utters, exhales, expels its ghostly imprecations. But from what does the ghostly emanation of the daemon arise? What enables it to utter obligations that have constricting, binding power?

In Martin Heidegger's history of being and its relation to the ought and the realm of moral values, the Kantian opposition between nature and the categorical imperative, which is experienced through the sublime relation that Kant calls "respect," opens the way to the modernist, technological understanding of a realm of universalizing rational values that is "set *above* being": "To this end being was attributed to the values themselves. *At bottom* this being meant neither more nor less than the presence of something already-there."[1] To decide that moral values have being somewhere, whether in a material or a spiritual element, is already to forget the daemon's ghostly undecidability by trying to bring it into the light of day. The modernist metaphysician reconstructs the spiritual realm of traditional ontotheology within the realm of natural law and discovers in the forces of nature a ground for the energies and vacillations of human willing. The *question* of the ought and the daemon cannot, however, be transcended through either nature or what lies beyond it. The daemon resists efforts to demonize or sanctify it. It haunts despite attempts to dispel or surpass it. The history of being is the history of philosophy's attempt to achieve a certain purity or unity within the operations of spirit by purging or cleansing it of the necessarily contingent impurity of the daemonic ghost, and by ridding the meaning of being of the burden of a persistent and inextinguishable secret.

1. Martin Heidegger, *An Introduction to Metaphysics*, 197–98. It is in the context of this discussion of the relation between being and the ought that Heidegger made his infamous distinction between those philosophers of National Socialism who thought in terms of values and "totalities" and his own sense of "the inner greatness and truth of the movement (namely the encounter of global technology and modern man)" (199). Is not this tactless and disingenuous phrase Heidegger's way of saying that his own Nazism in 1933–34 was precisely the expression of such an "encounter," which the subsequent history of Nazism betrayed through its monstrous effort to totalize technology's will to power by invading every aspect of human existence? That Heidegger introduced this idea in a 1953 edition of a work that ostensibly follows the text of lectures from 1935 may attest to the urgency he felt to explain himself to the daemon of his conscience.

To the extent that spirit remains a question and resists univocal interpretations, whether material or ideal, we might say that spirit remains daemonic. The daemon is what remains unthought in the history of philosophy's effort to think the meaning of being and spirit. The daemon is spirit's other. As Jacques Derrida asks in *Of Spirit: Heidegger and the Question,* "When one says of spirit or of the spiritual world that it both has and does not have force—whence the haunting and the double—is it only a matter of contradictory utterances? . . . Would the ghost vanish before thought like a mirage of the understanding, or even of reason?"[2] The answer to both questions is, of course, "no." We might say further that the daemonic (or *daimonic* in the primordial sense Heidegger seeks to activate within the unthought potentiality of Greek thinking) becomes demonic precisely to the extent that spirit is subjectivized by univocal interpretations. Indeed, Heidegger's thought is constituted by the instability between a demonic Nazism and a daemonic understanding of the enigma of conscience and the questions of a first philosophy. The project of *Of Spirit* is that of remarking the proximity of the demonic to the daemonic in Heidegger's thinking. As Derrida says of the idiomatic sense of the French exclamation *de l'esprit!*—"what the devil!"—there is, in both this Latin expression and in Heidegger's thought, the "return of the devil in a moment, and of the double at the heart of *Geist.*"[3] Heidegger's thought is throughout a crisis of conscience in which the human being's struggle with the limits of its own will to power must repeatedly run the risk of demonic subjectivization and technologization. Derrida's strategy is always that of affirming the daemonic, ghostly double of spirit, affirming the resistant power of the ghost to exert its force upon thinking and being precisely *as a ghost,* an obligating, binding daemon that presides over an intractable secret.

The essence of the essent in its totality is what remains concealed,

2. Jacques Derrida, *Of Spirit: Heidegger and the Question,* 62.
3. Ibid., 69. This doubleness is played out in an "irreducible hauntology" between *Geist* and *Gespenst* or *Spuk* in Jacques Derrida, *Spectres de Marx.*

withdrawn, and withheld behind the ghostliness of the secret that the daemon bears along with its every utterance. On the threshold of the unthought and the undecidable, on the edge of a secret, hovers the specter of the daemon, the figure of a still-hidden relation to origin and end. And that is why, as Derrida remarks, the "force of law" is always the effect of a ghostly secret: "The undecidable remains caught, lodged, at least as a ghost—but an essential ghost—in every decision, in every event of decision. Its ghostliness deconstructs from within any assurance of presence, any certitude or supposed criteriology that would assure us of the justice of a decision, in truth of the very event of a decision."[4] This "essential ghost" haunts every notion of spirit, *esprit, spiritus, pneuma,* breath, exhalation, ghost, *Geist,* gas, and flame. Derrida's writing, no less than that of Heidegger, relies on the invention of figures and metaphors through which this ghostly daemon can be made visible and thinkable as precisely the other of vision and thought. The ghost appears, for example, as *la cendre,* the Cinder, the Cinderella figure whom Derrida apostrophizes in *Cinders (Feu la cendre),* where the withheld essence of conscience is figured as a feminine phantom whose "unforeseen visits" and "comings and goings" orient Derrida to the fundamental questions and experiences of his thinking.[5] What Maurice Blanchot calls "the call of the Other," what Derrida calls the trace of a memory that "does *not* lead us back to *any anteriority*," what Heidegger calls *Holzwege,* the dead-end paths that bring us into the daemonic region: these are all daemonic figures for the question of conscience.[6]

"*There is something secret,*" writes Derrida:

But it does not conceal itself. Heterogeneous to the hidden, to the obscure, to the nocturnal, to the invisible, to what can be dissim-

4. Jacques Derrida, "Force of Law: 'The Mystical Foundations of Authority,'" 25–26.

5. Jacques Derrida, *Cinders,* 22.

6. Maurice Blanchot, *Le pas au-delà,* 173; Jacques Derrida, *Mémoires: For Paul de Man,* 137; Martin Heidegger, *Holzwege.*

ulated and indeed to what is non-manifest in general, it cannot
be unveiled. It remains inviolable even when one thinks one has
revealed it. Not that it hides itself for ever in an undecipherable
crypt or behind an absolute veil. It simply exceeds the play of
veiling/unveiling, dissimulation/revelation, night/day, forgetting/
anamnesis, earth/heaven, etc. It does not belong therefore to the
truth, neither to the truth as *homoiosis* or adequation, nor to the
truth as memory (Mnemosyne, *aletheia*), nor to the given truth,
nor to the promised truth, nor to the inaccessible truth. Its non-
phenomenality is without relation, even negative, to phenomenality. Its reserve is no longer of the intimacy that one likes to call
secret, of the close or very proper which sucks in or inspires
[*aspires ou inspires*] so much profound discourse (the *Geheimnis*
or, even richer, the inexhaustible *Unheimliche*).[7]

The daemonic secret of the Freudo-Heideggerian "uncanny" is at
once the most material and most ideal thing, and yet it is neither
the empirical nor the ideational. It is that in the midst of which we
find ourselves; it is the medium in which we come to ourselves as
precisely that which is divided from itself, daemonically other than
itself from the outset; we are the thing that feels the force of that
division. Conscience is a figure of the pressure that "the call of the
Other" exerts upon us in the radically material but nonempirical
medium that is language. Daemonic figures enable us to glimpse
the contours of the ghost.

As Jacques Lacan has remarked, the Kantian moral law involves
"the paradox of an imperative that presses me to assume my own
causality"; it is a paradox because at the same time it presses me to
realize that "I am not the cause of myself."[8] The division within
subjective willing infinitely displaces and divides the agency of will
itself. Derrida's "secret" is a daemonic figure no less than is Lacan's
notion of the phallic signifier, the signifier that brings loss and
absence to presence, makes them *felt*, brings them into the realm of

7. Jacques Derrida, "Passions," 21.
8. Jacques Lacan, "Science and Truth," 13.

experience precisely as loss and absence. It is from the position of the infinitely divisible phallic secret that conscience speaks: it is from this enigmatic topology that law derives its force. By finding our way into the vicinity, into the neighborhood, of this ghostly place, we obey what Derrida calls the "injunction that prescribes deconstruction" and enjoins us to "a responsibility that transcends this or that determination of a given context," because the "limit of the frame of the border of the context . . . always entails a clause of non-closure," and it is through this path, opening, trace, or signifier that the voice of conscience makes itself felt.[9]

Daemonic figures name the relation between language and the forms of moral judgment. To have a good or a bad daemon, a good or a bad conscience, is to mark a difference in the economy of guilt and language. It marks as well a difference in character or personality, in *ethos* as Heidegger explicates the word in the famous saying of Heraclitus, *ethos anthropoi daimon,* which is usually translated "Character for man is destiny" but which Heidegger renders: "The (familiar) abode is for man the open region for the presencing of god (the unfamiliar one)."[10] The daemonic is uncanny, unhomelike, because the most intimate site of human habitation is also the strangest of places, for it is there that the (unfamiliar) god comes to presence through the language of moral judgment that tells us *that* we are and that because we are what we are we should act thus, should think and feel in this or that way. The opening through which the daemon enters into that most proximate nearness of human dwelling occurs in language itself. The daemon is a figure for the god that dwells in language and, by virtue of this daemonic function of language, allows human beings to be called into their humanity or, inversely, allows them to fail to respond to the call. The necessity of freedom is an effect of language in the most fundamental sense. One has a bad daemon insofar as one fails to enter into the site whence the daemon calls. Inversely, one has a

9. Jacques Derrida, *Limited Inc.,* 152.
10. Martin Heidegger, "Letter on Humanism," 234.

good daemon—that is, a "happy" or "eudaemonic" relation to the god (*eudaimonia* means "happiness")—insofar as one responds to the call and enters into the otherness of human dwelling, which is precisely what makes it truly human. Derrida's reference to being "free otherwise," or to "a liberty freer still" concerns our capacity to actualize the possibility of affirming the presence of a lack or gap in our relation to Being.[11]

It is all a question of how near or far we are from the place in which the daemon brings the language of judgment to presence. To the extent that we cannot judge, we cannot be human, we cannot hear the daemon, or we hear the daemon poorly. It is a question of distance and nearness within the topology of language itself. The semantic and linguistic confusion between conscience and consciousness (for example, in *conscientia* and *la conscience*) makes obvious the incontrovertible problem of whether we can ever be conscious of that most certain and yet most ineffable thing that is the sense of existence itself and, more precisely still, the unique sense of existence that is specific to the being that dwells in language. It remains problematic whether we can ever bring to consciousness that of which we are most certain, which is the sheer facticity of our existence. It is this sentiment of existence that accompanies and underlies all our perceiving, sensing, knowing, and reflecting; it is that with which we know (*con-scientia*) ourselves and everything else we know. It is at the root of all our *savoir* and our *con-naissance*. The daemon names and figures that for which the hyphen stands as an enigmatic cipher. It is up to poets and thinkers to say the figures and to think the names for that which at once conjoins and disjoins our being, our Dasein, with and from Being itself. Daemonic figures and names, the poetry and philosophy of conscience, describe the (non)relation of Dasein to Being as precisely at once the most impossible and yet the most necessary of

11. Jacques Derrida, "Privilège," 107–8 (my translation).

relations, the one with which we are most intimately connected and yet the one that remains irreducibly unfamiliar and remote.

Whatever the relation of Dasein to Being, our sense of existence is the most compelling testimony to the fact that such a relation may exist, even though it happens to be a relation of absolute absence, an absolute nonrelation. The task of thinking is the task of thinking what is other than either ontotheology or nihilism, what is other than a relation of either presence or absence, for that is where we are now; that is where human "being" has been situated throughout its history thus far, even though human beings have tried mightily to dissuade themselves from this knowledge.

What is apparently our most proximate and secure possession—namely, our sense of existence—is also the most mysterious property of all, even though it is the property upon which all our other notions of property and possession are based, be they juridical, legislative, philosophical, poetic, or fictional. The Greek *ousia* means both philosophical substance and everyday property for precisely this reason. The act of appropriation, of making something our own, of constituting our property, is possible only on the basis of that most mysterious appropriation that is our coming to our sense of existence. And that is where the daemon enters the scene; that is where we encounter daemonic figures of the unfigurable itself, linguistic traces of that which lies beyond and deep within all that is presented as knowable phenomena. The daemonic figure marks the point where the ensemble of acts that constitute subjective appropriation (for example, of the body, of language, of the things and beings in the subject's world) finds itself disappropriated from itself by an otherness that lets itself be known only as a daemonic figure. Daemonic figures enable us to grasp the extent to which we fail to grasp the ground of appropriation and the essence of what it is that gives to consciousness its most certain and nearby, yet most uncanny and distant, sense of its own existence.

The transformation of classical *daimon* into Christian conscience is one of the most important events in the history of Western thought. This is the subject of my first chapter, but let me say at the outset that the decisive result of this momentous cultural translation is the victory or dominance of Christian and Latin subjective certainty over the irresolvable undecidability of the *daimon* of Greek antiquity. As we shall see, Plato's account in *The Republic* of the origin of the *daimon* incorporates and reworks the mythic conception of the daemon as the allotment or apportionment of fate to the individual soul, at the moment of its creation, by the three Fates or Moirae—but with this important difference: that in Plato's myth of Er the individual soul chooses its own daemon and thus in effect allots its fate to itself.[12] As Heidegger argued, Plato's thinking anticipates the subjectivizing turn of Christian theology in which conscience becomes the measure of the soul's self-certainty. In the reading of *The Republic* that follows, we shall discover that although it anticipates the Christian epoch of interiorized subjective certitude concerning the essence of existence itself, Plato's *daimon* is still haunted by the ghostly otherness of an irreducible exteriority. More precisely, we shall see that the resistant indeterminacy of the daemon is very much a question of the sheer materiality of language, since it is language that brings the remoteness of our sense of existence into the proximity of our most intimate self-relation. As Gregory Vlastos has noted, the daemon in Plato's thinking never has a divinatory function of revelation but serves rather as an inner voice or silent sign that must always be interpreted in its turn.[13] The daemon is the name and the figure of the inexhaustible hermeneutics of interpretation that separates and conjoins the sense of existence from and to that which brings existence to presence.

Much of my attention is turned toward the mediating, transitional role of the apostle Paul's Greek notion of *syneidesis,* which Je-

12. See the entry under *daimon* in F. E. Peters, *Greek Philosophical Terms: A Historical Lexicon,* 33–34.
13. Gregory Vlastos, "Socrates' *Daimonion.*"

rome rendered as *conscientia*. Following Freud's diagnosis in *Moses and Monotheism*, I read the Pauline intervention as part of a larger cultural crisis and as the most notable of many related efforts to find a solution for a widespread cultural anxiety and despair. Moreover, Paul becomes, in my reading, the hero not only of his own historical moment but of *Moses and Monotheism* itself and emerges as Freud's most significant and most unacknowledged precursor. In the wake of Pauline *syneidesis*, conscience seems securely internalized, subjectivized, and spiritualized. It was also, correspondingly, at this historical moment that the daemon was demonized, since any un-interiorizable residue of language or thought pertaining to our self-certain sense of being had necessarily to be cast out into an unredeemable exteriority—which is to say, the uncanny world of the daemon became the evil realm of the demon. The Pauline strategy is infinitely repeated throughout Western history: the unacknowledged daemon or ghost that haunts the self-relation we call conscience is cast out into the darkness and recognized as a demon, a derivative or secondary force.

As Paul Tillich has observed, the Pauline notion radicalized the notion of *syneidesis* that existed in Greek culture:

> The basic Greek word *syneidai* ("knowing with," i.e., with oneself; "being witness of oneself") was common in popular language long before the philosophers utilized it. It described the act of observing oneself, often as judging oneself. In philosophical terminology it received the meaning of "self-consciousness" (for instance, in Stoicism, the derived substantives *syneidesis, synesis*). Philo of Alexandria, under the influence of the Old Testament, stressed the ethical self-observation in *syneidesis* and attributed to it the function of *elenchos*, that is, accusation and conviction.[14]

14. Paul Tillich, "The Transmoral Conscience," 66. This brief essay, first published in 1945, is perhaps the most reliable and informative sketch of the history of conscience available. For an elaboration of some issues raised by Tillich, also consult Edward Westermarck, "The Supposed Objectivity of Moral Judgments."

"Knowing with Christ in one's conscience" has the effect of splitting the moral self off from the demonic possession of a bad conscience that can be cleansed only by the blood of the Savior. The radical spiritualization and certitude of Pauline *syneidesis* exiled the daemon to the realms of heresy by formalizing the binary division that had always lurked within the ontological instability of the ancient *daimon*. In the Pauline tradition through Luther and German idealism, the daemon becomes the demonized bad conscience that can be purified by following the model of Christ's sacrifice. The comings and goings of the Greek *daimones* between gods and humans became the internalized struggle of Christ and the devil, and the ghostly indeterminacy of the daemon became the harrowing scene of bearing witness before the fiery tribunal of the inner court of conscience. As spirit becomes increasingly univocal and determinate, conscience becomes a means of attaining self-certainty and of acquiring mastery over the otherness that would undermine the illusion of self-presence and certitude concerning the proximity of the divine.

So immense is the field over which the history of conscience unfolds that we can do little more than offer fables that may at best provide a glimpse into scenes of a still unwritten history. The institutionalization of conscience through ecclesiastical practice and casuistry succeeded over the centuries in reexternalizing the scene of witnessing through a complex theological apparatus. With the Reformation, all the vexed questions that faced the early Christians resurfaced with new intensity. Protestantism is an event in the history of the interpretation of conscience because it insisted on universalizing the *for intérieur* of conscience and bypassing both the intersubjective scene of confession and the bureaucratized situational ethics of Catholic casuistry. In light of the work of Max Weber and R. H. Tawney, we might also recognize that transformations in European social and economic life produced so many new situations (for example, the moral implications of making a profit, speculation, and all the other elements of emergent capitalism) that traditional moral casuistry was simply not up to the task.[15] The Protestant emphasis on the intrasubjective scene created new structures of interiority, identification, and internalization which sustained the emergence of so-called "possessive individualism." The proliferation of discourses on conscience in the early modern period may also have functioned to deflect the thinking of the emergent capitalist away from the social context and consequences of his actions and toward the inward scene where the question of grace and salvation has been replaced by a desire to tally up one's economic will to power. The incessant examination of one's economic existence, which Weber aptly names a "worldly asceticism," reduces theological questions to their economic core: "This peculiar idea [of earning money, combined with a strict avoidance of all enjoyment of life] is what obliges one to feel obligation toward one's professional activity."[16] Mediating between these transformations in the public sphere and private experience were the new Protestant theology of conscience and the literature and drama that tested its applicability and relevance vis-à-vis both the cultural inheritance of the past and the exigencies of the present.

Elizabethan literature generally and Shakespeare's work in particular constitute something like the afterlife and the apotheosis of casuistry. Catholic casuistry seemed to Elizabethans merely an equivocal effort to evade moral obligation; the new theology and the new literature of the Elizabethan Anglican settlement, which sought a via media between Catholic orthodoxy and Puritan extremism, between the institutionalization of conscience and its radical interiorization, set out to forge a new (and perhaps paradoxical, if not impossible) social contract in which the individual's freedom of conscience would be defined by and preserved within the con-

15. Max Weber, *The Protestant Ethic and the Spirit of Capitalism;* and R. H. Tawney, *Religion and the Rise of Capitalism.*
16. Weber, *The Protestant Ethic and the Spirit of Capitalism,* 54.

straints placed upon it by the absolute sovereignty of the monarch.[17] But the crossings between private conscience and public
duty are never made easily, if at all, and every effort to resolve the
relation of public and private, of the absolutist state and the individual whose conscience is free, was impaled on the contradictions
it sought to reconcile or overcome. To absolutize the state was to
encroach upon the divinity within, while to absolutize conscience
was to challenge the authority of the state. The Elizabethan settlement relied upon a "both . . . and" *and* a "neither . . . nor" formulation with respect to these absolutizing claims: in the abstract
there must be sovereignty of both the individual's and the monarch's conscience *and* in the concrete circumstances of practical life
there must be sovereignty of neither the individual's nor the monarch's conscience. As they shuttle back and forth between the ab-
stractions of state-sponsored poetic theology and the concrete particulars of an ethical situation, Shakespeare's daemonic figures
remember something that generally gets forgotten, which is that
something has always been forgotten. Shakespeare's figures of the
relation of language to moral law are daemonic rather than demonic because they remember the secret and the question of conscience.
The monarch as the outward, public conscience is always folded
into the depths of the citizen's private daemon, and vice versa.
Shakespeare's daemonic figures reflect upon the historical event of
Protestant literary culture, and they explore and transform many of
the new technologies and discourses of (self)-appropriation.

The daemon is neither good nor evil. It names the barely discernible shadow that falls upon present beings, cast by the flickering
withdrawal of the elusive thing that brings things and beings to
presence. The daemon is the name of the disjunctive conjunctive of
their (not) belonging together. Whatever is present and whatever

17. See Keith Thomas, "Cases of Conscience in Seventeenth-Century England,"
which surveys the Elizabethan scene and provides many useful references. For additional
background, see also W. K. Jordan, *The Development of Religious Toleration in England: From the Beginning of the English Reformation to the Death of Queen Elizabeth,*
esp. 251–59.

brings presence to the present are joined by virtue of their very disjunction. The withdrawal, the self-concealment, the self-denial, or refusal of the thing that presences leaves behind only a ghostly, daemonic, uncanny, whisperlike, shadowlike trace.

Shakespeare names and thinks this trace effect through his meditation on the question of conscience. Heidegger thinks and names it throughout his writing, and throughout the history of philosophy's efforts to name the essence of Being, for the daemon always leaves a trace to be read or thought within all the names for Being. This remarkable passage from his reading of the pre-Socratic philosopher Anaximander indicates Heidegger's general way of deciphering the daemonic trace of a disjunction that binds; in addition, it succinctly suggests a theory of tragedy that I hope to make explicit in the course of this book:

> The [Anaximander] fragment says: what is present as such, being what it is, is out of joint [*aus der Fuge*]. . . . The fragment speaks from the essential experience that *ādikīa* [disjunction] is the fundamental trait [*Grundzug*] of *eonta* [what is present]. . . . We discover a trace of the essence of tragedy, not when we explain it psychologically or aesthetically, but rather only when we consider its essential form, the Being of beings, by thinking the *didōnai dīken . . . tes adikīas* [letting order and reck belong to one another].[18]

To fail to read this daemonic trace is to fail to conceive of the possibility of tragedy. It is also to demonize the daemon. For Shakespeare, the effort to think the daemonic forms of conscience is a radical effort to depsychologize the relation of language to moral law. Insofar as we allow the thought of the disjunction of what is present from what presences to reach us, we enter the daemonic realm in which tragedy is one of the incontrovertible possibilities. As soon as we try to convince ourselves that the daemon that

18. Martin Heidegger, "The Anaximander Fragment," 41–42, 44.

speaks to us of such things must be an agent of evil, the trace effect goes under erasure. What has passed under the name of conscience has often very little to do with the thing itself. Our ability to hear, to glimpse, or to read the daemonic traces within what is present is the sine qua non of the question of conscience.

In *The Tempest* Prospero forgives his brother for having stolen his dukedom, but he knows that such forgiveness is without consequence for a man like Antonio, who is without a conscience. Antonio makes that clear earlier in the play in response to Sebastian, who asks whether the betrayal of his brother weighs on his conscience:

> *Sebastian.* But for your conscience?
> *Antonio.* Ay, sir, where lies that? If 'twere a kibe
>   'Twould put me to my slipper, but I feel not
>   This deity in my bosom.
>   (2.1.273–76)[19]

In Shakespeare, conscience names a relation into which not every human being is called a priori. Wandering disguised among his troops on the eve of battle, Henry V asks his men to call themselves to account before their own consciences: "Every subject's duty is the king's, but every subject's soul is his own" (4.1.166–68). It is up to the individual, not to the king, to enter into a relation with conscience and then to decide, as Henry says, whether or not to "wash every mote out of his conscience." In Antonio's case, it is a question not of having a clean or dirty conscience but of simply being out of range of the call of conscience. The question of whether it calls from within or beyond the subject, and what the topology of the inside/outside distinction might possibly describe, we shall postpone for later. Antonio has less regard for his conscience than

---

19. The Fool in *King Lear* remarks in a similar vein: "If a man's brains were in's heels, were't not in danger of kibes" (1.5.6). The editions of the plays from which I cite line numbers are those listed under Shakespeare in Works Cited.

he would for a callus on his foot. Other Shakespeare characters, as we will see, believe themselves immune from conscience only to find themselves subsequently in its grip; still others have damaged their consciences to the point that they no longer function. Whether conscience goes unheeded or has been scorched into unrecognizability, Shakespeare always makes it clear that it is up to the individual whether or not to want to have a conscience. Hamlet's "To be or not to be" pertains, in the final analysis, less to the act of suicide than to the possibility of coming into a relation with conscience that is always at the same time a relation with our fundamental sense of existence. Shakespeare not only is echoed but actually helps open up the philosophical terrain on which Heidegger is able to soliloquize (though somewhat less famously than Hamlet): "Dasein always understands itself in terms of its existence—in terms of a possibility of itself: to be itself or not itself [*es selbst oder nicht es selbst zu sein*]."[20]

Looking and listening into the abyss of time and care are, according to Nietzsche, specifically the prerogatives of the Dionysian man, whose exemplar is, of course, Hamlet: "In this sense the Dionysian man resembles Hamlet: both have once looked truly into the essence of things, they have *gained knowledge,* and nausea inhibits action; for their action could not change anything in the eternal nature of things; they feel it to be ridiculous or humiliating that they should be asked to set right a world that is out of joint [*aus den Fugen*]."[21] To come to conscience is to respond to the call of the belonging-together of order and ruin, of jointure and the out-of-joint. For Nietzsche the history of conscience is the history of a certain impatience with ethical indecision. There is always, he writes, "a conscience behind your 'conscience.'"[22] Nietzsche's genealogical deconstruction of the ontotheological interpretation

20. Martin Heidegger, *Being and Time,* 33; *Sein und Zeit,* 12 (all subsequent references in the text provide page numbers of the English translation and the German original respectively). On Shakespeare/Heidegger, see Derrida, *Spectres de Marx,* 43–57.
21. Friedrich Nietzsche, *The Birth of Tragedy,* 60.
22. Friedrich Nietzsche, *The Gay Science,* 263.

of conscience, which is his fundamental and lifelong project, proceeds in truly Shakespearean fashion by peeling away one interpretation after another but never, for all that, having done with
conscience once and for all. No less than Shakespeare, Heidegger,
or Freud, Nietzsche was haunted by the comings and goings of the
daemon. As he argued in the second essay in *On the Genealogy of
Morals,* the moral pieties of conscience are the residue of the most
barbarous cruelties and of the enforcement of the most brutal mne-
motechnics. The internalization of the herd instinct and the implantation of the sting of conscience were decisive to the formation of
civilization and yet at the same time a menace to it. (I discuss elsewhere Nietzsche's analysis of the errors and the violence that have
accompanied the effort to interpret conscience solely as a mode of
internalization [*Verinnerlichung*] and his own effort to resituate the
question of conscience in connection with the presencing power of
language.)[23]

While the force of Nietzsche's historicist genealogy of conscience
has been widely influential, above all in the work of Michel Foucault, the persistent afterlife of conscience in his thinking has been
less widely recognized. Like Nietzsche, Heidegger and Freud realized that we have not finished with conscience simply because we
have dedivinized and historicized it. The early modern insistence on
the ideality of conscience slowly but inexorably yielded to a modernist historicism. In both instances, however, the question of conscience goes under erasure, for while the forms of self-certainty
change their mode and genre, the epoch of self-certainty continues
to undergo transformations and refinements. Inspired by Nietzsche
and by Heidegger's critique of the subjectivization of Western philosophy and society that has culminated in the epoch of the *Gestell*
(which means framing, frame-up, framework, installation, or simply the setup), Foucault has analyzed modernity's obsession with
the technologization of the "inspecting gaze" of conscience which

23. See Ned Lukacher, "The Ring of Being: Nietzsche, Freud, and the History of
Conscience."

works by dividing individuals against themselves and by turning them into their own sentinels. The theology of conscience provided the architectonic for both the internalization and the externalization of disciplinary technologies that are increasingly turning the whole of modern society into a Panopticon, or "House of Inspection," which no longer needs external surveillance because its denizens have all been efficiently programmed.[24] Foucault's writings chronicle the various ways in which the modernist will to power has tried to surmount the unpresentable "thing," the secret, at work in the act of self-reflection. And like Heidegger, Foucault wants to reinvent our understanding of the ancient sense of the *daimon* as a "moral agent regulating private life" by discerning in ancient writing a notion of the ethical life that is not yet caught up in the grid of internalization, where the aesthetics of existence have not been overtaken by an ascetic imperative.[25]

The Shakespeare who emerges in the following pages anticipates Heidegger, Nietzsche, and Foucault in his awareness of the dangers of the conscience police and of the bureaucratization of moral judgment. In lieu of a readable utterance, what Shakespeare's protagonists discern is a disjunction at the very heart of the language of moral law. Shakespeare would have agreed with Rousseau's Savoyard Vicar in *Emile* when he remarks, apropos of the impasse to which he has been led in his discourse on conscience: "He who reads in the depth of my heart well knows that I do not like my blindness."[26] In his reading of the Vicar's "Profession of Faith," Paul de Man sees the Vicar's dilemma as an allegory of "the impossibility of reading," by which he means the self-canceling effect that the figural language of will and desire has on the Vicar's stated objective to demonstrate the autonomy of the voice of conscience, whose power to call us to account despite our will is rendered unreadable by the very pleasures of the will that such a pious

---

24. Michel Foucault, "The Eye of Power," 155.
25. Michel Foucault, *The Care of the Self*, 89.
26. Jean-Jacques Rousseau, *Emile; or, On Education*, 311.

explanation affords us.[27] "Virtue," writes de Man, "becomes finally justified in terms of an erotic pleasure principle, a moral libido
that seems not easily compatible with the piety of the inner voice of
conscience but that consistently acts out the rhetorical system of the
text."[28] What the Vicar calls "the spectacle" of disinterested judgment and conscience becomes a spectacle of the eudaemonic interests of the will to produce pleasurable sensations. The Vicar succeeds, in de Man's estimation, precisely by failing to answer the
question of conscience, for to answer the question one must know
the relation of will to nature and, above all, the relation of the
individual will to the essence of willing. The inside/outside asymmetry that the Vicar posits constitutes a strange topology in human
existence and its experience of will and language. Conscience becomes paradoxically synonymous for de Man and for Rousseau
with what de Man calls "the ethical indecisiveness" to which the
Vicar is led. Were the Vicar to say just what conscience is, he would
no longer be conscientious. That would be the unrestrained eudaemonic interpretation of conscience, which is how Nietzsche
read Rousseau and why he held him in contempt. De Man, however, reads in Rousseau the persistent trace of the question of conscience.

Homo Castus

Death and disjunction belong to human existence, and while we
resist the thought and experience of the nonknowledge to which we
are bound, it is the task of art to overcome this resistance. In a
passage from "The Theme of the Three Caskets," Freud describes
the way the artist, in this case Shakespeare, overcomes the repression of the figure of death by the figure of love:

27. See Paul de Man, *Allegories of Reading*, esp. 237–45.
28. Ibid., 243.

There are motive forces in mental life which bring about replacement by the opposite [*Ersetzung durch das Gegenteil*] in the form of what is known as reaction-formation; and it is precisely in the revelation of such hidden forces [*verborgener Motive*] as these that we look for the reward of this enquiry. The Moira were created as a result of a discovery that warned man that he too is a part of nature and therefore subject to the immutable law of death. [But man's imagination rebelled and he] constructed instead the myth derived from it, in which the Goddess of Death was replaced by the Goddess of Love and by what was equivalent to her in human shape. . . . It is by means of this reduction of the distortion [*Entstellung*], this partial return to the original, that the poet achieves his more profound effect upon us.[29]

The "theme" (*das Motiv*) or "motive" of the tragedy of *King Lear* and of the barely avoided tragedy of *The Merchant of Venice* is Freud's word in this essay for the pressure exerted by the daemonic trace of the enigmatic disjunction of time and death. Portia and Cordelia are aesthetic, psychological motivations that try to keep this deeper "motive" at bay. It is as though Freud were suggesting that between writing *The Merchant of Venice* and *King Lear* Shakespeare became possessed of a daemonic insight that allowed him to reduce "the distortion" that usually conceals the profound concealment that is this *Motiv*. Nothing could be further from a "theme" than this irreducible nonknowledge that comes to us through the daemonic genius of the artist; for the content of this *Motiv* is the force of an absence and the experience of the limits of the human.

All the force of the uncanny is released in "this partial return" to the "law of death." The power of tragic catharsis arises from our identification with the lifting of the repression on what was in fact a gap or hole in our self-relation and in our relations to others and to the Other. We have no idea what shape the Goddess of Death may

29. Sigmund Freud, "The Theme of the Three Caskets," in *The Standard Edition of the Complete Psychological Works*, 12:299–300 (hereafter, all volume and page references to the *Standard Edition* are given in the text, abbreviated *SE*).

actually possess, or whether it has any real resemblance to a human face, regardless of the poet's anthropomorphic turn of phrase. In turning toward the face of death, of being, of finitude, of poetry, or of conscience, Freud seems to assume that what the poet addresses (in Shakespeare at least) no longer has a human face. What, asks Keats in "Sleep and Poetry," is "more serene than Cordelia's countenance?" (line 9).[30] Freud believes that Cordelia's face is but "the equivalent in human shape" of something nonhuman, something that lies in the unconscious depths of poetry and sleep. Catharsis is the result of the terrifying confrontation with the facelessness of the Other, with something that is there as the most palpable absence, what Lear's Fool calls "an O without a figure" (1.4.152), something that lies between something and nothing, something like "the quality of nothing" (1.2.33).

The experience of the cathartic separation of the human and its other, finitude and its ground, time, being, and that which gives them, creates what Freud calls *King Lear*'s "profound effect," which results as the poet brings us into proximity with the gap between a human face and an unthinkable force. Lear himself experiences tragic catharsis as a purification by fire. Keats also recognized this when he wrote "On Sitting Down to Read *King Lear* Once Again": "once again, the fierce dispute / Betwixt damnation and impassioned clay / Must I burn through" (5–7). Keats's figure for reading *King Lear* is the experience of being "consumèd in the fire," and also of being reborn with "new Phoenix wings" (14).

King Lear is the tragedy of a dying man's fearful demand for love in the face of death. Humiliated by the senility of his desire and by the libidinous, incestuous, excess his demand belies, the old King suffers the onslaughts of the storm, the lightning, and the "burning shame" that stings his "mind so venomously" and "detains him from Cordelia" (4.2.43–45).[31] Recognizing that he himself is the

30. All citations from Keats follow the *Complete Poems*, ed. John Barnard, 3d ed.
31. These lines were canceled in the folio text of the play and appear only in the quarto of 1608.

one he rails against, the "perjured . . . simular of virtue," the one that is "incestuous" (3.2.53–54), he experiences his guilty conscience as a "wheel of fire" and his tears as "molten lead" (4.6.43–44). Lear's fiery catharsis and Gloucester's purification by oedipal blinding are both daemonic figures for the experience of the secret of human finitude and conscience. But what does it mean to be purified? Might it not mean the experience of an intractable *im*purity and an insoluble question?

The mad Lear and the blind Gloucester are versions of the purgatory of bad conscience, versions of the liminal experience of the human on the threshold of the disjunction between being and the ought. They are instances of the tragic disjunction between what has been and what could or should have been. It is Lear who first speaks of plucking out eyes when he vows to "cast" out his own eyes before he sheds another tear over Goneril's ingratitude (1.4.258). And so it is Goneril who advises Regan and Cornwall to pluck out Gloucester's eyes (3.7.5).[32] The plucking out and casting away of

32. Several literary genealogies may illuminate the sources of Shakespeare's turn to the dramatic event of Gloucester's blinding. Shakespeare was clearly thinking of bk. 2, chap. 10, of Philip Sidney's *Arcadia,* which depicts an encounter with the king of Paphlagonia, blinded by his bastard son Plexirtus, whose role anticipates Edmund's. Oedipus, of course, blinds himself. But what is the source for Shakespeare's emphasis on the cruelty of the sisters? Although it is Cornwall who manually casts out the "vile jelly" (3.7.82), he is acting at the instigation of Goneril and Regan. Gloucester's blinding is expressive of the depravity of their wills.

We might take a clue from Lear's extraordinary comparison of Cordelia to the "barbarous Scythian" who preys upon her own "generation" (1.1.110). The cannibalistic and vulturelike attributes of the sisters are uppermost in Lear's language throughout the play. Shakespeare's admiration for Florio's translation of Montaigne's *Essays* is well known, and here is Florio's rendering of what Montaigne in "On Some Verses in Virgil" has to say, via Herodotus, about the cruelty of Scythian women: "The Scythian women were wont to thrust out the eies of all their slaves and prisoners in warre" (Montaigne, *Essays,* trans. Florio, Essay 5, 3:91). Montaigne's explanation, again from Herodotus, is still more compelling; they blinded them (predominantly the men, it would seem) in order to "have their way with them": *crevoyent les yeux . . . pour s'en servir* (Montaigne, *Essais,* ed. Rat, 3:88). Is not the horror of Gloucester's blinding finally that, although it is Cornwall's act, in fact Goneril and Regan are casting out their father's eyes, and in a perversely sexual way?

Whatever the historical facts (and Plutarch argued that the real reason why Scythian

eyes permeate the play to the extent that not only do Goneril,
Edgar, and Lear speak of it; even the messenger who brings Goneril
word of Cornwall's demise refers to death itself as the experience of
being "plucked" (4.2.47).

In lieu of purity, the catharsis of *King Lear* entails the necessity of
a contaminant that incurably poisons the self-relation. There is a
secret that we absolutely cannot see, that lies in the realm of madness and blindness. All we can do is to be ready to confront the
enigma of a faceless secret, to be ready for death, to be ripe for it:

> Men must endure
> Their going hence even as their coming hither:
> Ripeness is all.
>
> (5.2.9–11)

Though Lear goes mad from this nonknowledge, and though
Gloucester is blinded by it, they have both felt the truth of Edgar's
notion. Though Shakespearean tragic catharsis has nothing to do
with securing moral purity, it has everything to do with re-marking,
with putting back into place, the contaminating question and the
impurity of a secret.

The *homo castus,* the "pure man," of the Latin moralists becomes in Shakespeare's hands the human experience of being *cast*

---

women blind their prisoners was to stop them from stealing milk; cf. Montaigne, *Essays,*
trans. Screech, 978), I believe Shakespeare grasped from Montaigne the strange energies
at work in the barbarous reaches of the unconscious will to power. To cast out one's eyes
is an effort to cast out an oedipal demon, to rid oneself of the bad conscience that
accompanies oedipal desire. In *King Lear* father and daughter are locked in a fatal
struggle to cast out the demons of sexual guilt and sadism. If the tumultuous sexuality of
father and daughters is finally what is at stake in *King Lear,* then perhaps Cordelia is a
new Antigone, for in effect it is she who, though absent for most of the play, guides Lear
and his party across the heath. And this is literally what happens in Seneca's *Thebais*
(also known as the *Phoenissae*): Antigone leads her blind father across the heath and
toward the cliff from which he wants to cast himself. Though devoured by a remorse that
"doth gnaw and grype [his] conscience" (*Thebais,* 111), Oedipus is finally persuaded by
Antigone to live.

into an enigma only to be *plucked* out of it by the even more impenetrable mystery of death. "How fearful," says Edgar on the Dover cliffs where he stages Gloucester's mock suicide in an effort to purge his father of his death wish, "How fearful / And dizzy 'tis to cast one's eyes so low" (4.5.12). Shakespeare and Edgar share the same project, which is to trifle with our despair in order to cure it (cf. 4.5.33–34), to bring us before what Edgar calls "the clearest gods" (4.5.73) and Gloucester the "ever gentle gods," in order to relieve the spirit of its anxiety in the face of death. Gloucester proclaims the efficacy of his cure:

> You ever gentle gods, take my breath from me.
> Let not my worser spirit tempt me again
> To die before you please.
>
> (4.5.207–9)

The "worser spirit" that Gloucester believes he has "parted from" on his (imaginary) leap from the cliff is, of course, the demon, the "thing," "the fiend" (4.5.68–69, 79). Edgar appears to Gloucester as a possessing demon, when in fact he plays the role of cathartic daemon. In his disguise as an indigent lunatic Edgar impersonates a victim of demonic possession, while vis-à-vis his father he impersonates a Jesuit exorcist, the tutelary spirit or genius that purges away evil. Purification means casting one's eyes into the imponderable depths over which the uncanny face of the cliff presides. From the sacrifice comes the possibility of looking upon the unimaginable, the impossible. The gods, says Edgar, "make them honours / Of men's impossibilities" (4.5.73–74), which means we respect the gods precisely because they are the impossible itself. It is the fear of death that is demonic, while Edgar's "ripeness" and Hamlet's "readiness" are Shakespeare's daemonic figures for a conscience that has been cast and purified before the fiery law of the secret.

"The syllable 'cast-,'" write Julia Lupton and Kenneth Reinhard, "operates as a master signifier that represents *King Lear* in and to

the discourses of psychoanalysis and classical tragedy."[33] We can
say further that "cast-" is literally the phallic signifier of *King Lear*
insofar as it names the presencing of absolute absence, loss, and
separation; it is the sound and the mark Shakespeare uses in this
play to name the obligatory, binding disjunction between the human and the divine. "Cast-" names the aporia in *King Lear,* the
impasse between worlds. This is the topology of the daemonic
world and the Freudian uncanny.[34] Two apparently separate ety-
mologies (Anglo-Saxon and Latin) cross in the Shakespearean *cast,*
where thrownness, separation, and disjunction overtake purity and
chastity, where the chastened man is synonymous with the one who

33. Julia Reinhard Lupton and Kenneth Reinhard, *After Oedipus: Shakespeare in
Psychoanalysis,* 209–10. From the Lacanian applications of the "cast-" motif in Lupton
and Reinhard to the historical analyses by Stephen Greenblatt and F. W. Brownlow of
the play's relation to the Jesuit exorcism ritual and to the anti-Catholic, antitheatrical
rhetoric of the dominant Anglican state ideology, the issues of purification, truth, and
conscience all come together around the question of the casting, and the "casing" or
setting, of what Edgar calls the "eyes' anguish" (4.5.6) (cf. Greenblatt, "Shakespeare and
the Exorcists," and Brownlow, *Shakespeare, Harsnett, and the Devils of Denham,* which
includes Harsnett's account in its entirety).

34. Freud's notion of the uncanny is perhaps more indebted to *King Lear* than is
generally thought. What remains hidden in Freud's essay "The Uncanny" and more
precisely in his appropriation there of E. T. A. Hoffmann's "The Sandman," what
"ought," as Freud says, "to have remained secret [*im Geheimnis*] and hidden [*im Ver-
borgen*]" but must nevertheless "come to light" (*SE* 17:224), is the fact (which Freud
does not himself consider) that "The Sandman" is a reading of *King Lear.* Hoffman's
story is about Nathaniel's attempt to foreclose the signifier of a lack (here caught up with
the names Coppelius and Coppola) and to resist castration. When Nathaniel can no
longer avoid having to sacrifice his eyes, he dies. To avert total blinding he is willing to
allow his eyes to be installed in Spalanzini's mechanical doll Olympia in the expectation
that he will get them back. The story's leitmotif is the "blazing circle of fire" into which
Nathaniel is invariably drawn as he approaches castration ("The Sandman," 108, 120),
in this case by Coppelius who steals the doll. In *King Lear* Hoffmann discovered the
daemonic figures of the unconscious complexes that are the essence of poetry. He transforms the "wheel of fire" into a proto-psychoanalytic allegory and grasps the grim
cunning of exchanges such as the one between Lear and Gloucester on the heath about
reading without eyes (4.5.138–41). The reemergence of "previously surmounted primi-
tive beliefs" and "infantile complexes" of the general Freudian topology of the daemonic, admits Freud, finally comes down to a question "of the material reality of the
phenomena" (*SE* 17:249, 248). What is uncanny about "The Uncanny" is that Freud
did not recognize that it was also a question of "the material reality" of reading *King
Lear.*

has been cast out into a zone where the relation between the human and the divine can be reinvented.

The post-Christian ethos of the play's pre-Christian setting is essential to both *King Lear* and Shakespeare's daemonic understanding of the question of conscience. As I argue throughout *Daemonic Figures,* Shakespeare's understanding of the cathartic separation of human and divine, while immersed in the arguments and images of Anglican poetic theology, differs radically from the state religion. In the place of a realm of moral values that is endowed with being and substance, Shakespeare experiences only the daemonic fires of a most palpable absence of such a realm. He finds himself very much in Lear's position in his lyrical, and still faintly amorous, "Come, let's away to prison" speech to Cordelia, where, despite the deprivation of being caged, he imagines "tak[ing] upon's the mystery of things, / As if we were *Gods'* spies" (5.3.15– 16; my emphasis). In neither the quarto nor the folio text of the play is there an apostrophe, which means, as Kenneth Muir remarks, that "Shakespeare intended the plural [possessive] since he was writing of a pagan world."[35] As we will see, in *Hamlet, The Merchant of Venice, Measure for Measure, Coriolanus, Macbeth,* and other texts, Shakespeare makes exactly the same point regarding the gods as a cipher of the sheer inaccessibility of the other of finitude in both ancient and modern settings. To take upon us "the mystery of things" *as* a mystery is to enter into the daemonic world of Shakespeare's writing. His writing, in *King Lear* and throughout, is in fact a kind of "*Daemono-poiia,* or devil-fiction," but not in the abusive sense that the Anglican bishop Samuel Harsnett used that expression to characterize an exorcism performed by Jesuit priests on members of a household in Denham.[36] While Harsnett is

35. See Kenneth Muir's edition of *King Lear,* 200 (annotation, in Muir's lineation, to 5.3.17). Jay Halio's otherwise helpful edition amends the word to read "God's," as, unfortunately, have so many editors before him. I use Halio's lineation because he prints the folio text and indicates differences from the quarto, rather than conflating the two as does Muir.

36. Samuel Harsnett, *A Declaration of Egregious Popish Impostures,* 319. The Den-

concerned to identify the "devil-burning heat in the priests," not with "natural innate fire" or "caelestial fire," but with the infernal "coales of Gods wrath,"[37] the fires of the spirit remain daemonically heterogeneous and unreadable in *King Lear*. Rather than "devil-fiction," I hope that we will come to think of Shakespeare's *Daemono-poiia* as daemonic figures of the question of conscience.

To rethink Shakespeare's place in the history of conscience is also to recognize the extent to which he anticipates the formulations of subsequent thinkers and opens a path toward contemporary issues. My main interest is in the relation of his writing to the articulation of the question of conscience and finitude by Heidegger and Derrida. But I am also interested in Shakespeare's debt to the Pauline tradition as well as to Plato's mythography of the *daimon*. Shakespeare's writing provides a pretext for a diverse series of excursions into the history of conscience.

Perhaps the best example of Heidegger's "debt" to *King Lear* in particular is his account of Dasein's "ripeness" (*Reife*) in *Being and Time,* where he writes that it "is *not* its end or its death": "This does not signify that ripeness as an 'end' and death as an 'end' coincide with regard to their ontological structure as ends. With ripeness, the fruit *fulfils* itself" (288/244; original emphasis). Dasein's self-fulfillment takes place through its "anticipatory resoluteness," which is its recognition of the impossibility of coming into relation with any totalizing structure. Echoing Edgar's notion of "ripeness" here, we will turn later to Heidegger's ruminations on Hamlet's idea of "readiness." By following Heidegger as a reader of Shakespeare, we will be able to illuminate the work of both writers. Lear's prison speech to Cordelia is a paradigmatic instance of what

---

ham case was widely publicized during the 1590s, though Harsnett did not publish his account until 1603. Shakespeare clearly had it in mind while writing the quarto *King Lear,* probably in 1604–5. Edgar's Harsnett-inspired expressions and incantations were removed for the folio.

37. Harsnett, *A Declaration of Egregious Popish Impostures,* 256–57.

Heidegger calls "an impassioned *freedom towards death*" (*Being and Time*, 311/266;[38] original emphasis).

In everything that follows here I will, in effect, be speaking of the letter *a* and of its reinscription in the demon; or rather, I will decipher the letter *a* that has always been there waiting to be read, under erasure but not indiscernible. The *a* that transforms the demonic into the d*a*emonic is, like Jacques Derrida's famous *différance*, a purely graphic intervention that cannot be heard in the vocal utterance.[39] It is a marker for the silent and invisible play of the letter that makes both self-consciousness and moral judgment possible. Without this trace effect of the d*a*emon there is no presence of the present, nor are there any present beings. The uncanny graphic *a* marks the strange disjunction that binds the question of being to the question of conscience and the moral law. Whatever enigma sustains their coming to presence, it relies somehow upon the sheer materiality of this silent graphic *a*.

38. See Jacques Derrida's reading in *Aporias*, esp. 26–42, of these passages in Heidegger.

39. See Jacques Derrida, "Différance."

1 From the Daemon to Conscience

I am unwilling that you should be partners with daemons.
—1 CORINTHIANS 10:20

The *daimonion* determines the basic relation of Being to man.
—MARTIN HEIDEGGER, *Parmenides*

The question of conscience is the unanswered and the unanswerable within all the doctrines and teachings, all the theologies and philosophies, all the literatures and figurations that there have ever been concerning the daemon and conscience. In all the attempts to define the topology and the temporality of the daemon, to determine the origin of the voice that silently judges and passes sentence, there has always also been the unanswerable, irreducible question of conscience, which lies at once far outside and deep within all the laws (moral, aesthetic, scientific, judicial) that human beings have ever given themselves or have had imposed upon them. Beyond all these laws and before the truth of conscience lies the question of conscience. We will never know the Law that gives conscience other than as a prohibition that bars access to itself. All we will ever know are the figures of conscience, its language and its arguments.

Overview

In this book I place several philosophical and psychoanalytic interpretations of conscience (those of Freud, Heidegger, Derrida) in conjunction with Shakespeare's poetry of conscience in order both to sketch the outlines of a history of conscience and to analyze the language and logic of some of the most important accounts of conscience in Western culture. One of the central issues to emerge in my presentation of these diverse texts is the relation of conscience to time. Canonical discourses in the Judeo-Christian tradition have attempted for two millennia to establish the certainty and the authority of the voice of conscience. Secular discourses have at once echoed this concern with certainty and begun the inexorable process of its unraveling. The question of time is invariably the undoing of the certainty of conscience. Through a consideration of the essential "historicality" (what Heidegger calls *Geschichtlichkeit*) of the discourses of conscience, we will begin to discern their fundamentally allegorical character. Conscience is the name of the shadow and the instability that is cast on all that is present by the mystery of what brings it to presence and holds it there. What is in fact certain about both the theological and the secular depictions of conscience is the uncanny uncertainty surrounding the topology and the temporality that underlie them. Amid all the names, dates, and places in the history of conscience, amid all the attestations of the divinity or the naturalness of conscience, there is invariably an irreducible allegorical kernel that points to a shadowy topology and an uncertain temporality.

Resisting the temptation to absolutize the sheer contingency of the event of conscience, of the comings and goings of its (un)certain voice, and refusing as well to absolutize the unthinkable "before" and the inconceivable "elsewhere" to which the voice of conscience would bear witness, the daemonic figures of my readings are concerned with the temporal and spatial instability at work in the discourses of conscience, with a persistent uncertainty that continues to make its appeal even after its ontotheological authority has vanished.

Like the ancient daemon in the Platonic dialogues, who communicates between gods and humans, the daemonic figures of the history and discourses of conscience communicate between the his-

torical and the allegorical character of language. In the history of
conscience a general pattern emerges. It begins in the genealogy
that leads from the daemon to conscience, and from Plato to Shakespeare. The ancient daemon whose temporality and topology were
enigmatic, elusively at once inside and outside the human being,
became, as a result of the New Testament, fully internalized in the
human psyche. More important still, the pagan daemon was demonized, and in its place the Apostle Paul substituted his epoch-
making notion of *syneidesis,* which defined a new way of casting out
the demon, a new experience of inwardness and self-knowledge,
and a new sense of self-certainty. The subsequent history of conscience systematized this internalization and institutionalized the
certainty that it had established. The Christian theology of conscience became a complex set of terms and arguments focused on
the task of administering the various faculties and components of
conscientia. The Protestant Reformation challenged the ecclesiastical administration of conscience and sought to recover the individual experience of inwardness of the Pauline epistles. The challenge
was not so much to the certainty of conscience as to the manner of
achieving such certainty. It is at this point that Shakespeare entered
the scene.

Shakespeare is the crucial figure in this history, for he calls conscience into question both as a matter of natural law and as a
matter of theological or intellectual certainty. The political and
ideological dimensions of his intervention and his relation to the
so-called Elizabethan settlement, are immensely important. I allude
to these questions and focus on Shakespeare's figures and allegories
of conscience in several of the plays. I read Shakespeare's role in
early modern European culture as an intensely ambivalent one,
marked above all by an anxiety about the danger of the authori-
tarian claims concerning conscience that were made by Catholics
and Puritans. The ensuing history of conscience in the modern
world has withdrawn from the tensed ambivalence of Shakespeare
and has been more willing to acknowledge the certainty afforded by
conscience. The secular modern world has continued to rely on the

theological internalization of conscience, which it has simply historicized without ever challenging its underlying self-certainty.

The challenge to the self-certainty of conscience, as a manifestation of natural if not divine law, begins very slowly and often inadvertently in Rousseau and Kant. A more substantial challenge comes from Hegel, though the full-scale assault on modernity's subjective appropriation of ontotheological certitude does not begin until Nietzsche, who initiated the protracted deconstructions of conscience and moral law that continue to the present day.

In my second chapter I relate this history, and especially the crisis of Shakespeare and early modern metaphysics, to Heidegger's "history of Being"; succeeding chapters present readings of Shakespeare's daemonic figures of conscience. In this chapter I offer a theoretical orientation to the question of conscience that draws on Freud, Heidegger, and Derrida. From analyses of the language of conscience and various scenes in the history of conscience, a general pattern emerges that might be described as follows: the genealogy leading from the daemon of the ancient world to the Christian and ultimately the modern interpretation of conscience, after contributing decisively to the formation to modern subjectivity, begins to call into question and then to reverse the techniques of internalization on which it had relied; the result has been a late modern or postmodern turn to the daemonic figures of conscience that cannot be internalized and that are prior to and irreducible to the moral law as it has been traditionally understood. *Daemonic Figures* is thus an account of those transformations in the history of conscience that have led to the internalization of moral law, as well as those that have challenged not so much the process of internalization itself as the self-certainty to which that process has led.

The Language of Historicality

By demonstrating the fundamental continuity and the fictionality that join natural, moral, and aesthetic law, I am not only historicizing the law (which has, of course, always pretended to stand outside history), for by absolutizing the historicity of law we simply mirror the essentialism we set out to escape. Rather, by referring to the "historicality" of the daemonic figures of conscience, I mean to mark their difference from the preliminary step of historicization, or what Heidegger calls "historizing": "To lay bare the *structure of historizing* [*der Geschehens-struktur*], and the existential-temporal conditions of its possibility, signifies that one has achieved an *ontological* understanding of *historicality* [*Geschichtlichkeit*]" (*Being and Time,* 427/375). By suggesting that Shakespeare's daemonic figures of conscience constitute such "an *ontological* understanding of *historicality*," I am suggesting that such figures, far from providing a new foundation, are themselves irreducibly allegorical, compulsively condemned to repeat the fate that must befall every effort to determine the Law before the law, the light before the beginning, the noumenon before phenomenality.

One fundamental issue should not be ignored in the historizing that follows: the question of the temporality of moral law and the strategies for its concealment. While it may appear that moral imperatives precede an act and that moral conscience follows it, we must also ask how it is that conscience should already be there waiting to be retroactively put into effect. This is to suggest only the obvious fact that moral conscience is inseparable from the imperative function of language and that conscience operates by reactivating the memory of a moral imperative that has been forgotten or rendered passive during the act itself. The task of historicizing the moral law is that of discerning the context in which our feelings and dispositions interact with the imperative character of language. Determining the historicality of the figures of moral law involves placing the historicity of conscience in conjunction with the irreducibly allegorical character of language and history. Guilt is a linguistic as well as a temporal problem. The fundamental question in reading the historicality of conscience and moral law is that of determining the relation between time and being-guilty and of understanding the role of language in that relation.

The leitmotif of our genealogy from the daemon to conscience is perhaps best stated by Rousseau in *Julie, ou La nouvelle Héloise:* "Is it not known that the disordered affections corrupt judgment as well as the will, and that conscience is altered and modifies itself unnoticeably [*insensiblement*] in every age, in every people, in every individual, according to the inconstancy of opinion and the variety of prejudice [*préjugés*]?"[1] Though there is no escaping the eye and the voice of conscience, its operation is everywhere different and perpetually in transformation. A book could be written on this extraordinary letter by Julie, which lies at the heart of Rousseau's project in that novel and in all his writing and experience. Of the diversity of these *préjugés*, there is also much to be said, for they are not only "prejudices" but also "pre-judgments," as though all judgments of conscience are the effects of a potentiality for judgment that withholds itself even as it empowers all the actual judgments that are issued, passed, sentenced in historical time. These "pre-judgments" operate *insensiblement:* "insensibly," outside the world of sensation. The realm of the Kantian moral law, with which the senses have nothing to do, is very close at hand at such moments in Rousseau's writing. It is as though there are at least two levels at which conscience operates: first, its palpable judgments, which we can hear and feel and which determine all the legally binding codes of law in every domain to one degree or another; second, its nonsensible aspect, which underlies the historicity of law but remains rigorously outside it, in the realm that Kant would call that of pure, practical reason. These are yet other terms for the historicality of the moral law.

Moving very rapidly here, and only in order to anticipate the articulations of the question of conscience that lie ahead, I would like to indicate an essay by Jacques Derrida entitled "Before the

1. Jean-Jacques Rousseau, *Julie, ou La nouvelle Héloise,* 2:358 (my translation).

Law," which is a reading of Kafka's parable of the same title. In an earlier form this essay was called "Préjugés: Devant la loi," which draws explicitly (as Rousseau's usage does not) upon the ambiguity between "pre-judgment" and "prejudice." Derrida draws on the ambiguities of the terms that lie on both sides of the colon of the French title. First, what he says of Kafka's man from the country, who spends his life standing before the guardian who at once indicates and obstructs the way to the law, goes to the heart of the "question" of conscience:

> There is some law, some law which *is not there but which exists.* The judgment, however, does not arrive. In this other sense, the man of nature is not only a subject of the law outside the law, he is also, in both an infinite and a finite way, the prejudged; not so much as a prejudged subject but as a subject before a judgment which is always in preparation and always being deferred. Prejudged as having to be judged, arriving in advance of the law which only signifies "later."[2]

Second, the positionality of being "before the law" is at once temporal and spatial, which means that the man who stands "before the law" is also a man who is prejudged by that which precedes the law; he is, as Derrida writes, "un homme d'avant la loi," a man who belongs to, who is of, that which is temporally "before the law."[3] The fables I offer in lieu of a history of conscience attempt to take into account the degree to which the various expressions of the law acknowledge or conceal the belonging-together, indeed the inseparability, of conscience and the strangely irreducible retroactivity of the law "before the law," which is utterly without content and whose only trace is to be found in its daemonic figures.

2. Jacques Derrida, "Before the Law," 205–6.
3. As the translator's note (ibid., 200 n. 3) points out, although the English "before" and the German *vor* can indicate both spatial and temporal relations, the French *devant* is exclusively spatial and *avant* is temporal, forcing Derrida to have recourse to the inventive locution *d'avant la loi.*

Pauline *Syneidesis*

The Pauline notion of conscience (or *syneidesis*) internalized the external strictures of Jewish law within the framework of the Greek culture of the self and created perhaps the most influential techniques of self-mastery and self-knowledge in Western history. The pagan and the Christian terms are both, however, efforts to respond to the same questions about the nature and origin of the silent voice that speaks inside our heads and reminds us of the debts, duties, and responsibilities that precede us and to which we feel bound. The daemon and conscience are both efforts to lessen the guilt and pain that arise from not knowing the whys and wherefores of either the voice that accuses us or the feelings it engenders. Paul's remarkable solution to his so-called "crisis at Corinth" provided not only a new name but a new answer to the question of the origin of the silent call of the inner voice. Against the horizon of the multiplicity and confusion of meanings attributed to the various daemonic cults and practices that flourished at Corinth, Pauline *syneidesis* provided a clear and compelling alternative: "That is why you are obliged to submit. It is an obligation imposed not merely by fear of retribution but by conscience" (Romans 13:5).[4] Quite suddenly, the immense chasm separating Jewish law and the Greek experience of Being appeared to have been bridged, and a new and continuous path had been created between all that exists and its heretofore concealed origin. The old law, which prohibited precisely such a crossing between Being and the Divine, or between Being and the Law, would now gradually be abandoned by Jews for whom Pauline conscience proved to be the irresistible way to a new covenant.

It appeared that Pauline *syneidesis* succeeded in collapsing the difference between human language and the Divine and thereby in relieving people of the guilt they felt as a result of this separation.

4. Biblical citations follow the *Revised English Bible*.

According to Paul, Christ promised an unprecedented cathartic deliverance from the guilt of separation from the Divine. Christ's blood "will cleanse our conscience" because he was without sin and because he had chosen of his own volition to sacrifice himself: "Through the eternal Spirit he offered himself without blemish to God" (Hebrews 9:14). The old offerings and sacrifices could not promise nearly so clean a conscience as that promised by the writers of the New Testament. On the one hand, Christian conscience intensified its focus on what was most essential to the Jewish law, which was precisely the sense of guilt it inspired. On the other hand, it offered at the same time a new cathartic mechanism for relieving the very burden it had so brilliantly redefined.

In his study *Conscience in the New Testament,* C. A. Pierce undertakes a philological reading of *syneidesis* in order to differentiate its "somewhat narrow idea" from the broader meanings that arose when it was translated as *conscientia* in the Latin Church.[5] In its New Testament usage *syneidesis* pertains specifically to a process of self-examination that internalizes the fundamental Pauline "principle of retribution inherent in the moral universe." In its everyday use in ordinary Greek, *syneidesis* meant to Paul's contemporaries what occurs "when, by his acts completed or initiated, [one] transgresses the moral limits of his nature."[6] To enter into a changed relation with oneself as a result of an act or an intention is not, of course, necessarily to be in the grip of a guilty conscience, but that is precisely what happens in the semantic revolution Paul introduced into the word *syneidesis*. In reflecting on the meaning of Paul's reinvention of what was a common Greek expression for the inward turning of the self upon itself, I am reminded of Matthew Arnold's famous observation: "The governing idea of Hellenism is spontaneity of consciousness; that of Hebraism, strictures of conscience."[7] What seems essential here is the substratum of guilt on

5. C. A. Pierce, *Conscience in the New Testament,* 118.
6. Ibid., 67, 54.
7. Matthew Arnold, *Culture and Anarchy,* 109.

which Paul invariably draws as he reinvents both the Jewish religion and the Greek *daimon*. It is this unconscious, compulsive component of *syneidesis* as the site of an almost intractable guilt that will slowly be winnowed away over the centuries as *conscientia* comes to mean an increasingly idealized self-consciousness that sees itself as the transparent site of the moral law. One might say that as *syneidesis* became *conscientia,* it gradually lost the traces of its Jewish origins and became reinvested with a certain Romanized Hellenic character.

Between the daemon and conscience comes Pauline *syneidesis,* which, paradoxically enough, even as it arises out of Jewish guilt—out of a certain agonizing experience of self-reflection—is nevertheless without precedent in the Old Testament, where retribution and guilt arise from outside the human subject rather than through the internal avenger that is *syneidesis*. Even where the Old Testament offers a clear anticipation of the Pauline notion, as in Psalm 119, where the psalmist has internalized the divine word, the fear of reproach and retribution still comes from outside and not from within the heart where the word (*imrah*) has been installed. As Pierce points out, only once in the entire Old Testament was the word *syneidesis* used in the Greek translation of the Hebrew: "Curse not the King in thy conscience [*syneidesis*]" (Ecclesiastes 10:20).[8] Paul's Jewish reinvention of Judaism as Christianity, and above all his internalization of the God of the Jews as *syneidesis,* which took place through the medium of the Greek and later the Latin language, was thereby destined to fall under erasure. Though we know the horrifying consequences of the obliteration of the Pauline connection between Christian and Jew all too well, we need constantly to be reminded of it. That there *is* a connection we must not forget, even though we cannot discern the causality behind it. Without such reminders we fall, at the worst, into anti-Semitism and, at the best, into borderline formulations like this from Adolf

---

8. Pierce, *Conscience in the New Testament,* 54.

Harnack's encyclopedic *History of Dogma* (1900): "To the question how such holy men appeared exclusively, or almost exclusively, among the Jewish people, the documents preserved to us yield no answers."[9] Research into the early history of Christianity is at a transitional stage as it considers the implications of the Dead Sea Scrolls, which provide a new glimpse into the transmission of scripture and its relation to rituals of self-cleansing and spiritual purification. At this difficult crossroads the fable to which I grant a certain explanatory privilege is Freud's *Moses and Monotheism* (1938), whose daring thesis—that the intensification of Jewish guilt was at once the price for maintaining the identity of the chosen people and the ultimate provocation for the emergence of Christianity—may well find substantiation in future biblical scholarship. In my argument, the importance of Freud's self-styled "historical novel" has little to do with his hypothesis that Moses was an Egyptian and everything to do with his reading of Paul's invention of what we might call the analytic situation of Christianity.

Having begun our fable of the history of conscience in midstream with the invention of *syneidesis,* we should have some sense of the Hebraic origins of Paul's accusatory internal daemon before considering the Hellenic genealogy of the daemon. Freud's thesis that the emergence of Christianity owed a great deal to a generalized feeling of guilt among Mediterranean peoples during roughly the period from Lucretius to Paul is already present in rudimentary form in Nietzsche. In a passage from *Daybreak: Thoughts on the Prejudices of Morality* (1881)—and, yes, it is precisely a question of "moral pre-judgments" (*die moralischen Vorurtheile*)—Nietzsche presents Epicurus and his disciple Lucretius, who died in 55 B.C., as the thinker and the poet who sought to deliver their contemporaries from a crippling guilt and thus from a terrible fear of punishment in the afterlife:

9. Adolf Harnack, *The History of Dogma*, 1:179. Whereas Matthew Arnold recognized the fundamentally Hebraic character of Christianity, Harnack concludes: "The Old Testament men of God were in certain measure Christians" (179 n. 3).

> *The "after death"*—Christianity discovered the idea of punish-
> ment in Hell throughout the whole Roman Empire: all the nu-
> merous cults had brooded on it with especial satisfaction as on
> the most promising egg of their power. Epicurus believed he
> could confer no greater benefit on his fellows than by tearing up
> the roots of *this* belief: his triumph, which resounds the most
> beautifully in the mouth of the gloomy and yet enlightened dis-
> ciple of his teaching, the Roman Lucretius, came too early—
> Christianity took the belief in these subterranean terrors, which
> was already dying out, under his especial protection, and it acted
> prudently in so doing![10]

Freud sees what Nietzsche does not: that "Christianity" was a
Jewish phenomenon that somehow managed to grasp a generalized
guilty conscience nearer the root than either Epicurus or Lucretius,
who nevertheless remain, as Nietzsche fully recognizes, prophets of
an enlightened culture and thinkers in a genealogy that includes
Nietzsche and Freud themselves. Because circumcision is central to
Jewish experience and psychoanalytic theory, we might glance at a
remarkable instance in Lucretius's poem that reveals the proximity
between Jewish guilt and the desperation of certain Roman cultists.
Lucretius describes those whose conscience is so guilt-ridden that
they believe only castration, literal or symbolic, will appease the
vengeful deities who await them in the afterlife:

> Some, burdened by the terror of death,
> lived by excision of the virile organ,
> some with the loss of the hand or foot remained
> alive, and some by sacrificing eyes.[11]

They castrate themselves, apotropaically, in order to ward off being
castrated by the punishing figures that are projections of their own
guilty conscience and of those demented cults and religions which

10. Friedrich Nietzsche, *Daybreak: Thoughts on the Prejudices of Morality,* 43.
11. Lucretius *The Nature of Things* 7.1208–14.

sought to capitalize on this reservoir of fear. Nietzsche's ironic characterization of the "prudent" manner in which Christianity capitalized on "these subterranean terrors" is not without an important kernel of truth about the nontruth or fictionality of such projections. This prudence consists precisely in abandoning the symbolic castration of the Jews and substituting for it the famous Pauline "circumcision of the heart" (Romans 2:29). The enlightened republicanism of the Lucretian *clinamen* or "swerve," which by the laws of chance and fate produced a cosmos from the directionless torrents of primal matter and energy, is too intellectual a promise to free human beings from the horrors of a world driven by the implacable destiny of revengeful gods. Pauline *syneidesis* addresses these fears with infinitely greater prudence than the erudite Epicurean *tetrapharmakon,* that poisonous remedy of "honey and wormwood" (Lucretius *The Nature of Things* 4.6) which would relieve humanity of its need to offer sacrifices to the theological "other" who spoke through one's own guilty conscience.

By the time of Lucretius and Paul the Greek daemon had become a grotesque figure out of the *Grand Guignol* of the ancient cults. Bereft of its philosophical and literary roots, it was ready to be demonized. For Paul the daemon was merely a medium of communication through which the fiery spirit of the avenging God of the Old Testament would henceforth pass. No less than Lucretius, Paul recognized that the daemons were empty vessels, but he put them to an infinitely more ingenious use. Through its internalization or implantation of a divine spark of the fiery breath of the divine spirit in the soul of every individual, Pauline *syneidesis* combined the most highly poetical elements of the Hebraic and the Hellenic traditions. Baptism and the "circumcision of the heart" were genial replacements for the Jewish circumcision of the flesh, but the New Testament imagery of *syneidesis* brought the fires of Jewish vengeance into the soul of the Christian convert. Paul and his colleagues realized that although their fellow Jews had to be relieved of some guilt, they had to be careful not to relieve them of too much. And, so our fable goes, *syneidesis* preserved a fundamental flame of guilt. Therein lies the difference between this remarkable Jewish invention by Christ and his apostles and all the other contemporaneous solutions: theirs preserved a modicum of guilt, now intensified in the most poetic imagery, and did so in order to make the ensuing purification more palpable and persuasive.

The imagery of Pauline conscience that proved so influential during the wars of conscience of Shakespeare's time centered upon this fiery imagery, the imagery of branding, of searing heat, of the tenderness of conscience and the fearful prospect of bringing it too near to the flame of the law, and of the inevitable knowledge that conscience must be held to the fire. The complex poetic psychology to which Pauline *syneidesis* gave rise during the English renaissance constituted one of the greatest resources for Shakespeare's art.

We will spend some time with Shakespeare in the smithy of the cauterized Pauline conscience. But first, we have to learn how Paul, Prometheus-like, brought the searing flame of the accusatory Jewish God into *syneidesis*. This fire and heat are for Shakespeare the central daemonic figures in his imaginative world. They are figures of guilt and of the enigmatic origins of guilt and the law, of temporal and spatial origins, of what lies outside the finitude of the world, and of what lies deep within the mystery of human nature; these daemonic figures are the cinders of what remains from the fire that burns before the beginning and after the end.

But whence the feelings of guilt that create this burning within? The solution provided by my fable combines Heidegger's analysis of the temporality of Dasein and Freud's fabulous thesis of the murder of the primal father. These daemonic figures for the origin of the law do not forget (or perhaps, to be more precise, they do not forget too often) the originlessness they daringly approximate.

Freud's *Moses and Monotheism*

Moses and Monotheism is the historicizing culmination of psychoanalytic theory's long effort to analyze the nature and origins of

conscience and moral law. In the course of this book I rehearse
most of Freud's analyses of conscience, many of which arose in the
context of his reading of Shakespeare. But for now let us begin at
the end of his career, and with what is perhaps his least influential
and most outlandish speculation: his thesis that the murder of
Moses the Egyptian lay at the origin of Judaism and therefore at the
origin of Christianity as well.

In this passage Freud explains why the solution to the ambient
guilt of the Mediterranean world could only have come from a Jew:

> The sense of guilt of those days was very far from being any
> longer restricted to the Jewish people; it had caught hold of all
> the Mediterranean peoples as a dull *malaise*, a premonition of
> calamity for which no one could suggest a reason. Historians of
> our day speak of an ageing of ancient civilization, but I suspect
> that they have only grasped accidental and contributory causes of
> this depressed mood of the peoples. The elucidation of this situa-
> tion of depression sprang from Jewry. Irrespectively of all the
> approximations and preparations in the surrounding world, it
> was after all a Jewish man, Saul of Tarsus (who, as a Roman
> citizen, called himself Paul), in whose spirit the realization first
> emerged: "the reason we are so unhappy is that we killed God
> the father." And it is entirely understandable that he could only
> grasp this piece of truth in the delusional disguise of the glad
> tidings: "we are freed from all guilt since one of us has sacrificed
> his life to absolve us." (*SE*, 23:135)

What perhaps gets lost in the boldness of the speculation is a certain resemblance that emerges here between Paul and Freud himself. It is as though in 1938, nearly two millennia later, another Jew
has come on the scene and has elucidated another depression: is not
psychoanalysis itself one of the most radical innovations in the
history of conscience since Paul? But while there is a principle of
recurrence at work here, there is also an immense historical difference, for Freud's later work reflects his realization that modern

civilization demands simply too much instinctual renunciation, and that although Paul's innovations had a long and unsurpassable success, times have changed and humankind will soon rebel against the god of conscience it created and under which it has suffered for too long.

We might anticipate a bit here and reflect that Shakespeare's thinking follows a similar current. Consider the following passage from *King Lear:* "Man's nature cannot carry / Th'affliction nor the fear" (3.2.48–49). We will return to these connections between Freud and Shakespeare later. For now, we must note Freud's troubling but persistent emphasis on the fact that the nature of Jewish guilt was so deeply racially ingrained that only another Jew could ever hope to sort it out. This has the effect, among other things, of placing the Jew in a remarkable position vis-à-vis the analysis of Christianity and of the entirety of Christian culture. The problems that arise here warrant a separate study. I am interested in this book in only one of these problems, apparently a very small, actually quite an immense one in the context of Freudian psychoanalysis: how is it that Shakespeare, a non-Jew, could achieve his extraordinary insights into the nature of conscience and moral law? Unable to prove that Shakespeare was a Jew, Freud chose the next best solution: to subscribe, in a quite deluded fashion, to Thomas Looney's thesis that Edward de Vere, the seventeenth Earl of Oxford—not the man from Stratford—wrote the works of Shakespeare. Though this is a topic for a later chapter, it is important to indicate it here, for *Moses and Monotheism,* as the culmination of Freud's will to historicize conscience, is also the culmination of his insistence that the transformations the followers of Moses underwent made a constitutive racial impact upon the Jewish people. Though it does not begin as a matter of the blood (which is why it is so important that Moses be an Egyptian), conscience irreversibly becomes a matter of the blood.

Since for Freud conscience is not a matter of divine intervention, a conventional psychoanalytic reading would regard Pauline *syn-*

eidesis as merely a reaction formation, a cover-up and a repression of the racial memory of a murderous guilt. But may it not also be more? Might it not preserve the memory and the guilt and enable them to survive, however concealed? Though it is highly unlikely that the Lamarckian thesis concerning racial memory and the inheritance of psychological racial traits, to which Freud subscribed, will ever prove scientifically sound, we will not be able to understand Freud's conception of the history of conscience unless we consider how important such hypotheses were to his thinking. Pauline conscience would appear as at once the greatest effort to deny the nature of Jewish guilt and its purest expression. And what of the role of language here? Since according to Freud Moses was an Egyptian, what he enforced upon the Jewish people could not have been something indigenously Jewish but only something that became indigenously Jewish after centuries of reinforcement.

Freud attempts to answer some of these questions. Let us continue with the Jewish-Christian connection for a bit longer. The absolution afforded by Christ makes, of course, no allusion to guilt for having killed God, or Moses, or the primal father. Nevertheless, Freud argues, "a crime that had to be atoned by the sacrifice of a victim could only have been a murder" (*SE* 23:135). If, following Freud's logic, Paul's reasoning was predicated on an unconscious memory of the murder of Moses, then this would ensure that "the victim of the sacrifice had been God's son." But to whom would the son be offered in sacrifice if the father were already dead? Of course, Freud had made this clear a quarter of a century earlier in *Totem and Taboo* and in numerous works in the interim: once murdered, the father's power grows, rather than diminishes, precisely through the emergence of the psychological phenomena of guilt and bad conscience. For Freud the crucial piece of evidence that Paul's thinking is driven by Jewish parricidal guilt is the ingenious way Paul conceals the specificity of that guilt behind the delusional and nonspecific notion of "original sin": "The unnameable crime [i.e., the murder of Moses as God the Father] was replaced by the hypothesis of what must be described as a shadowy 'original sin'" (*SE* 23:135). This leads Freud to a recognition of the genius of the Pauline solution to the problem of the intractability of Jewish guilt: it had to be reinvented in a form that could then be successfully purged; otherwise, Christianity would have remained an obscure cult. This takes us back to the epigraph from 1 Corinthians in which Paul differentiates Christianity from pagan and Jewish rituals that involve animal sacrifice and hence remain merely daemonic: "I am unwilling that you should be partners with daemons." What must be concealed, Freud insists, is precisely the guilt and the historical memory of the parricide from which it arose, which is to say, what must be eliminated is the daemonic guilt of the totem feast. The father must not be allowed to return; he must be buried once and for all beneath Christ's cathartic powers of absolution.

And so we come to the great solution: the Jews who did not convert to Jesus, the Jews who persisted beneath the burden of their unacknowledged parricidal guilt, would not be openly blamed for the very crime that haunted both Jews and the newly minted Jewish Christians: they would be blamed for killing Christ. In an astonishing reversal, the Christians found themselves able to confront their heretofore repressed guilt for having killed the father, even though what made it possible for them to confront it was its distorted concealment beneath the fiction of the murder of the son. The Christians managed to confront their guilt as Jews by entirely reinventing it. In addition to this brilliant concealment, which allowed them a certain intensely aesthetic satisfaction denied the Jews who persisted in denying that they had killed God the Father, the Christians then blamed the murder of the son upon the Jews who refused to convert. The reproach against the Jews goes something like this, says Freud:

> "They will not accept it as true that they murdered God, whereas we admit it and have been cleansed of that guilt." It is easy to see

how much truth lies behind this reproach. A special enquiry
would be called for to discover why it has been impossible for the
Jews to join in this forward step which was implied, in spite of all
its distortions, by the admission of having murdered God. In a
certain sense they have in that way taken a tragic load of guilt on
themselves; they have been made to pay a heavy penance for it.
(SE 23:136)

Since these sentences were written, in 1938, the burden of penance
has grown incalculably. Will the time ever come when we might be
able to weigh this penance? Those Jews who refused to convert
were compelled by the same compulsion to repeat their guilt that
Freud confronted in so many clinical contexts. Freud enables us to
grasp the extent to which the history of anti-Semitism has always
been the inseparable corollary to the history of conscience. The
great accusation leveled against Jews throughout the history of anti-
Semitism has always been that it is the Jews who lack a conscience,
which is why they could find it within themselves to murder Christ.
Freud enables us to grasp the extraordinary irony that has fueled
the entire history of anti-Semitism: that far from lacking a conscience, the Jews chose to persist in their bad conscience instead of
embracing the wonderful eudaemonic solution offered by the wonderful aesthetic fables of the Christians. I do not use the word
"eudaemonic" by accident, for the Christian solution is to transform the daemons, the inner voices that say we are guilty, into
happy daemons that tell us we are absolved of our sins. In Freud's
presentation, Paul emerges as perhaps the most brilliant thinker
and writer of the ancient world. Paul's reinvention of Jewish guilt as
Christian absolution conceals the "question" of conscience behind
the marvelous, aesthetic, eudaemonic judgments of Christian faith.
    But for Freud the interesting thing about Paul's genius is that in
working these linguistic and philosophical miracles he is really Moses revisited, for his great step forward from Mosaic law, the invention of Christian conscience, would have been impossible without

his Mosaic precursor. Though this is Freud's own version of what *Moses and Monotheism* is ultimately about, I have never been struck by his presentation of Moses, which seems too clever by half and infinitely less compelling than the deep appreciation Freud shows for Paul. In other words, what I believe is most important in *Moses and Monotheism* is not the historicizing zeal with which it zeroes in on the exact moment and the precise reasons for the existence of Jewish guilt, but rather its presentation of the Pauline intervention in Jewish history, which changed the world in so extraordinary a way that, as Freud must have surmised, an even greater event had to be somewhere behind it. The important thing to grasp from the Mosaic section of the book is, I believe, *that* something unthinkable must have happened long ago to explain the Pauline transformation of the nature of Jewish guilt, rather than Freud's specific account of *what* happened.

One moment in particular in Freud's account reveals something essential about the inexhaustible guilt that he discerns at the very heart of Jewish existence. Moses had, you will recall, radicalized Akhenaton's solar monotheism (or "henotheism," as Freud calls it, the belief in the One—*Hen* in Greek): "Ideas, memories and inferences became decisive in contrast to the lower psychical activity which had direct perception by the sense-organs as its content. This was unquestionably one of the most important stages on the path to becoming human [*Menschwerdung*]" (*SE* 23:113). This great event in the history of truth constitutes for Freud what the inward turn of Plato's thought constitutes for Heidegger. Freud admires this spiritualizing subjectivization of truth; Heidegger sees in Plato's thought the betrayal of the promise of early Greek thinking. Heidegger's thought will occupy us later, but for now let us note that Freud's appreciation of the turn away from sensation to reflection seems a highly unwarranted idealization on his part, as though the enigma of sense perception had somehow been mastered in Mosaic thought. This may also have been, he speculates, the moment of the turning away from hieroglyphic script to alphabetic writing: "If [the scribes of Moses] were subject to the prohibition against pictures, they would even have had a motive for abandoning the hieroglyphic picture-writing while adapting its written characters to expressing a new language" (*SE* 23:43 n. 2). The invention of Mosaic law becomes the catchall for every possible innovation: it is the moment of the "beginning of philosophical thought," and, most important, from a society that was not overwhelmed by guilt to one that was. Moses forced his people to give up everything to which they had been accustomed, to renounce every instinctual satisfaction on which they had relied, including even and especially the solace of rewards in the afterlife, which were so prominent in ancient Egyptian religion. Akhenaton had tried something along these lines years earlier and failed. Moses intensified the rigors of renunciation but practiced his new religion only on the small band of the Jewish people.

Freud speculates that although Moses' followers tried to toe the line, they too reached the breaking point and found it impossible to "tolerate such a highly spiritualized [*vergeistigte*] religion and find satisfaction of their needs in what it had to offer. . . . The savage Semites took fate into their own hands and rid themselves of their tyrant" (*SE* 23:47). But, alas for them, it was too late; Moses had already implanted conscience in them, and they would never recover. In *Totem and Taboo* the murder of the *Urvater* is highly sexually charged, but here, at the founding moment of the consummate guilt in world history, there is no allusion to any sexual dimension save the passing reference to the turn away from the maternal body. This is difficult to explain except by saying that the omission is probably an expression of Freud's personal ascetic severity regarding sexual matters rather than the result of some belated veneration on his part for the Jewish religion. The omission of the sexual content may have resulted from the depth of his identification with Moses. In the murder of Moses the father by the "savage Semites" the sexual motive is reduced to a ghostly presence. Mosaic law stands, in the shorthand of *Moses and Monotheism,* for the primal scene of oedipal prohibition, and what makes the ensuing guilt for the murder of Moses so singular, so inexhaustible, so unlike that of any other race, is the fact of the absolute severity of Mosaic teaching. The murdered primal father returns to haunt all the tribes and all the peoples who underwent the oedipal cycle described throughout Freud's work. But in the case of the Jews the returning specter of the dead father was a ghost to end all ghosts, for in his return the rigor of all those countless renunciations returned as well, and the ensuing guilt was of a qualitative and quantitative nature unprecedented in world history. The ghost in *Hamlet* is for Freud part of this extraordinary genealogy.

Here, at last, is Freud's culminating account of the specificity of Jewish bad conscience and thus, in the light of Paul's subsequent intervention, the essence of Christian *syneidesis* as well:

> There was no place in the religion of Moses for a direct expression of the murderous hatred of the father. All that could come to light was a mighty reaction against it—a sense of guilt on account of that hostility, a bad conscience for having sinned against God and for not ceasing to sin. This sense of guilt, which was uninterruptedly kept awake by the Prophets, and which soon formed an essential part of the religious system, had yet another superficial motivation, which neatly disguised its true origin. Things were going badly for the people; the hopes resting on the favour of God failed in fulfillment; it was not easy to maintain the illusion, loved above all else, of being God's chosen people. If they wished to avoid renouncing that happiness, a sense of guilt on account of their own sinfulness offered welcome means of exculpating God: they deserved no better than to be punished by him since they had not obeyed his commandments. And, driven by the need to satisfy this sense of guilt, which was insatiable [*unersättlich*] and came from sources so much deeper [*soviel tieferer Quelle*], they must make those commandments grow ever stricter, more meticulous, and even more trivial. In a fresh rapture of moral asceticism they imposed more and more new instinctual

renunciations on themselves and in that way reached—in doctrine and precept, at least—ethical heights which had remained inaccessible to other peoples of antiquity. (*SE* 23:134)

The Jews had managed to transform the pain of instinctual renunciation into a higher pleasure. All the interest lies in Freud's notion of the "insatiable" nature of the Jewish sense of guilt. The Jews who refused to convert to Christ did not do so simply because they were unresponsive to the aesthetic satisfaction that the Christian confession of guilt afforded. No, they refused because they had already discovered new pleasures. At first it was painful for the ego to make all these sacrifices to the Mosaic superego they had introjected. But in the wake of the murder of Moses and through all the priestly concealments and subterfuges that followed, the people learned to transform their pain into a secret pleasure. And so they gave themselves more and more laws; they enjoyed nothing more than submitting to the arcane bureaucracy of the law. Like denizens of a Kafkaesque world in ancient times, the Jews reveled in the sadistic abuse administered by a superego to which they had finally allied themselves.

Paul's ability to collapse the distinction between poetic and sacred language, and thereby to produce great happiness in his flock, could make no appeal to the denizens of the deep structure of the Judaic world, for they had already learned to stop fighting the superego and had joined forces with it. The egocentric satisfaction of Christian law sought to overcome separation from the Law rather than endlessly reaffirm the intervening labyrinth of laws after the Jewish fashion.

Freud's *Trieblehre*

In order to proceed further in this argument, we must clarify certain elements in Freud's *Trieblehre* or "theory of drives." By doing so, we will also set the stage for understanding the difference between the Catholic and Puritan interpretations of Christian law. Freudian psychoanalysis is, so the fable goes, part of the very genealogy of the Judeo-Christian conscience that it takes as its central object of study. Psychoanalytic theory does not, therefore, stand somewhere outside the history of conscience but rather constitutes one of its more recent manifestations.

Freud's account of the "insatiable" character of Jewish guilt implies that it is a pathological formation. It also bears many similarities to the clinical phenomenon of the "repetition compulsion" that produces what Freud calls "negative therapeutic reaction": even when confronted with the origin of their illness, patients persist in their symptoms and in fact even get worse. Freud's experience as a clinician informs everything he has to say about the history of conscience. "In the end," he concludes in *The Ego and the Id,* "we come to see that we are dealing with what may be called a 'moral' factor, a sense of guilt, which is finding satisfaction in the illness and refuses to give up the punishment of suffering" (*SE* 19:49).

What we must understand is how this "satisfaction" is produced beneath the burden of a moral compulsion. The formation of conscience is beginning to appear as a somewhat morbid phenomenon. The old saw that opposes the man of action to the man of conscience would not be out of place here, for there is something perhaps more than slightly distasteful about the sort of person who continually agonizes with his or her conscience. As Kant remarks, "Conscience should not lord it over us like a tyrant; we do no hurt to our conscience by proceeding on our way cheerfully; tormenting consciences in the long run become dulled and ultimately cease to function."[12] The melancholic who, Hamlet-like, seeks incessantly for signs of evil is notoriously incapable of action. Nietzsche adduces Hamlet in *The Birth of Tragedy* because he is the quintessential Dionysian man who is loath to commit himself to action.

---

12. Immanuel Kant, *Lectures on Ethics,* 134–35.

Might not the discourses of anti-Semitism on the Jew's lack of conscience be an effort to capitalize on the parodic nature of the Jewish conscience itself, which, after having existed for so long in a hyperactive mode in its obsessive concern with guilt, shame, and atonement, laughs at its own pathological character? Anti-Semitism is a particularly banal but insidious misreading of the self-parodic mode of the Jewish conscience itself. We will try to deal with some of the many questions that emerge here in the course of our reading of *The Merchant of Venice*. Here it will be helpful to indicate some of the finer points of Freud's theory of conscience.

The relation in the German language between conscience and certainty, *Gewissen* and *Gewissheit*, is something we must consider very carefully. As Freud remarks in *Totem and Taboo*, the certainty of conscience involves "the internal perception of the rejection [*Verwerfung*] of a particular wish operating within us" (*SE* 13:68). What is certain is the "rejection," which "has no need to appeal to anything else for support," for it is "certain of itself." But then what exacerbates conscience? Why does it turn again and again upon itself? Is it not because its self-standing self-certainty is in fact never really certain and never really self-standing? A so-called "healthy" conscience would, in a good-natured Kantian way, simply cease raking itself over the coals and move on, whereas a pathological conscience that keeps examining the ground of its own functioning would invariably be caught in an infinitely recursive involution. And any effort to write a history or a fable of conscience could never hope to elude this latter eventuality. What I call the "question" of conscience names precisely this "need to appeal," which is at once inseparable from conscience and yet the very element that it must try to foreclose if it is to achieve its much coveted self-certainty. We are thus locating a certain Heideggerian reading of conscience in the midst of the Freudian analysis. Heidegger's task is explicitly that of separating conscience from certainty and thereby opening the way to the otherwise foreclosed "need to appeal," which leads him from the "call of conscience" in *Being and Time* to the enigmatic silent appeal of language itself in his later writings. The potentiality for this separation is already implicit in Freud's "need to appeal" (*zu berufen braucht*), even though it enters Freud's text only under the sign of foreclosure. In the twenty-five years that separate *Totem and Taboo* from *Moses and Monotheism* Freud himself in effect overcomes his self-imposed foreclosure on considering the irreducible need of conscience to appeal to its undiscoverable ground.

Like Shakespeare, Freud understands not only that conscience makes cowards of us all but that we enjoy being so abused. This process stands at the center of Freud's history of conscience and at the center of his sobering recognition as a clinician that the strangely pleasurable agonies of conscience are responsible for releasing within the patient the most destructive forces. As Freud comes to recognize the neurotic destiny to which conscience has condemned his patients, the psychoanalytic couch becomes itself the stage on which the death drive choreographs its own tragic action.

Let us trace Freud's theory of conscience as it relates to his theory of the drives or instincts from "On Narcissism: An Introduction" (1914) to *Civilization and Its Discontents* (1930). In Freud's first *Trieblehre*, which opposed the ego instincts to the sexual instincts, conscience is a formation within the ego instincts. More precisely, conscience monitors the extent to which the ego is living up to its ego-ideal. Freud assumes that its function is generally to reassure the ego that it is conforming to its ideal. Both the ego-ideal and the conscience have been introjected by the ego from parental and social models. The relation between ego-ideal, superego, and conscience is a complex and fluctuating one in Freud's thinking. We can generally assume that conscience is a faculty of measuring the relation between the ego and its ideal or superego. Conscience is not superego, however, for only the latter draws, in a normative fashion, upon the force of the id. When the superego draws excessively on the id, the ensuing force overspills into conscience and renders it pathological as well. The superego functions in Freud's thinking as something like the quantity of enforcing power that is operative through the ego-ideal. While conscience measures the ego's performance vis-à-vis its ideal, the superego enforces the judgment that conscience makes. We might regard the whole process in a rather Kantian juridical context where conscience is the judge and the superego is the authority of law that makes the judge's sentence binding.

Freud calls conscience both an "agency" (*Instanz*) that acts upon the ego and an "institution" (*Institution*) of the ego, one of the fundamental ego-structures. In "On Narcissism" he speaks of the other "major institutions of the ego," which include dream censorship, which is a kind of night watchman who takes over while conscience sleeps; and the faculty of reality-testing, which protects the waking ego from danger. What Freud discovers, however, is that the ego's capacity to set conscience over against itself as a critical faculty is always itself a potential danger from within, for it can cause a break of fissure within the ego through which destructive forces may enter and threaten the very integrity of the ego they were intended to serve.

Paranoid symptoms arise when the agency of conscience begins to speak no longer in a silent internal voice but in what the subject experiences as audible speech, and likewise when the sense of being watched, which is also part of normative conscience, is projected into the external world and experienced as a pathological sensation (see *SE* 14:95–98). Freud cannot at this point explain how it is that conscience has begun to function independently and without its customary allegiance to the ego. He recognizes only that the internalization of the moral law can in certain instances trigger a process in which the subject's own aggressive sexual drives are somehow turned upon the ego.

In his essays and case histories from 1914 to 1918, Freud focuses increasingly on the instability created by the various deformations of the ego that occur in the process of its internalization of the moral law and of the imperative character of language generally.

(His reading of *Macbeth* becomes decisive to the transformation of his thinking about the role of conscience during this period, and I discuss it in a later chapter.) The crisis concerning conscience is full-blown in *Beyond the Pleasure Principle* (1920), in which Freud attempts "a clarification of the theory of the instincts" that he himself regards as a failure (*SE* 18:55 n. 1). The aggressivity that is released on the ego through conscience persuades him that there is a destructive force at work in what he thought were the forces governing life and sexuality. This extraordinary reversal reaches its culmination when Freud writes that sadism, which had always appeared to him as part of the sexual instincts, is now revealed as being "in fact [*eigentlich*] a death instinct" (*SE* 18:54). The essential effort of his theory to distinguish those drives that are directed to objects from those that are directed to the ego now no longer appears tenable. As the faculty through which the ego tortures itself, conscience becomes the switching station through which the ego appropriates the energy of the sexual drive for its own internal pleasure; it is a pleasure, however, that lies "beyond the pleasure principle" in the realm of the *Todestrieb* or "death drive."

But what is the exact nature of this peculiar pleasure that the ego derives from its incessant self-torture? We recall that conscience looks back at the act and holds the ego to account. In doing so, the ego-structures (conscience and the superego) draw libido away from objects in order to direct it upon the ego itself. And the more this happens, the more the ego anticipates the repetition of what happened the last time. We began this account from the end of Freud's career when conscience and instinctual renunciation had become uppermost in his thinking. In *The Ego and the Id*, written shortly after *Beyond the Pleasure Principle*, Freud still regards the process by which the ego-structures appropriate the object-libido of the id for their own peculiar purposes as an enigma: "With the aid of the super-ego, in a manner that is still obscure to us, [the ego] draws upon the past ages stored in the id" (*SE* 19:45). He had spoken on the same page of the "harshness and cruelty" of the ego-

ideal and "its dictatorial 'Thou shalt,'" and of the strange way in
which it seems to draw strength from the deepest sources of the id.
By the time of *Moses and Monotheism* this mysterious resource
appears as the "inherited property" of racial history on which each
succeeding generation will henceforth be able to draw (*SE* 23:132).
Freud could not be clearer about this: the repetition of the demands
of conscience creates an expectation of pleasure, of the higher pleasures derived from repeatedly submitting to conscience, of a pleasure that lies beyond the pleasure principle, a pleasure that is derived from the inherited power of ego-structures to appropriate the
force of libidinal object-cathexes that formerly served the sexual
drive. This is the work of Thanatos, of the death drive.[13]

We said earlier that being-guilty is an irreducibly temporal question. And that is just how Freud puts it in *Beyond the Pleasure
Principle* when he describes the process by which he has traced
"the origin of an instinct to *a need to restore to an earlier state of
things* [dem Bedürfnis nach Wiederherstellung]" (*SE* 18:57). Freud's
thinking has responded to a need, to an appeal, that draws him to
the enigma of time itself. The *Trieb* names the link between the
human subject and the irreducible mystery of time which, through
the drive mechanism, makes its appeal, its call upon the subject,
who responds through the subjective sensation of feeling to the
need to repeat what it had felt before. That is exactly what the
higher pleasures of conscience, the peculiarly compulsive pleasures
of repetition, are all about: they take the subject back to an earlier
state of things, to what the subject is finally most familiar with,

13. The cruel pleasures of conscience result from a regression to the primal unity of
Eros and Thanatos, to the founding sadism that enables the narcissistic ego to incorpo-
rate the object. Mikkel Borch-Jacobsen's account is penetrating: "Everything begins and
opens itself in that primal double band which is doubly primal, since it is only in the
amorphous destruction of the 'object,' in the cannibal-like (non)relation with the other,
that death *and* life are born" (*The Emotional Tie*, 12). Conscience once again exposes
the ego to the possibility of its absolute annihilation without remainder. It is in this sense
that Slavoj Žižek defines the "death drive" as "the radical annihilation of nature's
circular movement, . . . the destruction of the *symbolic* universe" (*The Sublime Object
of Ideology*, 135).

despite the apparent oddity of the regression and of the sensation it involves. The "uncanny" is another term for this temporal phenomenon, for the experience of feeling the call of what is absolutely earlier; whatever was "there" is still "here" in the call of the drive mechanism, in the call of conscience, and in the call that calls the subject back beyond conscience to the "question" that dwells uncannily within it.

In *The Ego and the Id* Freud speaks of the deadly game of conscience in terms of "instinctual defusion" (*Triebentmischung*) and offers a novel account of what happens when moral imperatives are internalized. At one stage in our development, he surmises, Eros and Thanatos are bound together and only gradually become disengaged or "defused." The formation of conscience and the superego is the primary scene of that separating-out of the instincts. In the act of identifying with a parent or with some element in the external world, the erotic component of the drive is sublimated, leaving the destructive component unbound; and it is this unbound drive, Freud speculates, that gives the categorical imperative its "compulsive character." Echoing Heidegger and Lacan, we might say that this is the scene of the coming of language or of the "instance of the letter." Rewriting the language of *Beyond the Pleasure Principle,* Freud here speaks of the ego's submission to the superego as a process of "decomposition" (*Zersetzung*) very much along the lines of what happens to protozoan life forms that are "destroyed by the products of decomposition that they themselves have created. From the economic point of view the morality that functions in the super-ego seems to be a similar product of decomposition" (SE 19:47). Can one imagine a more anti-Kantian formulation of the nature of moral law? But as I have demonstrated by adducing the temporal index that is never absent from Freud's language, his account is in fact more Kantian than he suspected. Despite the destructive character of Freud's sometimes Nietzschean-sounding rhetoric, there is an extraordinary honesty and a meticulous presentation of the issues. And Freud concludes this discussion in *The*

Ego and the Id by admitting that the formation of conscience necessarily demands running the risk that the ego might be overwhelmed by *Gewissensangst,* "fear of conscience" or "conscience
anxiety"—none of which, Freud adds, can be "grasped analyt-
ically."

In the course of his very exacting and revealing reading of *Beyond
the Pleasure Principle,* Jacques Derrida provides some crucial terms
that illuminate the curious nature of the higher pleasures of conscience. I have called the movement back to an earlier state a "recursive" one, in the sense that the ego turns back upon itself in a
temporally regressive direction. For the work of the death drive
Derrida employs the ambiguous expression *le pas de mort,* "the
step/stop of death," entailing a heterogeneous or plural function
which, though it ultimately leads toward death, is also programmed
to make many stops and delays along the way. As we have already
indicated, it is not the case in Freud's text that there is a simple
opposition between life and death. There is instead what Derrida
calls "life death," a disjunctive conjunction that no longer opposes
one to the other but rather relates them to each other through the
repetition compulsion, which at once holds life in place *and* moves
it toward death. "Life death" is configured through what Derrida
calls the "differentiated relay" of "the drive of the proper," which is
the organism's most fundamental drive to preserve itself for the
death that is proper to it: "In the detour of the step/stop, in the
step/stop of the detour, the organism keeps itself from the other
which might still steal its death from it. It keeps itself from the
other who might give it the death it would not have given itself. . . .
The drive of the proper would be stronger than life *and* than
death. . . . The most driven drive is the drive of the proper, . . . the
one that tends to reappropriate itself."[14]

"The drive of the proper" is Derrida's idiom for the nonpresent
trace of that which brings things to presence and which, while it lies

14. Jacques Derrida, *The Postcard,* 356.

beyond what is present, leaves its mark on present beings. It sustains and underlies "the auto-affective structure of time (that which there gives itself to receive is no present-being)."[15] "The drive of the proper" names the organism's relation to time, which is stronger, "more driven," than its relation to death. And Derrida places all of this under the sign of the daemon, which he writes as "demon," though without any diabolical suggestion. The daemon is not *what* returns in the "differentiated relay" of "the drive of the proper"; rather, the drive is itself the daemon:

> Truly speaking, there is not a return *of the* demonic. The demon is that very thing which *comes back* [*revient*] without having been called by the PP [Pleasure Principle] from one knows not where ("early infantile influences," says Freud), inherited from one knows not whom, but already persecutory, by means of the simple form of its return, indefatigably repetitive, independent of every apparent desire, *automatic*. Like Socrates' demon—which will have made everyone write, beginning with him who passes for never having done so—this automaton comes back [*revient*] without coming back [*revenir à*] to anyone, it produces effects of ventriloquism without origin, without emission, and without addressee. It is only posted, the post in its "pure" state, a kind of mailman [*facteur*] without destination. Tele—without telos. Finality without end, the beauty of the demon.[16]

This persecutory, Freudo-Socratic daemon is, of course, conscience as the figure of the relation of the auto-affective structure of time to time's other. In order to affect oneself, one must internalize what is absolutely other. The auto-affective structure of time thus includes a moment of irreducible hetero-affectivity. The time of the self is constituted precisely around its internalization of time's otherness. Daemonic figures are figures of the sending and receiving of the otherness of time and Being. The daemon is the *envoi* par excel-

15. Ibid., 359.
16. Ibid., 341.

lence. These figures of another temporality produce in us the subjective, affective experience of being-guilty. If there is original sin, it is simply a misreading or, rather, an overdetermined reading of the comings and goings of the daemon.

The very drive by which the ego appropriates object-libido to itself also disappropriates or exappropriates the ego from itself. The ego takes into itself precisely that which can never be appropriated: the daemonic structure of repetition, the other of "life death" itself. The ego sends its destructive drive toward an object, but meeting resistance of one sort or another (love, hate, sublimation, identification), it appropriates that destructive drive into itself and creates conscience. And this is how "the drive of the proper" functions as it conjoins and disrupts life death's relation to time's other.

Derrida's daemonic figures of sending and receiving have, of course, Lacanian and Heideggerian echoes. In a remarkable passage in *Civilization and Its Discontents* (1930) Freud anticipates them all:

> [The individual's] aggressiveness is introjected, internalized; it is, in point of fact, sent back to where it came from [*aber dorthin zurückgeschichkt*]—that is, it is directed towards his own ego. There it is taken over by a portion of the ego, which sets itself over against the rest of the ego as super-ego, which now, in the form of "conscience," is ready to put into action against the ego the same harsh aggressiveness that the ego would have liked to satisfy upon the other, extraneous individuals. The tension between the harsh super-ego and the ego that is subjected to it, is called by us the sense of guilt; it expresses itself as a need for punishment. Civilization, therefore, obtains mastery over the individual's dangerous desire for aggression by weakening and disarming it and by setting up an agency [*Instanz*] within him to watch over it, like a garrison in a conquered city. (*SE* 21:123)

The ego is like a conquered city watched over by the garrison tower of conscience. It is a wonderful image with a rich typology in the history of conscience. What is novel here, however, is that the domination of conscience takes place through a process that is like nothing so much as the post office's return of undeliverable mail to the sender. As Lacan recognized, "The Purloined Letter" is an allegory of conscience; indeed, all of Poe's writing is given over to the daemonic figures of conscience. The letter of conscience is precisely what returns in reverse form, as the ego's delusions of the grandeur of appropriation turn out to be the very means of its own expropriating demise. Poe's marvelous definition of conscience as "the unfathomable longing of the soul to vex itself"[17] might serve as a cipher of the abyssal temporality that is so essential to the effort to think the inexhaustible "question" of conscience.

A few pages later in *Civilization and Its Discontents,* Freud turns to what he calls here the "paradoxical" problem surrounding "the history of the origin of conscience." The problem is that although he knows "that conscience (or more correctly, the anxiety which later becomes conscience) is indeed the cause of instinctual renunciation to begin with, . . . later the relationship is reversed. Every renunciation of instinct now becomes a dynamic source of conscience and every fresh renunciation increases the latter's severity and intolerance" (*SE* 21:128). All these issues will return again in *Moses and Monotheism,* but the interesting thing is Freud's insistence here on the fundamental connection between conscience and the idea of return and reversal, of a recursive cycle of delays and concealments all of which are inexorably moving the subject back to a more primordial temporality.

Freud's articulation of his notion of the "uncanny" (*Unheimliche*) revolves around the motif of returning to the maternal body and its homelike (*heimlich*) incarnations (cf. "The Uncanny," 1917). But what does it mean to return home, to return to another time and place, to "an earlier state of things"? It means, above all, encountering obstacles and resistances that prevent us from such an

17. Edgar Allan Poe, "The Black Cat," 393.

intense satisfaction; it means, in other words, encountering the daemonic figures that stand between us and the possession of the primordial essence. Conscience is an inseparable part of the uncanny, the point of an irreducible doubling between what is most familiar and what is most unfamiliar, and the split within the ego between the demand for satisfaction and the sometimes even more powerful internal refusal of such satisfaction.

Conscience is always linked in Freud's thinking with the internal resistance to oedipal desire. We feel guilt because we have internalized the oedipal interdiction, which effectively functions, as Derrida remarked, like an automaton. All object-cathexes that hold out the promise of oedipal satisfaction become potential candidates for appropriation by the ego-structures and for transformation into the destructive force of conscience. Any object of desire can theoretically become the occasion for a crisis of conscience, since anything that approximates the ideal oedipal homecoming can trigger the most intense resistance. This is the thesis Freud pursues in his reading of *Macbeth* and other works of art in "Some Character-Types Met With in Psycho-Analytic Work" (1915), in which he discusses patients and literary figures who suffer the crippling effects of the "forces of conscience" (*Gewissenskräfte*) precisely at the moment of their greatest success, because the achievement of a long-sought goal can bring with it a return to the severity of the oedipal prohibition. Conscience denies one the pleasure of success precisely because the satisfaction achieved reactivates the unconscious memory of one's oedipal wishes, which must in effect be repressed all over again.

In the contemporaneous paper "Thoughts on War and Death" (1915), Freud predictably describes the invention of spirits and daemons in primordial human history as the result of oedipal guilt. But what is interesting about his account is the way it links the invention of the daemon to the work of mourning. We mourn in order to work through the ambivalence of our feelings for the dead, to work through the tangle of love and hate, of conscious and unconscious memory that is reactivated by death. Though this essay precedes the theory of the death drive and Freud's related speculations on mourning and conscience in the Wolf Man case history and in the closely related essay "Mourning and Melancholia" (1917), we may see his account here of the invention of the daemon as already naming the work of death. For what is the death drive, finally, but the incessant, interminable work of mourning for the loss of that which is absolutely earlier than all origins, the relentless effort to idealize this absolutely unidealizable loss? And is that not what our effort to give ourselves moral imperatives is all about: an impossible effort to bring the endless work of mourning to an end? In "Thoughts on War and Death" it is precisely the ambivalence of the mourner's feelings that produces the daemon:

> It was beside the dead body of someone he loved that he invented spirits, and his sense of guilt at the satisfaction mingled with his sorrow turned these new-born spirits into evil demons that had to be dreaded. . . . His persisting memory of the dead [*Die fortdauernde Erinnerung*] became the basis for assuming other forms of existence and gave him the conception of a life continuing after apparent death. . . . What came into existence beside the dead body of the loved one was not only the doctrine of the soul, the belief in immortality and a powerful source of man's guilt, but also the earliest ethical commandments. The first and most important prohibition made by the awakening conscience was "Thou shalt not kill." It was acquired in relation to dead people who were loved, as a reaction against the satisfaction of the hatred hidden behind the grief for them; and it was gradually extended to strangers who were not loved, and finally even to enemies. (*SE* 14:294–95)

This wartime essay rehearses the thesis of *Totem and Taboo* concerning the idealizing return of the murdered *Urvater,* who was hated precisely because he barred access to the females, including the mother. The daemon emerges as a figure for the internalized resistance against any simulacrum of the satisfaction that one might attain by overcoming this prohibition. Now that the prohibiting agent is dead, the promise of satisfaction returns only to be repressed once again by the internal daemon of conscience. Freud's thesis is clear: we give ourselves moral laws in the process of idealizing the ambivalence we experience in the work of mourning. But the very effort to bring mourning to an end succeeds only in continuing the struggle of ambivalent feelings—only now the struggle has been fully internalized as the individual becomes convinced that the law originates within the self. The subsequent history of philosophy and religion continues this concealment of the temporal index of the law by reaffirming its timelessness or its divine origins. Freud depicts the work of mourning as the demonization of the daemon, the idealization of ambivalence, and the transforming reversal of oedipal guilt into the higher pleasures of the moral law. But all this can, of course, be undone, and the revenging daemon can return as the destructive conscience of the troubled patient.

The Freudian account of the daemon remains in the shadow of the Hebraic, Judeo-Christian tradition even as Freud radically reinvents that tradition and enables us to grasp more fully the natural and historical origins of the moral law and the dynamics of internalization. Despite the naturalizing and historicizing motivations of Freud's analysis, we have throughout focused on the persistence in his writing of a temporal question concerning the origin of conscience, which can be reduced neither to historical nor to natural time. We have, in other words, constantly indicated those points in Freud's texts where guilt is linked to time and Being. Might we regard this as the persistence of a certain Hellenic orientation within Freud's thinking?

Heidegger and Plato's *Periakteon*

I alluded earlier (in "The Daemon's Ghostly Secret") to Heidegger's innovative rendering of the saying by Heraclitus concerning the *daimon* as the *ethos* of human existence: "The abode of man contains and preserves the advent of what belongs to man in his essence. According to Heraclitus's phrase this is *daimon, the god.*"[18] This topological interpretation of the daemonic world, the *daimonion,* is pursued at greater length in Heidegger's 1942 seminar on Parmenides, where he suggests that the ancient Greek understanding of *daimonion* is best rendered by the German *unheimlich.* In view of the 1946 comment on the Heraclitean daemon, we might say that man's essential abode is the uncanny and that the task of thinking the ancient Greek daemon requires a certain homecoming to the strangest of all dwelling places.

Heidegger's brief but extraordinary discussion of the daemonic dwelling place in his 1942 seminar occurs in the context of a reading of the myth of Er at the end of Plato's *Republic.* Because the objective of this chapter is to present a theoretical horizon against which to project Shakespeare's place in the history of the fables about conscience, I want to approach Heidegger's contribution very carefully by first setting, as it were, the Platonic stage. I do not use this expression by accident; to the contrary, what I mean to suggest is precisely that Plato's *Republic* is organized around a dramatic and theatrical device whose importance has never, to my knowledge, been recognized. That it culminates in the *daimonion topos,* in the "daemonic place," might lead one to conclude that the place of the stage is the "daemonic place" par excellence. Neither Shakespeare or Heidegger is interested in this aspect of Plato's text, and I am not concerned with the question of influence. What I mean to suggest is something at once far more sweeping and far more intricate: namely, that the place of philosophical thought and the place of the stage are not in fact the traditional enemies that the Platonic tradition has always assumed them to be. The question of returning to an irreducible but enigmatic temporality, to what Heidegger and Freud both (though for very different reasons) call "the uncanny," defines the context in which my reading of Shake-

18. Heidegger, "Letter on Humanism," 233.

speare's poetic dramaturgy can be most fully realized. The massive and decisive turn that Heidegger wants to put into effect in our thinking about the nature of conscience, the utter and complete turning away from the spiritual, Pauline reading of the divine spark in the human breast, is an effort to return to an ancient sense of the daemonic world that Plato had already begun to abandon. And for Heidegger the primal scene of that tragic turning away from the daemonic place was, of course, *The Republic,* the very text where the daemon makes one of its last curtain calls.

Shakespeare, as we will see, is caught in a caesura, a break or interval between the Hebraic strictures on guilty conscience and the Hellenic affirmation of humankind's uncanny home in the daemonic world. Freud was a great reader of Shakespeare and tried to pull him into the gravitational field of Judeo-Christian guilt. But Heidegger also read Shakespeare, and we will look closely at his subtle and hitherto unnoticed Shakespearean allusions.

According to Heidegger, Plato's *Republic* sets into motion a "turning in the determination of the essence of truth" in Western philosophy.[19] Plato begins to turn away from the daemonic place to which Heidegger is trying to return. In view of our discussion of Freud, such a return would be tantamount to reversing nothing less than the internalization of the oedipal prohibition itself, or, what may amount to the same thing, insisting that such an internalization never really occurred. From a Freudian perspective, Heidegger would be insisting that the imperative character of the language of moral law, regardless of what deep structural transformations it may have worked in the human mind over the centuries, is capable of being substantially erased. And once that is out of the way, the delusory guilt under which we have labored, with all its inbuilt obstacles and resistances, would no longer block our access to the oedipal object par excellence: Being itself. This is basically Jean-François Lyotard's assessment of Heidegger: that in his cultivation

---

19. Martin Heidegger, "Plato's Doctrine of Truth," 251 (translation modified).

of Being, Heidegger "totally ignored" the Mosaic law that prohibits access to the Law.[20] This is an appealing reading that lends itself readily to any number of convenient oppositions, such as the Hebrew/ Hellene opposition to which I have alluded. The problem is that such oppositions are never adequate to the actual nature of the texts in question. As we have seen, Freud's Hebraism crosses silently but decisively into Hellenism. This is true as well for Heidegger, who is perhaps more concerned with the Mosaic prohibition of access to the Law, and with the incontrovertibility of the ensuing separation, than is any other thinker of modernity, including Freud. Heidegger thinks the "beyond" of Being as an untraversable gap or default. When Heidegger is determined to overcome is the delusory internalization of a nonexistent spiritual principle that has always posed as law. By advocating that we surmount this historical aberration, he is by no means suggesting that we thereby surmount the default of Being itself. Heidegger introduces Oedipus to ontology.

In seeking to turn back to the daemonic place, Heidegger is not advocating the intellectual equivalent to incest but, on the contrary, is reinscribing the resistances and the obstacles to grasping the maternal body of Being, and of what gives Being and time, in radically new and desubjectivized ways; he is resituating the very place of the law of separation, which can no longer be conceived psychologically. In this sense, it is Freudianism that remains under the sway of the domination of *aletheia,* or the unconcealment of truth, by the *eidos,* or the intellectual activity of the human subject. We needed a great deal of close reading and some ideas from Derrida to extricate Freud from this unhappy scenario. What we are going to do now is to extricate Plato from Heidegger's animadversions.

In order to appreciate Heidegger's commentary on the daemonic *topos* at the end of *The Republic,* we will have to backtrack to the initial appearance of the daemon in *The Republic.* It occurs just

20. Cf. Jean-François Lyotard, *Heidegger and the "jews,"* esp. 80, 85, 89.

after Socrates begins to announce the terms that will organize the allegory of the cave, which he is about to unfold. It is the allegory of (at least) two suns: the physical sun that rules over the sensory *topos* that is the world of nature, and the invisible sun that Socrates calls "the idea of the good" (*agathon idean*), 508E), which illuminates the realm of intelligibility. When Socrates claims that this latter sun is as generative in its world as the physical sun is in the natural world, Glaucon cries out, "Oh Apollo, what daemonic hyperbole" (*daimonias hyperboles,* 509C). Paul Shorey's translation reads: "hyperbole can go no further," and Glaucon surely means something like: "what an outlandish hyperbole." But the allusion to the daemon is crucial, for it is precisely toward the outer reaches of the daemonic world that Plato will take us from this point on. We come closest to Plato's sense here by reading Socrates' allegory of the cave as not only anticipating but in fact situated in the daemonic underworld to which we will be led by Er's story or *muthos*. Both myths are daemonic in the fundamental sense that Heidegger will describe later.

Though the allegory is very familiar, I am going to focus on some very unfamiliar elements. Socrates describes a cave whose inhabitants are bound, unable to move, and permitted to look only at the wall of the cave in front of them: "Picture further the light from a fire [*pyros*] burning higher up and at a distance behind them" (514B). Between the denizens of the cave and the fire behind them is a kind of partition or parapet on which other, unbound denizens are moving back and forth holding various objects. The visual world of the bound prisoners consists solely of the shadows of these objects. For reasons Socrates does not go into, certain prisoners are freed from their chains and are dragged "by force up the ascent [and] out into the light of the sun [*helios*]" (515E). In the terms of the allegory, the *pyros* is the natural sun, while the *helios* is the intelligible sun beyond nature. *Helios* is, in other words, at once the sun and not the sun. It is important that we note the slippage that takes place in Plato's use of *helios:* in the allegory it is a visible light; in Socrates' interpretation of the language of the allegory what was a visible, and indeed blinding, *helios* becomes the "hardly visible" (*mogis horashthai*) sun of "the good." We have, then, two turns in the allegory: the first, from the wall to the fire; the second, from the fire to the sun. The allegory depends, of course, upon a turning, through language, from the natural to the intelligible world. Without this turning we do not reach the daemonic world, and this turning depends, as we have seen, on the double or allegorical meanings that are attributed to *pyros* and *helios*. Everything relies upon the efficacy of Socrates' metaphoric use of *helios*, which means that the word itself is the site of a turning from the merely figurative nature of sensation to the literality of intellection. We will want to focus first on the nature of the turning within the sun beyond the world of things and physical sensation, and second on the metaphor Socrates will use to clarify what he means by this culminating inward turn toward "the good beyond being." Socrates' insistence on the inadequacy of the allegory of the cave and on the need for the true metaphor will result not only in the emergence of a theatrical metaphor that will interest us throughout the rest of *Daemonic Figures* but also in an essential insight into the nature of metaphor itself.

Derrida's observation about the heliotropic nature of the sun as the paradigmatic metaphor, the metaphor of metaphor, could not be more relevant here: "[The sun] is the paradigm of the sensory *and* of metaphor: it regularly turns (itself) and hides (itself). . . . Thus, metaphor means heliotrope, both a movement turned toward the sun and the turning movement of the sun."[21] The sun is the sensory object par excellence and yet at the same time, as Derrida remarks, is always "improperly known" and thus always "improperly named." The concealment of the essence of the sun is itself essential and insurmountable. That turning away of the essence, its gathering of itself into itself, is constitutive of the paradigmatic.

21. Jacques Derrida, "White Mythology," 250–51.

Language cannot reverse the fundamental concealment of that turning but can instead turn toward it. Insofar as all metaphor is based on the sun, all metaphor is based on this concealment, which renders null and void the very promise of metaphor to enable us to "cross over" via the transport of resemblance. We can always, of course, pretend that our metaphors are literal and that our poetic language is really scientific or sacred. But to do so is to fail to recognize the truth of the resistance to knowledge that metaphor really does illuminate. Since heliotropic metaphor is actually based on an incontrovertible nonresemblance, (because we do not know the essence of *helios*), it initiates a turning without any possibility of either closure or knowledge. What metaphor does provide, however, is the quite literal nonknowledge and resistance of the turning in which the sun itself is seized; metaphor enables us to turn, through language, toward the literality of that primordial and irreversible turning of essence away from knowledge and language. In this sense, metaphor does "bring across" the truth of its nontruth.

In the Parmenides seminar, Heidegger will call this the essence of the daemonic. It allows things to appear not simply before the mind but in the world. But in the midst of all that comes to presence is a fundamental concealment, and that is the realm toward which Socrates turns via his "daemonic hyperbole" par excellence, which, as we shall see, is not the inward turning of the mind in the allegory of the cave but a piece of stage machinery called the *periakteon*. The inward turning of the eye of knowledge toward "the good beyond Being" (*agathon epekeina tes ousias,* 509B) is an irreducibly metaphoric turn toward an insurmountable concealment. Metaphor turns us toward a literal turning in which what lies beyond Being turns away from all that is in Being, and which we are perfectly free to misrecognize, which we can pretend to see as something present, as Socrates and many others have. The turning of metaphor within *helios* and toward *agathon* leads us toward Plato's culminating allegory of language, which involves the *periakteon.* In its turning away from the light of *helios* as the sun and toward the allegorical signification of *helios* as *agathon,* the eye presumably becomes itself the source of light or draws on an inner light source no longer dependent on the sun of nature. This is the effect of metaphor, but it is not simply a nontruth or error, for what has literally occurred is a turning toward the power of metaphor itself to posit a world that lies beyond phenomenality. The positing power of language to reveal that *there is* the "other" of phenomenality, the realm of the hiddenness of the sun's essence, is metaphor in the fundamental sense that Heidegger calls daemonic. Metaphor in the weak sense presumes to describe the resemblance between the phenomenal world and its other, when in fact it is literally turning us toward an intractable nonresemblance.

Diogenes Laertius, in his *Lives of the Philosophers,* tells the proverbial story of Socrates demanding that Plato commit himself to philosophy by burning the manuscript of his tragedy. It is a wonderful story and perhaps not unrelated to the extraordinary thing that Socrates says as he turns, once again, to yet another metaphor in order to make it still clearer exactly what he means in the allegory when he speaks of the turning of the eye toward the realms of thought. The following passage contains perhaps the most paradoxical metaphor in the Platonic corpus and certainly the most decisive one in *The Republic:*

> But our present argument indicates that the true analogy for this indwelling power in the soul and the instrument whereby each of us apprehends is that of an eye that could not be converted to the light from the darkness except by turning the whole body. Even so this organ of knowledge must be turned around from the world of becoming together with the entire soul, like the scene-shifting periact [*periakteon*] in the theatre, until the soul is able to endure the contemplation of essence and the brightest region of being. (518C–D)

There were two turnings in the allegory of the cave, and both of them were figures for the heliotropic turning of metaphor. And now

Socrates turns to yet another metaphor: "the scene-shifting periact in the theatre." The daemonic figures of language are turning toward the irreducible yet undiscoverable realm beyond Being itself, and what comes to Socrates' mind, to what does he turn? A piece of long-forgotten machinery of the ancient Greek stage. The theater provides at this critical moment the metaphor for the metaphor of metaphor. The *periakteon* is the daemonic sun of language itself. There can be no end to reading this passage, for there is no end to the literal turnings that this metaphor sets into motion. The periact is the primary daemonic figure in *The Republic,* for all comings and goings between sensation and intellection depend exclusively upon its functioning. At the center of Platonism's primal scene burns the slowly turning heliotropic sun of the tragic stage.

At the decisive juncture in Plato's text, at precisely the point where one would expect a metaphor of subjectivizing interiority, Plato turns not to an image that describes the dialectical sublation of self-consciousness into its self-negating realization as a higher form of knowledge but rather to the sheerly mechanical operation of the periact. In the place of the internalizing, uplifting imagery of dialectical recovery, at the point of the crucial turning toward the *eidos,* Plato's thinking turns to what is, in effect, the automatic functioning of stage machinery. Further still, since the entire allegory describes the workings of language that make it possible for human cognition to turn to the sun of truth, the periact, as Plato's quintessential daemonic figure for the comings and goings between gods and humans, is nothing other than a metaphor for the materiality of language itself, which remains utterly external to cognition and sensation even as it makes possible the translation from one to the other. At the moment of the greatest event in the Platonic corpus, what comes on the stage is nothing less than the mechanical structure of the stage itself. The periact is the daemonic figure of an irreducible otherness that dwells at once deep within and yet at an impossible distance from self-consciousness.

For Plato the eye becomes sunlike, when in fact it is language, and more precisely metaphor, that literally becomes sunlike; and of course being sunlike is itself a metaphor for whatever it is that a sun could possibly be like, for whatever it is that lies beyond the sun, beyond all the suns, beyond Being itself. Plato forgets the positing power of metaphor, its absolute otherness, its daemonic character, and appropriates it for subjective reflection. But his text gives it to be read in all its mystery. And he will not forget the periact through which he forgetfully turned away from the turning of metaphor, for it will re-turn as the ur-metaphor in the myth of Er.

But what is a periact? Its unfamiliarity to modern readers has left this crucial passage in Plato essentially unread. Though Socrates alludes to the singular *periakteon,* there were apparently two *periaktoi* at the front of the stage, one on either side. Since they are for Socrates analogies for the turning of the eye inward, he might just as easily have alluded to two periacts, one for each eye. This movement from two eyes to one "organ of knowledge" is part of the turning itself in which the power of language to make entities appear becomes confused with the physiology of the human body. Plato might have been thinking of two periacts because of the anthropomorphic analogy they afforded but reduced them to a singular periact in recognition of the singular turning that was in fact at stake here. In their still definitive account of the ancient Greek theater, A. E. Haigh and A. W. Pickard-Cambridge describe the *periaktoi:*

> These were huge triangular prisms, revolving on a socket at the base. Each of the three sides of the prisms consisted of a large flat surface, shaped like an upright parallelogram. One of these prisms was placed at each end of the stage, in such a manner as to fit exactly with the scene at the back, and continue it in the direction of the side-wings. Each of the three sides was painted to present a different view, but in every case the painting should coincide exactly with the painting in the back-scene. As the periaktos was turned round, it presented a different surface to the

spectators. . . . The principal use of the periaktoi must have been to produce a change of scene in cases where the prominent feature of the background remained the same.[22]

In their learned and arcane list of references in the ancient world to the *periaktoi,* Haigh and Pickard-Cambridge do not mention *The Republic,* though it is infinitely better known than all the texts to which they do allude. Everyone remembers the exile of the poets, but no one remembers the periact. We must learn to reverse the pattern and henceforth take the former much less seriously than the latter.

Haigh and Pickard-Cambridge also note that one or both periacts could be employed to indicate a scene change on only one side of the stage or to distinguish a change of scene within a district from a more radical change of scene. But I find particularly fascinating their description of an additional use of the periact beyond the shifting of scenes: "Besides their use in effecting a change of scene, the periaktoi were also employed to introduce sea-gods and objects too heavy for the mechane. It is not said how this was managed. But it is possible that, of the two sides of the periaktos which were out of sight of the audience, one contained a small ledge or balcony, on which the sea-god took his stand. As the machine rolled round, he would suddenly come into view."[23] Is it not possible, or perhaps even likely, that Plato, the former tragedian, might have been thinking of this "small ledge or balcony" when, in the allegory of the cave, Socrates speaks of those mysterious figures carrying objects on the parapet behind the prisoners?

Regardless of such speculations, what is certain is that the periact gives us an entirely new sense of that celebrated "old quarrel" (*pallai diaphora,* 607B) between philosophy and poetry. The disjunctive conjunction or *diaphora* between philosopher and poet consists not so much in the latter's inability to restrain the emotions he excites as in the former's pretense to be in possession of the

22. A. E. Haigh and A. W. Pickard-Cambridge, *The Attic Theatre,* 197–98.
23. Ibid., 199.

daemon, to have internalized it and placed it in the service of the *eidos*. The poet is more tolerant of the daemon's unpredictability and its irreducible externality. In the myth of Er, Plato the poet once again—and perhaps for the last time in his career—gains the upper hand over Plato the philosopher and acknowledges the un-internalizable enigma of the daemon. Socrates has the temerity to say that poetic mimesis is poisonous for those "who do not possess as a *pharmakon* a knowledge of its real nature" (598B). Everything Jacques Derrida has said about the *pharmakon* in Plato's thinking is applicable here,[24] for all philosophy's ruses of subjectivization can be exposed as soon as the daemonic figures of language, like the *pharmakon* and the *periakteon,* once again become readable as figures of a fundamental contamination of philosophy by poetry.

Conscience is one of the names for coming into relation with the daemonic power of metaphor and for being drawn into its field of force. It is in the myth of the warrior Er that Plato returns to the turning of the periact, which has now become part of the most immense turning imaginable, the rotation of universal space-time around the spindle that Er calls the *atrakton*. From the *periakteon* to the *atrakton,* from the theater of the mind to the theater of the cosmos itself, the power of language to turn the mind becomes itself one of the effects, one of the wheels, motors, and springs, in a larger turning that originates beyond Being and that causes all the regions of Being to rotate at its bidding. Er describes the passage of his soul after death back to the "daemonic region" (*topon daimonion,* 614C) from which all souls originate. On the way to this region, Er and the souls glimpse the cosmos in its entirety, which appears as they approach it like a "revolving vault," a spinning pillar of light:

> They discerned, extended from above throughout the heaven and the earth, a straight light like a pillar, most nearly resembling the rainbow, but brighter and purer. To this they came after going forward a day's journey, and they saw there at the middle of the

24. See Jacques Derrida, "Plato's Pharmacy."

light the extremities of its fastenings stretched from heaven; for this light was the girdle of the heavens like the undergirders of triremes, holding together in like manner the entire revolving vault. And from the extremities was stretched the spindle of Necessity [*Anankes atrakton*], through which all the orbits turned. (616C)

As they approach the pillar of light, they can see that it consists of many streams of light that hold the entire cosmos together the way the ribbing and "undergirders" reinforce the hull of a ship ("trireme"). All of the orbits, which include that of the Earth, the Sun, the stars or fixed planets, and the planets themselves, all of which constitute separate disks or whorls, eight in all, rotate around the cosmic periact. The vault of the cosmos, ribbed with girders of light, turned by the periact-like *atrakton,* as though the periact were no longer on the side of the stage but had now become the driveshaft turning the stage itself. The transformations of time and space, of the natural world, and of human history and thought would thus all appear as shifting scenes under the direction of the enigmatic dramaturgy of the force that turns the spindle.

The goal, however, is the daemonic fields of *lethe,* or oblivion, where, as Heidegger says, "the whole wandering is gathered."[25] As the souls move beyond the cosmos toward the daemonic underworld and toward the origin of the spinning of the world spindle, they pass through fire before they reach what Heidegger calls "the district of the uncanny." The souls reach the fields of the daemonic place and drink of the waters of its river. Heidegger reads the myth as an allegory of the attainment of philosophical vision. There are some elements of the myth itself to which he does not attend, but we shall. And it is precisely these mythic, poetic elements, these traces of Plato the tragedian, that seem to me worth mentioning, especially because Plato employs them to describe the origin of the daemon.

25. Martin Heidegger, *Parmenides,* 118.

The *atrakton* extends beyond the whorls that it sets into motion. One end of the spindle lies in the lap of Necessity and is turned by the daughters of Necessity. It is in this "turning of the spindle" (*epistrophe ton atrakton*) that we find the mythic origin of the daemon: "And Lachesis sent with each [of the souls], as the guardian of his life and fulfiller of his choice, the *daimon* that he had chosen, and this divinity led the soul first to Clotho, under her hand and her turning of the spindle to ratify the destiny of his lot and his choice" (620E). Lachesis sends the daemon in response to the soul's choice; Clotho ratifies the choice; and Atropos makes the bond between soul and daemon irreversible. In lieu of an idea or a concept concerning the origin of the daemon, Plato leaves us with an enigmatic myth, the revelation that at the origin of the daemon and its relation to the soul lies a fundamental concealment that remains outside time, space, and subjectivity.

For Heidegger this myth is something like Plato's parting glance at the moment of a great change: "About the time that the Greeks departed from their essential history, they expressed once more the legend of the counter-essence of *aletheia*, the *muthos* of *lethe*."[26] This is an extraordinary insight into the beauty and pathos of *The Republic*, for at the culminating moment of the dialogue's inexorable turning toward the origin of the daemonic place, Plato presents not the unconcealment of the daemon but its intractable "counter-essence," the trace of an absolute oblivion. By attending to the "scene-shifting periact," we sought not so much to counter as to stagger and complicate Heidegger's characterization of *The Republic* as the site of "the unstated occurrence whereby the idea became master of aletheia."[27] By linking the *periakteon* to the *atrakton*, we confirm Heidegger's notion in the Parmenides seminar that *The Republic* indeed poses the "question" of the daemon precisely by refusing any internalization of the meaning of Being and by affirming the "counter-essence" that belongs to the *lethe* of the *daimon*:

26. Ibid., 100.
27. Heidegger, "Plato's Doctrine of Truth," 265.

"*Lethe,* in Plato's 'myth,' is the *daimonion* of a field that resides not in the here but in the there. This field is the ultimate thoroughfare, where the wanderers must stop immediately prior to their transition out of the there into the here."[28]

Heidegger also insists that the unmasterable counter-essence of *aletheia* cannot be characterized as something specifically "literary."[29] Perhaps, though, as we have seen, it was a specifically literary experience that enabled Plato to write his account of the turning toward philosophical vision. Plato's memory of the stage becomes, however, entirely transformed and placed in the service of a philosophical inquiry, and more important, in the service of thinking. I want only to mark the crossings between literature and philosophy without privileging either vis-à-vis the question of conscience. The realization that conscience and the daemon lead toward a fundamental concealment can be achieved or obstructed by both philosophy and literature. The task in any case is that of thinking the question rather than presuming to have discovered an answer.

Plato teaches us that the daemonic place is the stage of thinking, which is to say that theater in the essential sense is the region of the uncanny. What comes to light in the appearance of the light is the invisible, uncanny, counter-essence of what light makes visible: "That which is lighted, however, is not only what is visible and seeable, but prior to that—as the emerging—it is what surveys everything that comes into the light and stays in it and lies in it."[30] The daemon is that invisible uncanniness which "looks out" (*deion*) at us from the visible itself. The truth of madness and the madness of truth are stretched along the continuum of the *to deion* as Being itself, fundamental concealment, looks out at us from the extraordinariness of the ordinary. Maurice Blanchot calls it "the madness of the day." All of Lacanian psychoanalysis is contained

28. Heidegger, *Parmenides*, 123.
29. Ibid., 122.
30. Ibid., 102.

within these pages of Heidegger's seminar, which provide, among other things, a philological understanding for the daemon as the witness, the one who watches: in other words, conscience in the most conventional sense. For it is above all in the daemon as "the *silent word*" that Heidegger is interested. Art brings us before the daemon, but it does so only because the word is already there: "If there were not the *silent word*, then the looking god as sight of the statue and of the features of its figure could never appear."[31]

Here we revisit all the issues concerning the daemonic figures of language: "In *muthos* the *daimonion* appears. Just as the word and 'having the word' sustain the essence of man, i.e., the relation of Being to man, so in the same range of essence, i.e., in relation to the whole of being, the *daimonion* determines the basic relation of Being to man." For Plato and Aristotle the word for this relation is *eudaimonia,* not in Paul's sense but in the sense of "the appearing and coming into presence of the *daimonion*": "This is not a 'spirit' dwelling somewhere within the breast. The Socratic-Platonic talk of the *daimonion* as the inner voice signifies only that its attuning and determining do not come from the outside, i.e., from some being at hand, but from the invisible and ungraspable Being itself, which is closer to man than any obtrusive manipulatable being."[32] And the ungraspable place where this uncanny daemon appears from out of its absolutely enigmatic dwelling place is language itself.

31. Ibid., 116.
32. Ibid., 117.

2 Shakespeare in the History of Being

> The inner and invisible domain of the heart is not only more
> inward than the interior that belongs to calculating repre-
> sentation, and therefore more invisible; it also extends fur-
> ther than does the realm of merely producible objects. . . .
> The interior of uncustomary consciousness remains the in-
> ner space in which everything is for us beyond the arithme-
> tic of calculation, and, free of such boundaries, can over-
> flow into the unbounded whole of the Open.
> —MARTIN HEIDEGGER, "What Are Poets For?"

> (A closet never pearst with christall eyes)
> —WILLIAM SHAKESPEARE, Sonnet 46

In *Being and Time* conscience keeps silent because it has something
to say: "Only in keeping silent does the conscience call; that is to
say, the call comes from the soundlessness of uncanniness, and the
Dasein which it summons is called back into the stillness of itself"
(*Being and Time*, 342/296). Heidegger's interest is not in the everyday "existentiell" conscience of traditional ontotheology, which
gives moral judgments and which we experience as our most immediate and incontrovertible self-relation, but in the "existential-
ontological foundations of conscience" that sustain what Heidegger regards as the most primordial and essential ground of Dasein's
understanding of itself and its world. Although the ontotheological
interpretation of conscience adduced this mode of understanding as
a basis for "proofs of God or for establishing an 'immediate' consciousness of God" (313/269), Heidegger regards the silent discourse that comes to us in the call of conscience as the daemonic
figure for the fundamental mystery that is Dasein's relation to Be-

ing. Conventional interpretations identify the caller as God or family or the ambient values of the social-historical moment; Heidegger believes that these ways of posing the question "Who's calling?" are misleading and determines instead to regard the call as the cipher of Dasein's most fundamental relation to itself: "*What if this Dasein, which finds itself in the very depths of its uncanniness, should be the caller of the call of conscience?*" (321/276). It is thus that Dasein calls itself away from its "lostness in the they-self" and comes into its "ownmost potentiality for Being," which throughout *Being and Time* is synonymous with the enigmatic word *Sorge,* usually translated as "care." It is the keyword of *Being and Time* where it names the impasse that the existential analytic of Dasein invariably runs into as it tries to articulate Dasein's relation to Being: "The call of conscience—that is, conscience itself—has its ontological possibility in the fact that Dasein, in the very basis of its Being, is care" (322–23/278).

The Daemon and the Gift

As the translators of *Being and Time* remark in a footnote: "The etymological connection between 'Sorge' ('care'), 'Fürsorge' ('solicitude'), and 'Besorgen' ('concern'), is entirely lost in our translation" (157 n. 4). Dasein's relation to itself, to Being, to others, and to the things in its world are all characterized, in one way or another, by this cluster of terms, which are all generated from the root word *die Sorge*. Indeed, Division I of *Being and Time* culminates in a medieval Latin allegorical fable, *Cura:* "Since 'Care' first shaped this creature [the human being], she shall possess it as long as it lives" (242/198). "*Sorge,*" writes Heidegger, "as a primordial structural totality, lies 'before' [*vor*] every factical 'attitude' and 'situation' of Dasein, and it does so existentially *a priori*" (238/193). Dasein— which is not the self but rather our most intimate and enigmatic sense of existence, that which stands behind consciousness and selfhood and makes them possible—experiences its "thrownness," its "fallenness" in the world, as anxious anticipation, as a being that constantly awaits some clarification about how and what it is. Dasein's "being-in-the-world is essentially care" because Dasein is always "ahead-of-itself," always "beyond itself," always relating and assessing everything it does vis-à-vis its "ownmost potentiality-for-Being." The radical individuation of existence that is at the heart of *Being and Time* is itself suspended within the enigmatic structural totality of care, of that which holds together the always dispersed and fragmented bits of Dasein's being-in-the-world. Care holds together the disjointed fittings through which every Dasein confronts its irreducible uncanniness, but it does not, for all that, endow them with a unity.

It is care that stands in the way of the project of a fundamental ontology, and it is care that prevented Heidegger from completing *Being and Time* and ensured that his masterpiece took the form of an unfinished fragment. And so the call of conscience in which Dasein calls upon itself could only be the call of care. We expect, we wait, we are circumspect, we linger, we tarry, we are resolute, we do all of these things only insofar as Dasein experiences its world as care. But by the same token this strange thing called care, which destroys the possibility of any ontological determinations, marks the site of whatever it is that goes unthought in all our thinking and that remains unsaid in all our saying. Care is Heidegger's name for our relation to the persistent nonrelation between Dasein and Being. Care names our relation to a nonrelation, to something that is not there and that leaves no trace. Our dealings with other selves, other Daseins, with what is ready-to-hand, with equipment, and so on, are all suspended within the medium that *Being and Time* calls care. Whatever, in the final analysis, might be calling upon Dasein through the experience that Dasein has of its own inner voice must pass through the care in which Dasein is suspended.

To recognize the extent to which *Sorge* operates in *Being and Time* as a universal medium into which every other category of the existential analytic can be translated, to see at every turn that "the being of Dasein is care" (465/412), to realize that even Dasein's experience of space and time is a function of care, is to be reminded that Dasein's self-understanding can never get further than the almost mechanical repetition of the word *Sorge,* that Dasein is fundamentally cut off, suspended, curtailed, and limited from its ground. Because care stands at the center of the uncanniness into which Dasein is called by conscience, it is important to listen to this word and to try to hear the idiomatic tonality it gives to Heidegger's text in its fragmentary wholeness.

In the etymology of *Sorge,* the evidence is suggestive if not exactly compelling. This is what Friedrich Max Müller, the celebrated nineteenth-century philologist, had to say about *Sorge:* "*Sorrow* is the Anglo-Saxon *sorh,* the German *Sorge;* its supposed connection with *sorry* is merely imaginary, for the Anglo-Saxon for sorry is *sárig,* from *sár,* a wound, a sore." [1] To be sure, this is a fascinating cluster of root words, and their precise connection is doubtless a matter for debate. That *Sorge* is sorrow, if not a wound or sore, is suggestive of the general sense of lack and deprivation that is so central to *Being and Time*'s discovery about the radically individuated way in which we come to our sense of existence. "Relentlessly," writes Heidegger, "[the call of conscience] individualizes Dasein down to its potentiality-for-Being-guilty, and exacts of it that it should be this potentiality authentically. The unwavering precision with which Dasein is thus essentially individualized down to its ownmost potentiality-for-Being, discloses the anticipation of [*zum*] death as the possibility which is *nonrelational*" (354/307). The call of care "strikes" this nonrelational possibility into conscience. Conscience is the site whence care calls Dasein toward death. Could we call this "sore" the mark of castration, the inscription of the lack through which we come face to face with what we authentically are? Through the word *Sorge,* which is the essential

---

1. Max Müller, *Lectures on the Science of Language: Second Series,* 529.

daemonic figure of *Being and Time,* the lack in Being comes to presence as a sorrowful separation and, why not, as a wound in the text which never heals.

The wound has always been there; it is in the texts of the ontotheological tradition even as the unsaid on which what is said necessarily depends. Philosophy and theology have always been adrift in a sea of cares. We will look more closely at some of these poetic theologies in Chapter 3. But we should recall here that the medieval Schoolmen defined conscience as a kind of bifold entity in which conscience as natural law—that is, our dispositions and appetites and our ability to control them—was always at the mercy of conscience as *dictamen rationis,* the voice of theoretical reason sustained by the realm of the divine Idea. Our animal and rational desire were constantly being checked by the divine spark within us; natural law was constantly being put on trial before positive law. The elaboration of Pauline *syneidesis* by the Schoolmen (who introduced, as we shall see later, several quite irrelevant and regrettably influential complications) remained essentially intact until Kant, who utterly transformed this history and brought the interpretation of conscience to an entirely new level (see my final chapter). Kant begins to think the difference between theoretical and practical reason and between the spiritual and the corporeal thing. Though not yet the individualized event that is the Heideggerian call of conscience, the explicitly juridical setting of Kant's analysis provided a context in which the sorrow and care of the call somehow became discernible as something irreducible and pervasive—which is only to say that the scene of conscience is a scene of bearing witness and attestation. Conscience not only calls; it passes judgment, and it inflicts punishment. Conscience hurts, and if it doesn't, it's not conscience. That is what care and being-guilty are all about. The role of the daemon is that of bearing witness to the wound of care, for care is precisely the coming to presence of Dasein's irreparable sore.

While in *Being and Time* we are in the post-Nietzschean realm beyond good and evil, we are nevertheless still within the juridical scene of testifying and bearing witness. "The primordial 'Being-guilty' cannot be defined by morality," writes Heidegger, "since morality already presupposes it for itself. . . . And only because Dasein is guilty in the basis of its Being, and closes itself off from itself as something thrown and falling, is conscience possible, if indeed the call gives us *this Being-guilty* as something which at bottom we are to understand" (332/286). Although it is clear that, as care, the call "calls beyond the deed which has happened, and back to the Being-guilty into which one has been thrown, which is 'earlier' than any indebtedness" (337/291), what needs to be pointed out as essential to understanding the textuality of *Being and Time* is that care is like a judge calling Dasein to the bar. Not only does care name the enigmatic origin of the voice summoning us back to the primordial temporality that is properly our own; it names the very thing that does the summoning. In other words, the irreducibility of care and the summoning voice in the juridical scene are daemonic figures for the sheer materiality that is the summoning power of language itself as a radical nonpresence that enables Dasein to turn toward its abyssal essence. This is, of course, to read *Being and Time* in terms of the later Heidegger's thinking about the concealed essence of language.

"Characterizing conscience as a call," he writes, "is not just giving a 'picture,' like the Kantian representation of the conscience as a court of justice. Vocal utterance, however, is not essential for discourse, and therefore not for the call either; this must not be overlooked" (316/271). I am suggesting simply that the silent discourse that is the call of care is nevertheless inscribed within a juridical scene in a sense that depends on neither the visual nor the acoustic details but is juridical in the most fundamental sense, which involves the power of language to summon Dasein into its Being-guilty as care. The whole of Division II, section 2, of *Being and Time* is pervaded by the language of testimony and attestation, which Heidegger insists is not to be taken to mean that conscience is a court à la Kant. Heidegger does not believe "that the ontical way of understanding conscience must be recognized as the first court of appeal [*erste Instanz*] for an ontological Interpretation" (324/279). Despite his legalistic language of appeals and testimony, Heidegger seems convinced that his analysis is not inscribed within a courtroom setting. The alternating use of *Ruf* and *Aufruf,* call and summons, transforms the entire analysis into a play of the metaphorical and the literal. The question finally becomes, what is the difference between a literal courtroom and a metaphorical one? Dasein's attestation (*Bezeugung*) of its Being as care in the most primordial mode of Being-guilty is, among other things, an ontological *Instanz* of the law of Dasein's relation to language. The *for intérieur,* the inner court of conscience, is not something Heidegger either has escaped or should have felt a need to escape. On the contrary, he has traced it to its irreducible materiality as the invisible and silent power of the letter to call us to account.

Heidegger's court of conscience is situated in the uncanny, daemonic topology where Dasein is summoned to Being-guilty. This is, as Heidegger observes, a curious kind of summons: "Does not this way of interpreting the conscience lead to a complete perversion of its function? Does not a 'summons to Being-guilty' means a summons to evil?" (333/287). If I am called on to be guilty, then no doubt I am expected to go out and do something evil in order that my conscience will subsequently pass judgment on me: "Guilty!" But no, says Heidegger, this is not what he means: "Dasein need not first load a 'guilt' upon itself through its failures or omissions; it must only *be* 'guilty' *authentically*—'guilty' in the way in which it is." The nature of the call makes it possible to be misunderstood; the possibility of misunderstanding the call of care is fundamental. "Hearing the appeal correctly" calls forth Dasein's "authentic potentiality for becoming guilty": "This includes its *becoming free* for the call—its readiness [*Bereitschaft*] for the potentiality of getting appealed to" (334/288). Hearing the appeal incorrectly is tantamount to an incitement to riot. The call thus lies at the origin of good and evil. The word "readiness" will play a role in my reading of Heidegger and *Hamlet* in Chapter 3. We should note here, however, that Dasein's resoluteness before death and the enigmas of existence derives from a Shakespearean daemonic topology and that Heidegger recognized that it belongs in the secret court of care.

Care calls on Dasein to bear witness against itself, to impugn and accuse itself. The unfathomable origin of the call is not itself the witness but only summons Dasein's own capacity to testify against itself. "No one," writes Paul Celan, "bears witness for the / witness [*Niemand / zeugt für den / Zeugen*]."[2] Dasein as care, as that which bears witness against itself, is free-falling and groundless, without a principle of reason.

But Heidegger does provide an interesting characterization of the enigmatic "no one" who dwells near Dasein. The relevant passage does not, however, appear in the analysis of the call of conscience; it comes much earlier, in a discussion of Dasein's relation to discourse and, more exactly, within a discussion of the nonacoustic "hearing" that lies at the basis of Dasein's experience of language. "Hearing is constitutive for discourse, and just as linguistic utterance is based on discourse, so is acoustic perception on hearing," writes Heidegger. "Hearing constitutes the primary and authentic way in which Dasein is open for its ownmost potentiality-for-Being—as in hearing the voice of the friend whom every Dasein carries with it. Dasein hears, because it understands" (206/163). Dasein's ability to understand, to "hear," the silent voice of the friend lies at the basis of its ability to listen to discourse in the ontical world. Is it not this same friend whose voice will later call Dasein into the scene of conscience?

It is the friend that Dasein carries with itself, and not the voice, which rather lies between them: *der Stimme des Freundes, den jedes Dasein bei sich trägt*. By specifying that Dasein bears the friend with itself rather than the voice, Heidegger marks the irreducible

2. Paul Celan, "Ash-glory" (*Aschenglorie*).

otherness of the voice. Dasein carries the friend with itself, and the friend's voice lies somewhere between them. Might we not say that it is the friend who will subsequently "bear" witness against Dasein, precisely in its capacity as a friend, since its testimony enables Dasein to discover itself? Though Heidegger never makes the connection explicit, can there be any doubt that it is through the friend that care makes its call on Dasein, which is to say that it is through the friend's voice that Dasein calls upon itself? Derrida has recently suggested that this friend is not a "kind of witness," nor is it "the eye" or "the ear of conscience, for this voice is not interior."[3] But is not the topology of the voice prior to the very determination of the inside/outside binarism? As Derrida goes on to say, the topology of the friend "is neither the very close nor the infinitely distant."[4] The friend names the way Dasein and language are simultaneously articulated outside and inside each other; language is inside Dasein as its outside, and Dasein is inside language as its outside. The friend whom Dasein carries along with itself will, in bearing witness against Dasein, enable Dasein to realize the fundamental enigma of the "there" that it occupies.

Rather than disjoining the two passages, as Derrida's reading tends to do, I am suggesting that we juxtapose them in the fugal, recursive manner that characterizes the textuality of *Being and Time* in its fragmentary entirety, which proceeds throughout by introducing new terminology and categories in terms of an earlier terminology and thus slowly transforms its keywords while at the same time preserving them. It is because the friend cares about Dasein that it testifies against it. The friend occupies the enigmatic topology of Dasein's irreducible otherness. As Derrida remarks, the friend's voice "is really the voice of the other," and it is that voice in the fundamental sense of something that remains "other" within Dasein's very nature. The witness is the friend whom Dasein carries with itself into the abyssal temporality into which the call of care

3. Jacques Derrida, "Heidegger's Ear: Philopolemology (*Geschlecht* IV)," 175.
4. Ibid., 178.

leads it, leads them, together and yet separate. They are daemonic figures for the materiality of language that lies outside consciousness but enables consciousness to enter into its most intimate self-relation.

In his later works, Heidegger repeatedly juxtaposes the scene of the friend and what has now become the scene of poetic attestation, the scene in which, instead of Dasein's bearing witness to its uncanny otherness in the call of conscience, the poet recounts the coming to presence of the friend who bears language into the proximity of human dwelling. *Bezeugen* (testifying) becomes *dichten* (poetic saying). The poet bears witness to the friend who bears language, whose enigmatic essence makes it impossible for anyone to testify on its behalf. The friend has a prominent role in "Language in the Poem" (1953) and "Hebel—der Hausfreund" (The Friend of the House, 1958), where Dasein's Being as care becomes the poet's Being as the friend who "brings [*bringt*] the house of the world to language in order to make it habitable for human dwelling."5 Dasein's Being-in-the-world has become the burden of poetic saying. Heidegger's transition from the existential analytic of Dasein to the mission of poetic saying occurred by way of his extraordinary engagement during the 1930s with the poetry of Friedrich Hölderlin, and later that of Rainer Maria Rilke, Georg Trakl, and Johann Hebel.6

The lack in Dasein's Being that is *Sorge* or care has now become the fundamental concealment in Being, and just as care played a constitutive role in Dasein's coming into its own, now the task of the poetic friend is that of bearing the lack in Being into the language of human dwelling, which is precisely what makes that language a place in which humans can dwell. In the Hebel essay, for

5. Martin Heidegger, "Hebel—der Hausfreund," 147 (my translation).
6. Two recent general discussions of Heidegger's readings of the poets are Gerald L. Bruns, *Heidegger's Estrangements: Language, Truth, and Poetry,* and Véronique M. Fóti, *Heidegger and the Poets: Poiesis, Sophia, Techne.* See also Jacques Taminiaux, "The First Reading of Hölderlin," and Robert Bernasconi, "'Poet of Poets, Poet of the Germans': Hölderlin and the Dialogue between Poets and Thinkers."

example, the lack is called the "enigma" (*Rätsel*), and it is the task
of poetry to find words for the truth of this essential mystery.
Hebel, who flourished in the early nineteenth century, is adduced in
contrast to modern poets whose inability to find the words for the
richly luxuriant lack in Being has left their contemporaries wandering aimlessly in the house of Being that is language because they
have not been taught how to dwell poetically "there." The poet's
task is to enable us to dwell within this mystery by making the
uncanny demonic world into a familiar habitation through the
poetic saying of daemonic figures, by saying the mystery as a mystery and giving us the words with which to bring that enigmatic
lack to presence. The poetic world in which we dwell is itself a
"jewel case" or "treasure chest" (*Schatzkästlein*), which is the title
under which Hebel collected his poetry.

In lieu of the distress of Being-guilty, Heidegger is now concerned
with the pain of this poetic attestation of the incontrovertible power
and the irreducible otherness of the language of poetic saying. As
Dasein discovered its ownmost potentiality through the juridical
summons before language, now the speakers of a language come
into the mystery that is properly their own through the pain that
must be suffered when the poet brings into language the concealment or lack in Being that, in appropriating us for its own, expro-
priates us from ourselves and allows us to recognize the uncanniness in which we already dwell.

The pain of this appropriative expropriation is most carefully
elaborated in the two major essays on Georg Trakl: "Language"
(1950) and "Language in the Poem." The friend within poetic
language bears the constitutive and yet castrating division or gap
within language that binds Dasein to its own imponderable mystery. In the latter essay, *Being and Time*'s curious configuration of
Dasein and the friend has been transformed, through the refining
fire of Trakl's poetry, into the relation of the friend and the stranger; the friend has now become the stranger it always was. The
poet/friend "listens after" (*lauscht . . . nach*) the stranger, who

moves, through death, into the "earliness" of "apartness": "In listening, [the friend] follows the departed and thus becomes himself a wanderer, a stranger."[7] Poetry becomes the conversation between the friend and the stranger, and the conversation becomes a still more intimate relationship between death and the mourner.

In this remarkable passage, where Heidegger reinscribes the pathos of Trakl's poetry into his own idiom, care and mourning bring "apartness" (*Abgeschiedenheit*) into the friend's very existence and transform him into a brother of the departed (*Abgeschiedenen*): "The friend's saying is the singing journey down by the stream, following down into the blue of the night that is animated by the spirit [*Geist*] of the early dead. In such conversation [*Gespräch*] the singing friend gazes upon the departed. By his gaze, in the converse look [*Gegenblick*], he becomes brother to the stranger. Journeying with the stranger, the brother reaches the stiller abode in earliness [*der stilleren Aufenthalt in der Frühe*]."[8] Poetry is a conversation in this fundamental sense that the poet as friend becomes the poet as brother who shares, by virtue of the language he brings to presence, the lack and absence in which the departed dwell in the earliness of death. That the poet becomes the brother is, of course, essential in Trakl's case where the experience of poetry is synonymous with mourning for his dead sister.[9] Her absence is inscribed within him in the *Gegenblick,* the look back in which his gaze takes on the features of the now departed stranger. The poet becomes a stranger to himself at this literally incisive moment of poetic mourning and pain. This central experience of the *Gespräch* within poetry itself is what enables poets to enter into dialogue with thinkers and what allows them to reinvent the world of human dwelling. The friend's self-estranging conversation with the strangeness that dwells in un-

7. Martin Heidegger, "Language in the Poem," 186, and "Die Sprache im Gedicht," 68.

8. Heidegger, "Language in the Poem," 187, and "Die Sprache im Gedicht," 69.

9. David Farrell Krell, *Daimon Life: Heidegger and Life-Philosophy,* 288–91, discusses Trakl's figure of his sister as *ein flammender Dämon.* Also see my discussion of Trakl's sister in Ned Lukacher, "Mourning Becomes Telepathy," 3–4.

canny stillness in language's concealed essence lies at the basis of all poetic saying.

In Heidegger's later writings, *Sorge* and *Gewissen,* care and conscience, undergo numerous translations and elaborations as Dasein's relation to Being and time becomes no longer the domain of philosophical analysis in any traditional sense but the site of an innovative conversation between poetry and thinking. *Daemonic Figures* is an effort to develop some of the ramifications of this dialogue and more particularly to stage a conversation between Shakespeare, Heidegger, and Freud. As Shakespeare is an integral part of European culture, we can be sure that Heidegger, though he never explicitly cites or discusses Shakespeare, was nevertheless familiar with, at the very least, *King Lear, Hamlet,* and *The Merchant of Venice.* Freud, on the other hand, reads and cites Shakespeare at some length. A strange asymmetry will emerge in my presentation of Freud and Heidegger as readers of Shakespeare, for it appears that Freud's well-known positions on the poet are finally less intimately engaged with the central issues in Shakespeare's writing than Heidegger's more oblique meditations. Heidegger's silence belies the profound affinity between his thinking (*Denken*) and Shakespeare's poetic saying (*Sage*) of the words for Being, whereas Freud's self-certain pronouncements belie his wide divergence from the poet's fundamental orientation. Freud's misreadings are, however, both very revealing with respect to his own thinking and generative of many unpredictable and valuable insights.

As Heidegger remarks in *What Is Philosophy?* there is at once a profound affinity and an abyss between thinking and poetry.[10] Poets poetize and thinkers think, and together they manifest two intimately related yet widely divergent ways of corresponding, *ent-*

---

10. "Between these two there exists a secret kinship [*eine verborgene Verwandtschaft*] because in the service of language both intercede on behalf of language and give lavishly of themselves. Between both there is, however, at the same time an abyss, for they 'dwell on the most widely separated mountains'" (Martin Heidegger, *What Is Philosophy?* 95). Also see the important discussion of this relation in Heidegger, "The Nature of Language," esp. 85–90.

sprechen, co-responding, to the enigmatic lack in Being. Thinkers try to name "the essential experience of Being," as Parmenides does with the word *Moira,* the apportioning Fates, or Heraclitus with the gathering power of the *Logos,* or Anaximander with the dispensing of Being through *tō Chreōn* or "usage."[11] When it comes to poetry, however, what Heidegger emphasizes is "the care of the poet" (*die Sorge des Dichters*), which is the leitmotif of his reading of Hölderlin.[12] The poet takes upon himself the lack in Being in a more direct and self-sacrificial way than the thinker: "So for the poet's care there is only one possibility: without fear of the appearance of godlessness he must remain near the lack of the god [*dem Fehl Gottes*], and wait long enough in the prepared proximity [*in der bereiteten Nähe*] of the lack, until out of the proximity of the failing god the initial word is granted, which names the High One."[13] Note here not only the prominence of the proximity in which the poet dwells vis-à-vis the lack but also the role of the idea of readiness, preparedness.

Heidegger wrote that in 1943 in an essay on Hölderlin's poem "Homecoming" (*Heimkunft*). The title of one of his last essays, "The Lack of Holy Names" (*Der Fehl heiliger Namen,* 1974), which is drawn from "Heimkunft," suggests how pervasive this notion was in Heidegger's later thinking. The poet most resembles the thinker in his shared search for the words for Being's lack or default; he differs most from the thinker, however, in the proximity he takes up vis-à-vis the lack—the way in which, we might say, he lives the lack. "The poet," writes Heidegger in this late essay, "is obliged to speak by a [certain] distress. This distress conceals itself in the withheld coming-to-presence of the godly."[14] Our technological age, he continues, is incapable of "experiencing the power of

11. See Martin Heidegger, "The Anaximander Fragment," 54–55.
12. See Martin Heidegger, "Remembrance of the Poet," esp. 262–69, and *Erläuterungen zu Hölderlins Dichtung,* esp. 25–31.
13. Heidegger, "Remembrance of the Poet," 265 (translation modified), and *Erläuterungen zu Hölderlins Dichtung,* 28.
14. Martin Heidegger, "The Want of Holy Names," 264, and "Der Fehl heiliger Namen," 321.

the Exposition [*das Gestellnis*] which determines it in such a form
that it became apparent how—namely, in a distorted way—this
'lack' rules it, then the Dasein of man would be alloted participation in the open region of the saving [power]."[15]

The two greatest thinkers of the modern epoch, Descartes and
Hegel, for all their considerable contributions, Heidegger observes,
did not succeed in finding "a way," as opposed to "a method," that
would enable us to experience "the power" of the self-denial of the
origin that holds us in its grip. We need "to endure distress," and
for that we need not the thinkers and their methods but "the poet
who must enunciate the distress and urgency of what is withheld
in the task of understanding."[16] Because they do not dwell near
enough to the lack in Being, thinkers have failed to point the way to
this enduring distress. The corollary, as we have seen in the essay on
Hebel, is that poetry has also failed to confront the lack. What it is
that comes to presence remains withheld; it is that withholding
self-refusal of the origin that needs to be said; and Heidegger believes that it is still poets, rather than thinkers, who stand the best
chance of taking the risk of saying the words that would enable us
to dwell in the self-denial that is the opening of Being's self-refusal:
"This happened at the beginning of western thought *as* this beginning and has since then characterized succeeding epochs of the
history of Being up to the contemporary technological age in such
fashion that the oblivion of Being unknowingly adheres to the destiny of the clearing [*Lichtung*] as its principle. Yet the self-denial of
the clearing of coming-to-presence as such prevents the lack of 'holy
names' from being itself experienced as a lack."[17] And this is why
the poet's unique capacity to dwell near the self-denial of the origin
affords him the best chance of forging a path toward this desper-
ately needed experience. If the self-concealing refusal of Being is not
itself brought into the clearing, we run the risk of destroying ourselves in the epoch of the *Gestell;* that is why, in his famous inter-

15. "The Want of Holy Names," 264 (translation modified).
16. Ibid., 265.
17. Ibid., 265–66.

view with *Der Spiegel,* he remarked that "only a god can save us."[18] This enigmatic phrase simply means that we will perish unless a poet can save us, for the poet is the only god with whom Heidegger has ever been concerned. Unless there is a poet who has dared to think and say and dwell near the lack, the survival of Dasein itself is in question. This is what is at stake today concerning the question of conscience.

What we need is a poet who dwells nearest the lack in Being and who brings into the clearing the words of Being's self-refusal. We need a poet who says the names for the lack, whose poetic sayings, whose daemonic figures, enable us to experience "the want of holy names." *Es gibt Sein, Es gibt Zeit*—it gives Being, it gives time— but yet "it" refuses itself, conceals itself, remains withdrawn behind and within all that it brings to presence.[19] Only daemonic figures of the lack of what It is that gives its gifts can enable us to experience and endure the distress in which we have always already been. No wonder Heidegger is worried that we may never see the epoch of the expropriating event of appropriation that he (hopefully) calls the *Ereignis,* because the *Ereignis* will happen only if that poetic god comes in time.

This is the context in which I read Shakespeare: the poet of the end of the *Gestell* and the beginning of the *Ereignis.* Heidegger knew this without ever saying it; it resonates throughout all he has said. Freud comes to a similar recognition about Shakespeare but in a far more arduous though no less powerful way. "The *last* god," writes Heidegger in his second masterpiece, the *Beiträge zur Philosophie* (Contributions to philosophy), "is not an end, but the inner vibration of the beginning and thus the highest form [*Gestalt*] of the refusal."[20] Everything I have to say from here on is about nothing else but Shakespeare's place in the history of Being.

In the epigraph to this chapter Heidegger speaks of "the interior

---

18. See "Spiegel Interview with Martin Heidegger."
19. See Martin Heidegger, *On Time and Being,* 1–54.
20. Martin Heidegger, *Beiträge zur Philosophie* (*Vom Ereignis*), 416 (my translation).

of uncustomary consciousness" (*das Innen des ungebräuchlichen Bewussteins*), which is to say, the uncanny *topos* of the daemon that from this inner space (*Innenraum*) opens onto the immensity of the Open (*das Offene*).[21] The immediate context of the passage contrasts Cartesian certitude to Pascalian inwardness by way of prefacing a reading of the poet Rilke's experience of the clearing. The lack in Being comes to us through this uncanny inwardness whose nearness is incalculably remote from the inwardness of calculable self-certainty and the order of clear representations. Insofar as the history of Being is the history of Being's not being-there, of its being-gone, the task of poetic saying is one of turning our "uncustomary consciousness" toward Being's default.

In one of his most original descriptions of "Being's default" (*Ausbleiben des Seins*) Heidegger writes: "How are we to understand the fact that Being itself stays away? Perhaps in the sense that Being halts somewhere, like a being, and, for whatever reasons, perhaps because it has lost its way, does not reach us?"[22] But this "default" is not a simple lack or absence; it is rather the marker of something immense that remains withdrawn and concealed. If it should ever come to pass, the *Ereignis* would be the event in which Being's not-reaching us finally reaches us as a resonating non-negativity, the event in which we come into our own by dint of being expropriated by the self-refusal of Being. The *Ereignis* would signal the arrival of the call of conscience on a global scale.

But how would we experience what it might mean to belong to that which is itself lost and withheld? Heidegger's answer is the "releasement," the "letting be" (*Gelassenheit*), in which we might endure dwelling poetically—that is, daemonically—within what would have been the uncanny, demonic default where we had always (unwittingly) dwelt: "[Humankind and Being] are mutually appropriated, extended as a gift, one to the other. Only the entry into the realm of this mutual appropriation [*Übereignung*] deter-

---

21. Martin Heidegger, "What Are Poets For?" 127–28, and "Wozu Dichter?" 306.
22. Martin Heidegger, *Nietzsche*, vol. 4, *Nihilism*, 213.

mines and defines the experience of thinking."[23] By "clos[ing] all beings off [from Being],"[24] the *Ereignis* would enable beings to enter into the transforming space of this inwardness through which the outward lack in Being would take us in its power.

Jews, Ewes, and Uses of Will in *The Merchant of Venice*

"The essence of Being in the beginning of early modern metaphysics," writes Heidegger, "is actually ambiguous in that a manifold of essential possibilities of the essential completion of reality appears which later coalescces, developed from original unity. The ambiguity of the essence of reality in the beginning of modern metaphysics is a sign of a genuine transition."[25] By the time of Descartes and the *cogito ergo sum* the transition will have ended, and modernity will be in place. The certainties of the medieval world were sustained by faith, which Descartes will replace with the *lumen naturale*. The certainties of conscience and faith will be replaced in modernity by the notion of Being as *actus purus* into which the light of reason can penetrate. That is why, Heidegger says, modern culture remains a Christian culture even when it has lost its faith. What ensues is the inevitable "narrowing" (*Verengung*) of presence into self-presence, first through the divine moral law and then through scientific natural law. And like Freud, who insists that the *Urvater*'s power is greatest after his murder, Heidegger insists—quite rightly, I believe—that God and Christianity continue to dominate even after the "death of God" and the weakening of faith: "If the faith of the Christian Church has grown weary and has forfeited its worldly dominance, the dominance of God has not yet disappeared. Rather, its form has been disguised and its claims

23. Martin Heidegger, *Identity and Difference*, 33.
24. Martin Heidegger, "Overcoming Metaphysics," 110.
25. Martin Heidegger, "Metaphysics as History of Being," 25.

have hardened beyond recognition. In place of the authority of God and Church looms the authority of conscience, or the domination of reason, or the God of historical progress, or the social instinct."[26]

With the collapse of the realm of supersensuousness as the site of the highest values, which were slowly replaced by values that took and continue to take the form of mechanical utilitarian formulas, what transpires, as Nietzsche argued, is a "decline of cosmological values."[27] Shakespeare's prophetic soul bears witness to the impoverishment, the demonization, of the daemonic world and to the flaunting of moral certainties that provide cover for either comic or tragic exercises of the will to power. This is the provenance of any dramatist. Shakespeare's exposure of the ruses of the will constitutes an inquiry into the essence of willing as such. As mere self-certainty and willful posturing, conscience becomes simply an agent of will to power, one that must, as Nietzsche said, eventually lose its bite.

In a particularly difficult passage in "Overcoming Metaphysics," Heidegger writes of those who believe that the human will is itself "the origin of the will to will, whereas man is willed by the will to will without experiencing the essence of this willing." The passage continues: "In that man is what is thus willed and what is posited in the will to will, 'the will' is also of necessity addressed in its essence and released as the instance [*Instanz*] of truth. The question is whether the individuals and communities [*Verbände*] are in virtue of this will, or whether they still deal and barter with this will or even against it without knowing that they are already outwitted by it."[28] They are "outwitted" in the sense that the essence of willing has nothing to do with the imaginary "goals" and "missions" that such individuals and groups attribute to it. Such bartering with the

---

26. Martin Heidegger, *Nietzsche*, vol. 3, *The Will to Power as Knowledge and as Metaphysics*, 203.

27. Nietzsche cited by Heidegger, in *Nietzsche: Nihilism*, 227.

28. Heidegger, "Overcoming Metaphysics," 101.

will is part of what Heidegger calls the "historical struggle to *lead* the completion of nihilism." The notes that make up "Overcoming Metaphysics," dated 1936–46 and first published in 1951, give the strong impression of being highly critical of the Nazi cult of the will and in fact appear to characterize the Nazi community as less a community than a mere "band" or "association." What is peculiar about the passage, however, is that one does not usually think of the Nazis as "dealing and bartering," even with the will. The image here is that of merchants whose dealings are somewhat unsavory. Moneylenders and usurers would not, perhaps, be far removed from such transactions. In their deluded subjectivization of the will the Nazis appear somehow to have become like merchants, certainly, and perhaps even like the Jews. A strange tonality.

The Merchant of Venice was, for all the wrong reasons, among the most popular of Shakespeare's plays in Germany during the 1930s. Heidegger's allusion to those who have been "outwitted" (*überspielt*) has a slightly literary character—a mere fancy, perhaps, though there is something irresistible about the idea of the Nazis outwitting themselves after the fashion of the Jewish nemesis itself. Hitler as Shylock undone—amazingly paradoxical.

The anti-Semitism of *The Merchant of Venice* is not a problematic issue. Derek Cohen has counted seventy-four references in the play to Jew, Jewish, Hebrew, and so on, most of which have negative connotations.[29] Shylock's daughter Jessica is, however, an appealing character, largely because she handily shucks off her Jewishness and, furthermore, manages to steal most of her father's valuables, his mockingly sexualized "bags" in Shakespeare's ambiguous idiom (2.8.18). In a play fraught with images of blood identity, Salerio taunts Shylock by telling him that there is more difference between the blood of father and daughter than between "red wine and Rhenish" (3.1.36). The disorder of Shylock's will rather than some endemic disorder of Jewish blood is Shakespeare's

29. Derek Cohen, "Shylock and the Idea of the Jew," 305–16. See also John Gross, *Shylock.*

concern here. Nevertheless, none of Shakespeare's sources identify the race of the moneylender or are concerned with him one way or the other; it is part of Shakespeare's signature in the play, and an element in his "Will." The word "Jew" and the characterizations of the Jew, however improvisational they may appear, pertain to the specificity of Shakespeare's art in this play. The problem of reading the play arises as soon as we try to disengage anti-Shylockism from anti-Semitism, which is to say, to separate the individual will from the group will or from the nature of willing as such. We must decipher the relation of Shylock's will to natural law and from there proceed to the question of conscience and the inner disposition of the heart. The relations between the will, conscience, and Shakespeare's signature will open a path toward a general examination of the structures of Shakespearean expropriation.

Before attempting to bring something new to the already immense critical commentary on this play, I want to attempt an even more problematic contribution to Shakespeare studies by speculating on the biographical and historical context of *The Merchant of Venice*. How is it that Shakespeare comes to invent the character of Shylock, through whom he can consider such questions as the relation of Christian to Jew, usury to the gift, natural phenomena to money and language, and will power to love? Why in *The Merchant of Venice* does Shakespeare come upon the daemonic figures that define him as a poet who dwells in the proximity of the lack in Being? I speculate that perhaps his focus on the meaning of conscience in *The Merchant of Venice* was the result of a biographical event whose significance for the reading of Shakespeare's work has gone unnoticed for more than sixty years. It is striking that Shakespeare's biographers have not paid very much attention to this event since Leslie Hotson published his discovery of it in 1931.[30]

30. Even those few biographers who have noted Hotson's discovery have seen little significance in his findings. See, e.g., Samuel Schoenbaum, *William Shakespeare: A Compact Documentary Life*, 199–200; Russell Fraser, *Shakespeare: The Later Years*, 46; and Peter Levi, *The Life and Times of William Shakespeare*, 148. Hotson underestimated his own discovery, and biographers have followed suit.

In *Shakespeare versus Shallow* Hotson published court records indicating that on November 29, 1596, William Shakespeare was charged, along with Francis Langley (owner of the Swan Theater which Shakespeare's company, the Lord Chamberlain's Men, had used), and three others, with having threatened to kill one William Wayte.[31] Previously, players and theater owners had enjoyed the protection of the first Lord Hunsdon, until his death in July 1596 created an opportunity for the Puritans in the City who had continually opposed the theaters and had harassed Langley since 1594; Hunsdon's replacement as lord chamberlain was Henry Brooke, Lord Cobham, a Puritan sympathizer (who became the butt of the famous Sir John Oldcastle reference in *Henry IV, Part I*). In early November 1596, three weeks before the accusations were lodged against Shakespeare, Langley himself had filed a "surety of the peace" against Wayte and another exceptionally interesting figure, William Gardiner (or Gardener), whom Langley accused of having threatened to kill him.

Gardiner was a prominent justice of the peace and one of the most scurrilous characters one might imagine. Hotson's book chronicles the numerous embezzlements and schemes that Gardiner used during his long life to amass a considerable fortune by tricking friends, strangers, and family members—including his ill-fated nephew and flunky, William Wayte—out of money, property, inheritances, and anything else he could lay his hands on. In this particular instance he had offered his services to the lord mayor of London and the Puritan zealots who were determined to put theater owners and players out of business:

31. Leslie Hotson, *Shakespeare versus Shallow*, 8–9. Here is the Latin original of the entry of petition for sureties of the peace, with accompanying English translation: "Anglia ss Willelmus Wayte petit securitates pacis versus Willelum Shakspere, Franciscum Langley, Dorotheam Soer uxorem Johannis Soer, & Annam Lee, ob metum mortis &c. Attachiamentum vicecomiti Surreie retornabile xviii Martini. (England Be it known that William Wayte craves sureties of the peace against William Shakspere, Francis Langley, Dorothy Soer wife of John Soer, and Anna Lee, for fear of death, and so forth. Writ of attachment issued to the sheriff of Surrey, returnable on the eighteenth of St. Martin [i.e., November 29, 1596, the last day of Michaelmas term])."

The City's attack on the playhouses was at its height. Langley's most vulnerable point was therefore his position as owner of a theatre. Using his power as justice of peace in Southwark, and seconded by the lord mayor and the aldermen, Gardiner could piteously [sic] persecute Langley and Shakespeare and his fellow-actors at the Swan. The latter, however, though deprived of their strong support in the Privy Council, had nevertheless a present protector in their new patron, Sir George Carey, now Lord Hunsdon after his father's death.[32]

Langley and the players resisted Gardiner's plot. Gardiner died in 1598, and there are no other documents concerning the case.

But Hotson has found something incredible here: William Shakespeare under attack by the Puritans and their legal minions and enmeshed in a series of legal proceedings, involving death threats and petitions for protection, instigated by a very villainous old justice of the peace who would do anyone's bidding for a price. E. K. Chambers's *William Shakespeare* appeared in 1930 and so contains no reference to the case, yet it is odd that Chambers never subsequently remarked on the Gardiner incident. The linkage of Shakespeare and Langley should alone have triggered a great deal more interest than it has. Langley's reputation as a theater owner is at least colorful: Russell Fraser calls him a "usurer, extortioner," and Gerald Eades Bentley says that in 1597 Langley forced the Earl of Pembroke's players "to sign bonds forfeiting £100 if they left his Swan to play elsewhere."[33] Rather than a colleague of Shakespeare in the war of the theaters against the City, it may be that Langley himself embodied in the theatrical world something of Gardiner's mentality, or even Shylock's. Nevertheless, with Shakespeare's Globe Theater near London Bridge and Langley's Swan standing at either end of the strip of theaters on the south bank of the Thames,

32. Hotson, *Shakespeare versus Shallow*, 27–28.

33. Russell Fraser, *Shakespeare: The Later Years*, 61; Gerald Eades Bentley, *The Profession of Player in Shakespeare's Time, 1590–1642*, 16. See also William Ingram, *A London Life in the Brazen Age: Francis Langley, 1548–1602*, esp. 139–50.

it is difficult not to see Gardiner's involvement in this litigation as part of the City's attempt to contain the social energy of the theatrical world. *The Merchant of Venice* is an allegory of the struggle between the Hebraic conscience of the Puritans and the spirit of art. The topology of Shakespeare's critique of conscience is partly the expression of a struggle for control of the means of representation: a struggle between city and suburb, between pious cant and apparent godlessness.

Hotson says nothing about the possible connection between his discovery of Wayte's suit against Shakespeare and *The Merchant of Venice*. The only significance he sees in the documents he has discovered is in connection with Justice Shallow in *The Merry Wives of Windsor*, whom Hotson believes London audiences would have recognized as a swipe at Gardiner. In my Shakespeare fable, however this is a defining moment, for whether or not Shakespeare seriously threatened the lives of Gardiner and Wayte or whether they threatened his, the incident must have made him realize with greater urgency and immediacy that the Puritans in the City were serious in their war against his livelihood in the theater, if not his very existence. How could he not be interested in the justice who had tried to close down the Swan theater? Shakespeare probably recognized that Gardiner, whose habit was to lend money and then prevent debtors from meeting payments, was at once dangerous and ridiculous. Like Shallow and his cronies, Gardiner and his cohorts are figures of a depraved senility. In him Shakespeare saw the consciencelessness on which the economic and legal power of the City relied.

Since it was in July 1598 that James Roberts secured rights to print *The Merchant of Venice*, we may conclude that Shakespeare had by then written at least a preliminary draft of the play. But since the first quarto was not published until October 1600, may we not also surmise that in the intervening months Shakespeare had, with a new or renewed determination, entered the war of conscience on which the survival of not only the theater but the

Elizabethan settlement itself depended? Despite the Puritan di-
atribes against usury, Gardiner's villainy might have shown Shakespeare the usurious essence of the Puritan mentality. Shylock is the
result of Shakespeare's analysis of Gardiner's obsessive economic
individualism. Gardiner was not, of course, a Jew, but I hypothesize
that Shakespeare nevertheless reworked Gardiner's indomitably
usurious will within a specifically Jewish register.

Why did he choose a Jew as the figure for Gardiner's English
vice? Shakespeare may have been predisposed to scapegoating the
Jew as a result of two events involving the Earl of Essex and his
circle. The first is the well-known trial and execution of the Queen's
Jewish physician in 1594, which was largely perpetrated by the
Earl of Essex. The second is less well known and remains, like the
foregoing speculations, hypothetical. It requires some additional
background.

The Earl of Southampton, Henry Wriothesley, was in the Essex
circle and spent two years in the Tower for his participation in the
abortive rebellion of 1601, for which the Earl of Essex was exe-
cuted. The historian G. P. V. Akrigg has made an exceptionally
suggestive and coherent case for regarding Shakespeare's relationship with Wriothesley as an indispensable element, if not the leitmotif, in the emergence of Shakespeare's art.[34] Akrigg relates the
homoeroticism and what he calls the "submerged homosexuality"
of the sonnets and *The Merchant of Venice* to Shakespeare's relationship with Southampton. Though speculative, this seems to me
highly suggestive and not without considerable explanatory power.
Whatever the precise nature of their relationship, Wriothesley had
probably at the very least been a patron of Shakespeare and may
even, as Nicholas Rowe reported in 1709, have financed his artistic

34. See G. P. V. Akrigg, *Shakespeare and the Earl of Southampton*. Also see Neil
Cuddy, "The Conflicting Loyalties of a 'Vulgar Counselor': The Third Earl of Southampton, 1597–1624." Cuddy's account provides new information on Southampton's
career after his release from the Tower in 1603 when he became an adviser to King
James; it offers no opinion, however, on Southampton and Shakespeare.

career from the outset. Someone must have done so, and until there is a better candidate, Wriothesley seems the man of the hour. Since my interest is in the character of "the friend" in the sonnets and *The Merchant of Venice,* which in turns opens onto the question of Dasein's finitude, even the most speculative surmise as to how Shakespeare may have been led to think about the most poetic of all questions is worth pursuing, however tentatively.

Akrigg provides a basis on which to hypothesize that it may be Southampton who stands behind Shakespeare's decision to make the miserly moneylender in *The Merchant of Venice* a Jew. It may, of course, have derived from an earlier play called *The Jew,* to which Stephen Gosson refers in *The School of Abuse,* or it may have been simply a matter of adopting a conveniently available stereotype. But it may also have involved the Earl of Southampton's difficulties with moneylenders in 1597. Perhaps the "friend" who had financed Shakespeare's career was now himself in financial straights. He may have brought it upon himself by his generosity and by incurring the wrath of his guardian, Lord Burghley, whose granddaughter he refused to marry, for which he was forced to pay an immense fine to the queen. Akrigg speculates that in the sonnets Shakespeare took the conservative position by urging Southampton to obey Burghley. But this is by no means certain. In any case, Southampton's decision to marry for love rather than profit launched him on a career of debts and difficulties which had reached the critical stage by 1597, when his then considerable debts came due and he was pursued after the fashion of Antonio.

In his edition of the play, John Russell Brown cites a source to the effect that the name Shylock, which has never really been explained, may be an incorrect form of "Shallach," which is Hebrew for "cormorant," which was "often used of usurers."[35] Might not Shakespeare have come upon such knowledge, at just this time, through his familiarity with Wriothesly's ordeal? I suggest an addi-

35. John Russell Brown, Introduction to Shakespeare, *The Merchant of Venice,* 3.

tional though no less hypothetical explanation for the name. The Oxford English Dictionary notes that "shy" could in the sixteenth century be used of someone who was "of questionable character, disreputable, shady." Furthermore, the term "shy-cock" was slang for "a wary or cowardly person; also, one who keeps within doors for fear of bailiffs."[36] Or, we might add, one who stays indoors for fear of moneylenders. The name Shylock would thus draw together a number of apparently disparate but ultimately connected elements, all relating to Southampton's dilemma in 1597.

Two further biographical speculations are particularly apropos of a play that is so concerned with castration, circumcision, and other phallic configurations and, of course, with the Earl of Southampton. First, as Dennis Kay points out in his recent biography of Shakespeare, the name Shakespeare was apparently considered embarrassingly phallic in the late fifteenth century; Kay cites a certain Hugh Shakespeare who changed his name to Hugh Sawnders in 1487 because of his original surname's vulgar and provincial connotations.[37] Though we will never know whether William Shakespeare was embarrassed by his name, we can examine several instances in his writing where he inscribes it, plays with it, and puns on it at just those points where what is in question is the relation of historical experience to the unthinkable ground from which it arises —at the very point, we might say, where the proper name stands before the law.

What is the law of the name, or the relation to the law that is given in a name? Could it have been a coincidence that it was in late October 1596, just days before the uproar with Gardiner and Wayte, that the College of Heralds granted Shakespeare's petition for a coat of arms? And is it a coincidence that the coat of arms awarded to the Shakespeares, which depicts a silver falcon grasping

36. Cited in Eva Turner Clark, *Hidden Allusions in Shakespeare's Plays: A Study of the Oxford Theory Based on the Records of Early Revels and Personalities of the Times,* 195–96.

37. Dennis Kay, *Shakespeare: His Life, Work, and Era,* 22.

a spear and shaking his wings, repeats the leitmotif of Southampton's coat of arms, which depicts four silver falcons.[38] Might
not Southampton be linked to Shakespeare's understanding of his
own relation to the law and to the idea of legitimacy?

Samuel Schoenbaum provides what may be the final piece of
evidence to dispel the suspicion of even the most skeptical critic
that this exercise in speculative biography is no more than a tissue
of coincidence and irrelevant detail. The clerk who prepared the
documents concerning the coat of arms also left drafts of a motto
that read *Non, sanz droict* (Non, sans droit), which, though apparently intended to read, "Not without law," also means the opposite
as a result of the comma: "No, without law." Does Shakespeare's
motto place him inside or outside the law? Might Shakespeare be
some sort of outlaw? Did he cryptically scribble this on a piece of
paper in an effort to tease the poor clerk out of thought? No doubt
recognizing the incongruity, the clerk crossed it out and wrote *Non
sanz droict,* this time without the comma.[39] There is no record of
what finally became of this enigmatic motto, and the family seems
never to have used it. In the fall of 1596, considering Shakespeare's
problems with the Puritans and a maniacal justice of the peace in
Southwark, the ambivalence of the motto, even without the comma, might have appeared a bit too provocative. It cannot be denied,
however, that the immense and irresolvable enigma of Shakespeare's life seems strangely inscribed in this marvelously unreadable coat of arms. Here we truly have, among other things, a *Non*
without negativity and precisely in connection with the law. The
law is here in the *sanz,* in the "without." The law is precisely where
we realize it is still lacking, still withheld; the law is "there" where
its not-being-here makes its claim upon us, the claim of the pure
outside of the law inside the proper name itself, the law that divides
the name from itself and thus gives the name. This could only be
Shakespeare's motto. He stands, to be sure, in the *Non* of the law,

38. Akrigg, *Shakespeare and the Earl of Southampton,* 245.
39. Schoenbaum, *William Shakespeare,* 229.

which is also, of course, the *Nom,* the name of the law. With or
without the law (of his name) Shakespeare stands outside the law,
or rather before the law.

We have set the stage, then, for a reading of *The Merchant of
Venice* in which the play's anti-Semitism functions ideologically as
an assault on the Hebraism of the usuriously hardworking, antitheatrical Puritan capitalists. Although the Earl of Southampton
doubtless encountered Jews in his European travels, Shakespeare
probably had no familiarity with them. But then again, he didn't
have to; he knew all he needed to know about them through the
Puritans. We have saved for last the element in the play that Shakespeare must have known the Puritans in the City would have found
most appalling: the unabashed homoeroticism between Antonio
and Bassanio. The history of the (un)readability of Shakespeare's
homoeroticism in *The Merchant of Venice* would doubtless see
George Granville's 1701 adaptation of the play (and particularly
his prologue) as standing at the origin of a long history of homo-
phobic misreading in which Antonio's relationship with Bassanio is
the unreadable itself. The play's homosexual ethos needs to be
grasped at the root where the questions of will, interest, and conscience come together.

Marc Shell has already articulated the critical implications of the
play's pervasive contrast between sexual procreation in the natural
world and the unnatural generation of interest in the monetary
world of usury.[40] Anti-Semitism and homosexuality are the two
most notable imprints of Shakespeare's reinvention of his sources,
and they should tell us a great deal about his experience of the
world. I have tried to explain the politics underlying the anti-
Semitism. The homosexuality has a much more obvious function,
though it has been as misunderstood and as misconstrued as the
anti-Semitism. Antonio's homosexuality offsets the very opposition
between natural and unnatural generativity, for his desire, unlike

40. See Marc Shell, "The Wether and the Ewe: Verbal Usury in *The Merchant of
Venice.*"

that of Portia or Shylock, has no interest in generativity or productivity of any sort, animate or inanimate. For Shakespeare, his is a natural desire without any concern for interest, profit, or utility. In all the discussions I have read of the play, this simple fact goes unnoticed. Nevertheless, it is essential to understanding how Shakespeare conceives of the daemon and the gift and how, conversely, he opposes them to the will of the Jew, to the fecundity of the ewe, and to the principles of use and what he calls "usance" generally.

Shakespeare's concern is to differentiate the complexity of the "hues" (almost a homonym of "use") of human nature. (The term "hue," which is a homonym of ewe and proximate as well to the sixteenth-century orthography of "Iewe/Jew," does not appear in *The Merchant of Venice* but is prominent in the sonnets.) And like the three caskets from which Portia's suitors must choose, there are three hues, not two: not simply male or female, Venice or Belmont, monetary or natural production, and Jew or Christian. Antonio's hue names a third term, one that is linked to language (and which differentiates language from money) and that reaches back into the abyssal origins of Dasein's finitude. The daemonic figures of *The Merchant of Venice* reach back to that which is earlier than any indebtedness. We are moving inexorably closer to them.

Shylock is driven by a will so strong that Antonio compares it to nature's most fundamental forces: the inexorability of the ocean tide, the struggle for survival in the animal world, the power of "the gusts of heaven" themselves (4.1.70–77). Nothing is harder, Antonio insists, than Shylock's "Jewish heart." Since it is pointless to resist the inevitable, Antonio accepts his fate: "Let me have judgment, and the Jew his will" (4.1.83). In his retelling of the parable of Jacob's manipulation of Laban's flock, Shylock relates the Jewish genealogy of his will to power. The bond by which he hopes to eliminate Antonio, whose generosity in lending money and paying off the debts of his fellow merchants has sharply curtailed Shylock's profits, is the culminating expression of this willpower. That it specifies cutting precisely the pound of flesh that lies "nearest the heart (4.1.229) is a measure of Shylock's desperation, for Antonio dead is worth infinitely more to him than the three thousand ducats Bassanio has borrowed.

The hardhearted Puritans in the City, and their allies such as the demented miser Gardiner, probably lie behind Shakespeare's realization of Shylock's ruthlessly calculating will. But Shakespeare does not simply oppose to such force the inwardness of the loving heart. Shylock's force draws upon an inwardness far more powerful than that to which any other character in the play has access. Like a canting Puritan, Shylock cites scripture to justify his own venality. Antonio's allusion to "an evil soul producing holy witness" (1.3.94) must have recalled for Shakespeare his own recent experience of Puritan testimony. It is not a question of opposing the head and the heart, since the problem lies within the fiction of natural law itself. Through Shylock and Antonio, Shakespeare attempts to reinvent our fictions about will and natural desire. Shylock's will and Antonio's desire reinvent the relation between natural and human law by showing that they are contaminated by each other at their origins. The impurity of law necessitates the impurity of desire, and vice versa.

Shylock's most crucial line in the play is not the poignant question "Hath not a Jew eyes?" (3.1.52) but his claim in the courtroom: "I stand here for law" (4.1.142). The realization of his bond, which would legalize his revenge and eliminate his biggest business rival, would acknowledge a metaphoric resemblance between his will and the law itself, which is to say, it would signal the finality of the subjective appropriation of the law. Its force would thus appear as a natural force in a continuum with the will to power. In such a context "the quality of mercy" (4.1.180) can make no appeal. Shylock invokes a bond to natural law that he is certain will ensure him the victory in his litigation in positive, human law: "There is no power in the tongue of man / To alter me,—I stay here on my bond" (4.1.236–37). But it is, of course, the power of language that turns back Shylock's will, and he is allowed the privilege of uttering the very words that defeat him: "'Nearest the heart,' those are the very words" (250). It is the letter of the law itself that alone can cut into Shylock's hardened heart and that leaves not a drop of blood.

Shakespeare appeals not to the inwardness of the heart as the site of feeling and emotion but to the inner space of what Heidegger calls the heart's "uncustomary consciousness," which is that inner space where the materiality of language incises human existence and brings it before the impossible totality in which it has been thrown. This is the point of the incision of the lack in Being, near which only the poet dare dwell. Beyond even the most exceptional instances of will to power, beyond even Shylock's prodigious will, there is a still greater power that may appear synonymous with the quality of mercy but has much more to do with the power of language. Shylock's will is defeated by what it depends on: the letter of the law. Portia might have phrased her judgment along the lines of Shakespeare's motto: *Non sanz droict*. It is the bloodless letter of the law that constitutes for Shakespeare the essence of the law's inner mystery.

"No jot of blood," insists Portia (4.1.301). It is an interesting expression, since "jot" derives from *iota,* the smallest letter of the alphabet, and is thus a rather appropriate figure for the irreducible literality of language that here sustains the law. In the jot the letter of human law and the blood of natural desire come into an uncanny relation; the letter through which the will manifests itself has here become an absolute resistance to the will's most sought-after object, the blood of Antonio. The "jot of blood" is what Shylock could not read in the very contract he himself forged. It is the signifier of the unreadable itself, the phallic signifier or purloined letter that invariably returns to its sender. Shakespeare's daemonic insight in *The Merchant of Venice* is that the *jot* is the conscience of the play. In order to found itself the desiring will must enter the circuit of the letter, on which it must always run the risk of losing itself. It must divide itself in order to constitute itself; and it is that uproariously terrifying (non)knowledge that must always come back again to the sender, to the writer of the bond, to the overreaching mortgagor awaiting payment. Comedy and tragedy are names for the ways in which "the letters work upon [the] blood" (*Othello* 4.1.266), two ways of reading a jot. A jot, the very least thing imaginable, a mere letter, the most unnoticeable, insignificant thing—this is the only trace that this other law will ever leave behind. This "jot" is the gift of the law and the daemonic figure of *The Merchant of Venice*.

Heidegger remarks apropos of a line in Hölderlin's poem "Greece" that the movement toward the *Gering*, which means the "very least thing," the smallest and most insubstantial thing, is also the movement toward a great beginning.[41] The *Gering* enables us to enter into the bond that *rings* back to the beginning, the bond through which the silent call of the beginning *rings* and that is itself a most delicate *ring*, like Hölderlin's god, most nearby and yet most difficult to grasp. The very end of Act 4 and all of Act 5 of *The Merchant of Venice* literally *ring* with the poetry of the *ring*. It reaches a veritable din in 5.1.193–203, where nine out of ten lines end with the word *ring*. Shakespeare is having a great deal of fun with the passing of the gift of the ring: it becomes the play's central metaphor for the bonds of homoerotic friendship, heterosexual marriage, and the law (before the law). The figure of the ring is also a figure of the hymen, and to give the ring is to give the gift of virginity. As the hymen, the ring names that strange fusion of language and the body that determines the production of value and meaning. In Shakespeare's elaboration, however, the ring as hymen becomes the figure of irreducible deferral and delay, not only with respect to erotic pleasure but also in relation to human nature's place in the world. The "jot of blood" that will not be shed in the courtroom will presumably be shed in the hymenal sacrifice to which the play's gleeful closing pun on Nerissa's ring alludes. The

41. Martin Heidegger, "Hölderlins Himmel und Erde," 172–74.

ring/hymen becomes Shakespeare's daemonic figure for the reality
of conscience as the power of language beyond the will and the
machinations of self-reflection. Heidegger's playful pun on "the
ringing of the ring" (*das Gering des Ringes*), which "wrests free"
(*entringt*) what is most delicate and compliant in the coming-to-
presence of things and world,[42] describes quite independently and
in a different language and idiom what Shakespeare is doing when
he glories in this metaphoric bell-ringing in *The Merchant of Venice*.

It is also the ring that binds the theatrical world of Belmont,
which is now no longer simply the world of marriage and domes-
ticity, to something entirely other, something inaudible, what
Lorenzo calls the "harmony . . . in immortal souls" that "we cannot hear" (5.1.63, 66). The ringing of the ring is for Shakespeare
the metaphor of an absolute nonresemblance, the metaphor for
metaphor insofar as the audible ringing of poetry is itself finally
sustained by the silent bond that joins the souls of lovers to the
enigma of "soft stillness and the night" (5.1.57).

Shakespeare's unsettling of the claims of conscience leads him
into a parodic analysis of the silent voice of the moral law as it
falteringly tries to make itself heard in, of all the play's characters,
the person of Launcelot Gobbo, who is the clown of *The Merchant
of Venice*. It is through Launcelot that the connection between
Shylock's will and the voice of conscience becomes unmistakably
clear. His parodic soliloquy (2.2) comically anticipates the courtroom scene in its depiction of Gobbo as someone caught in a
hopeless litigation between conscience on one side and the fiend on
the other. Gobbo wants to have a good conscience about leaving
Shylock's employ, but conscience will not comply, and it is the fiend
who gives him the advice he wants to hear: "to be rul'd by my
conscience, I should stay with the Jew my master, who (God bless
the mark) is a kind of devil; and to run away from the Jew I should

42. Heidegger, "The Thing," 180.

be ruled by the fiend, who (saving your reverence) is the devil himself" (2.1.21–25). In the only reference to conscience in the play, conscience becomes a figure of Shylock's own voice, as though Shylock were the voice of guilty conscience and as though Antonio and the others were voices for other ego-structures in an essentially intrapsychic allegory.

Several surprising implications might be drawn from Launcelot's virtuoso judicial clowning. First, its attack on "hard conscience" is an anti-Puritan jab and a rather sharp one. Shakespeare had no interest in exciting animosity against Jews, but against Puritans he was relentless. Second, the moral law of duty here gets rather short shrift, and conscience itself appears as the expression of harsh commandments that we have internalized but that have no genuine right over us. Shylock would function in such an allegory as the avenging conscience who threatens the transgressing ego (Antonio) with castration or circumcision, and the guilty ego is willing to make the sacrifice to the superego and become the "tainted wether of the flock." But then, at the last moment, a transformation in the ego-ideal itself empties the conscience of its enforcing power and the ego-structures are able to gather in a ring no longer threatened either by a socially motivated demand for instinctual renunciation or by the destructive forces of the id. Shylock's defeat is tantamount to a victory over the burden of historical guilt and its role in enforcing a productive economy and in satisfying its needs. Shakespeare wants to gather us in a ring where, without guilt or anxiety, we wait before the law that will never come. Lorenzo speaks of the sweet ability of music to pierce Portia's ear and draw her home (5.1.67–68). Shakespeare's ear is pierced by the silent call that comes from the merest jot of language, and it draws him home to the impossible bond that its mere being there ensures will always be to come.

Once again the motto *Non, sanz droict* (this time with the comma) seems to apply uncannily well, for Gobbo in effect says to conscience and to the Jew, "No, I won't listen, for you have no right, and I would rather obey the devil than follow your sanctimonious edict." We must understand that for Shakespeare, Gobbo is a figure of fun but one whose message is quite jolting, penetrating, and serious in its implications. It is as though Shakespeare were saying, "We must have done with these Puritans and their canting conscience, and since they rely so heavily on the patriarchal law of the Jews, there is no harm in having done with them as well."[43] Shakespeare must take responsibility for writing a text that could be so easily appropriated by hatemongers, and he must be blamed for masking the bitter and politically risky pill of anti-Puritanism beneath the glib humor and theatrical effect afforded by a facile anti-Semitism.

The Friend in the Night of Language:
Will in the Sonnets

"Be it known that William Wayte craves sureties of the peace against William Shakspere, Francis Langley [et al.], for fear of death, and so forth [*ob metum mortus &c.*]." Thus reads the accusation of November 1596 that followed hard on the heels of Langley's prior complaint against Gardiner and Wayte. Bonds would have to be posed by the accused, which would be forfeit if anything came of the complaint within a year's time. This little adventure multiplies the already numerous enigmas that confront the reader of *The Merchant of Venice* (and other plays) and the sonnets. Might not the additional names in the Petition ("Dorothy Soer, wife of John Soer, and Anna Lee"), or others who have left no trace in the documents, stand along with Shakespeare, Langley, and, of course, Southampton behind the fantastic misadventures in the *Henry IV*

43. Max Weber's remarks on the Hebraism of English Puritanism are helpful here: "Old Testament morality was able to give a powerful impetus to that spirit of self-righteous and sober legality which was so characteristic of the worldly asceticism of this form of Protestantism." Weber also insists, however, on the differences between "Jewish speculative pariah-capitalism" and the "Puritan bourgeois organization of labour" (*The Protestant Ethic and the Spirit of Capitalism*, 165, 271 n. 58).

plays? But of course, the evidence that might substantiate such beguiling identifications has doubtless long been lost "in the dark backward and abysm of Time" (*The Tempest* 1.2.50), to which we might have been pleased to entrust it in any case.

Here is sonnet 134, whose link to *The Merchant of Venice* has often been remarked:

> So now I have confessed that he is thine,
> And I myself am mortgaged to thy will,
> Myself I'll forfeit, so that other mine
> Thou wilt restore to be my comfort still.
> But thou wilt not, nor he will not be free,
> For thou art covetous, and he is kind;
> He learned but surety-like to write for me,
> Under that bond that him as fast doth bind.
> The statute of thy beauty though wilt take,
> Thou usurer that puts't forth all to use,
> And sue a friend came debtor for my sake;
> So him I lose through my unkind abuse.
> > Him have I lost; thou hast both him and me;
> > He pays the whole; and yet am I not free.

Shakespeare was forced to secure a surety of the peace, which is to say to enter into debt to the law and to whoever might have paid his bond. In this poem it is the dark lady who seduces the friend, takes him as surety and bond in order to release the poet, who nevertheless remains bound to her. And her beauty enables her, like the consummate usurer, to lend all her capital (beauty, desire, sexual favors) at rates so high that the wills of both men remain hopelessly in debt. As Joel Fineman realized, this sonnet "not only renders explicit, at the level of theme and image, what is implicit in the young man sonnets, but also the way in which it supports this explication with the language that it speaks."[44]

44. Joel Fineman, *Shakespeare's Perjured Eye: The Invention of Poetic Subjectivity in the Sonnets,* 284.

Fineman's larger thesis for the sonnets as a group concerns the process by which Shakespeare was brought to reinvent poetic language in so highly intricate a dialectical and chiasmic fashion as to bring the tradition of visionary poetics to an end. Shakespeare's elaboration of what Fineman calls the irreducible "languageness of language" generated a new notion of subjectivity, one based no longer on the reliability of visual experience but on the inexhaustible mediations of the word and the letter. The testimony of the eye/I has thus been perjured, and its fundamental groundlessness has emerged from concealment. It is in this daemonic place that Shakespeare discerns the bond between the poet and the friend whom he, in effect, carries within himself and who, as Fineman remarks, "thereby divides the poet from himself." Fineman's reading of the sonnets reveals Shakespeare as the last god, the one who dares to dwell near the unfathomable lack in Being and thus discovers there the site of unparalleled riches. It is through his relationship with the friend that the poet is led toward the topology of poetic saying. But by no means does the poet find it easy to dwell poetically.

In our hypothetical biographical scenario, Shakespeare's actual bond may have been paid by Southampton, leaving the poet further in his debt. Southampton's adventures then went into high gear, for in 1597 he fought with Essex in the assault on Cadiz. By the time *The Merchant of Venice* was written, Southampton had married Essex's cousin and had converted from Catholicism to the Church of England in, of all places, Paris. By the end of 1598 his fate was inexorably linked to that of the ill-fated Earl of Essex. I present this concatenation of events in the life of Southampton that are contemporaneous with the writing of *The Merchant of Venice* and, I believe, the sonnets, in order to suggest that the poet's falling-out with the friend and the concern in both works with a certain corruption or decline may be the poetic consequences of Shakespeare's dismay at Southampton's increasing intimacy with the Essex circle.

Akrigg, who makes none of these connections and is, furthermore, unaware of the Gardiner incident, strongly suggests that Shakespeare came to regard Southampton as somehow flawed, blemished, and stained in some irreversible way. As the older man, Akrigg surmises, Shakespeare may have seen himself reflected in Antonio's guilt and self-loathing vis-à-vis his affection for Bassanio.[45] After 1598 what may have been a very remarkable relationship between Shakespeare and Southampton probably came to an end, and the young earl was seized by the whirlwind that would soon consume Essex and land Southampton in prison for three years. Shakespeare's doubt and loathing may have taken many forms. In both *The Merchant of Venice* and the sonnets something comes between the poet/Antonio and the friend/Bassanio: money, power, and marriage in the first instance, and the dark lady in the second. The relation between the poet and the friend devolves into anxiety and alienation. The effort to dwell near the lack slides from a profound accord to anguish and jealousy. But what is crucial to reading both the play and the sonnets is to understand that the crisis that overtakes the effort of Antonio and the poet to dwell near the lack reveals what a desperate struggle it is to think the difference between present beings and the self-concealment of Being. The incisive power of language—which is stronger even than Shylock's will—and the seductive power of the dark lady are figures for the division that joins and separates the poet and the friend; they are figures for the pain and distress into which language calls the poet.

The dark lady is the name of the instability within the sun; if the friend is stained, it is her fault, for it is her will that manipulates the wills of both the poet and the friend and draws them beyond the sun, beyond the world of phenomenality, and into the language beyond the language of consciousness. Her will is finally synonymous with the presencing power of language, its strange materiality, which, though invisible, lies at the foundation of our ability to see things and bring them to presence. Heidegger calls this the

45. Akrigg, *Shakespeare and the Earl of Southampton*, 236–40.

"apophantic" (*apophanesthai*) power of language to make things manifest (*Being and Time*, 56–57/32–33). Though it gives light and allows things to come into the light, it remains hidden and in the dark. Language gives its gift but keeps itself concealed. It is the dark lady who draws them on from deep within "death's dateless night" (sonnet 30), and it is she who "makes black night beauteous" (sonnet 27). Like Juliet when she questions the "contract" that binds her to Romeo and says that it is "Too like the lightning, which doth cease to be / Ere one can say 'It lightens'" (2.2.116–20), the poet of the sonnets is drawn into the enigmatic materiality that underlies the apophantic power of language.[46] What is it in language that enables us to enter into the clearing, into the invisible lighting of language? As soon as we glimpse it, it vanishes like Juliet's lightning. Night itself is only finally a metaphor for the

46. This passage from *Romeo and Juliet* may also have appeared to Oscar Wilde as a reflection on the nature of love and ethical obligation generally, for these are the lines that Sybil Vane utters so disappointingly in *The Picture of Dorian Gray* (chap. 7). Her love for Dorian makes it impossible for her any longer to experience the bond to the otherness of language and art. Wilde sees the connection of this passage to Dorian's fatal effort to kill conscience, for Dorian no less than Sybil fails to understand the obligation that the "contract" entails. The lightninglike trace effect that Juliet glimpses lies at the center of the strange clearing of language. Wilde himself recognized an intimate connection between *Romeo and Juliet* and the sonnets (see "The Portrait of Mr. W. H.," 176–77). Wilde's invention of the boy actor Willie Hughes as a cipher for Shakespeare's homoerotic identifications also marks the site of the poet's relation to the lack that remains from the still concealed name of Being. What Juliet glimpses is the bond between playwright and actor, between Romeo and Juliet, between the poet and language, and between Dasein and another hue/you.

One of the interesting side effects of Lord Alfred Douglas's effort to prove the historical existence of Willie Hughes, which he claimed to have authenticated in the records of the City of Canterbury (without offering proof), is a letter that appeared in the *Times Literary Supplement* for May 28, 1938, from A. C. Cripps, who points out that Douglas's insistence on the word "Hews" in sonnet 20 "might just as easily be understood as supporting the 'Southampton' theory of the Sonnets (on which Lord Alfred pours scorn) as the rival theory which he adopts. For obviously 'Hews' might stand for 'He.W.S.': which leads us directly to 'He[nry] W[riothesley Earl of] S[outhampton]'"; and, I might add, it might also stand for "He, W[illiam] S[hakespeare]." There was, as it so happens, a William Hewes who was apprenticed to Christopher Marlowe's father in Canterbury and who apparently maintained contact with the playwright when they resided in London (see William Urry, *Christopher Marlowe and Canterbury*, 24–25).

irreducible darkness and enigma that dwell within light itself. Shakespeare's ridicule in *Love's Labour's Lost* and elsewhere of the "School of Night" and of the pseudophilosophical poetry of Chapman and Ralegh derives from the fundamental insight that vision and ocular phenomena are themselves mired in shadow and that one need not affect the mystical transport of the night, since darkness rules even in broad daylight. The dark lady draws the poet and the friend into the dark night of language, which is to say into the enigma of language as such.

The young man does not respond to the poet's effort to persuade him to marry and, as the poet foresaw, they now both descend into "hideous night" and the "wastes of time" (sonnet 12). The young man becomes the friend that he always was. This is crucial, and I do not believe anyone noticed it before Fineman. Perhaps the most fascinating sequence in the sonnets concerns the transformation of the young man whom the poet has been urging to marry into the friend whom the poet has incorporated in language and who indeed becomes a figure for the most intimate relation to language. As the poet falls asleep in sonnet 27, the young man's image appears to him:

> my imaginary soul's sight
> Presents thy shadow to my sightless view,
> Which like a jewel hung in ghastly night,
> Makes black night beauteous, and her old face new.

In sonnet 65 the jewel that invents the night has become the poet's "black ink" that shines bright and keeps "time's best jewel" from being lost in the passage of time. In *The Merchant of Venice* Portia's ring is her treasured and "loved . . . jewel" (5.1.224). In sonnet 131 the dark lady has become the poet's "fairest and most precious jewel." Language for Shakespeare is the black jewel that illuminates the invisible bond that joins human finitude to the enigma of time and space. It is this allegory that organizes both the sonnets and

The Merchant of Venice, and the relation between them. The poet is always fearful of losing his relation to language; the friend names that relation, and they are both drawn ineluctably toward the dark mystery of language.

In sonnets 135 and 136 the relation between the poet's will and that of language itself—that is, the dark lady—is sexualized; the poet speaks of placing his will in hers (135) and then begins to play with his name. He realizes that the friend's assumption of the debt he owes the lady leaves him still hopelessly enamored of both of them, and this leads him to recognize in turn that he is entirely beyond the question of debt and has always been so, for all three of them are names for a continuous process of willing. From the illusion that the subject is the origin of its own will, the poet achieves the remarkable insight that the essence of willing lies not in subjectivity but in language and, beyond that, in language's withheld essence. His own name is a wonderful encouragement to the culminating moment of sonnet 136:

> Then in the number let me pass untold,
> Though in thy store's account I one must be,
> For nothing hold me, so it please thee hold
> That nothing me, a something sweet to thee.
>   Make but my name thy love, and love that still,
>   And then thou lov'st me for my name is Will.

This is the most exquisite philosophical eroticism in Western literature. It shelters the truth of its nontruth, the nothing of its willing in the (w)hole of its Will. No debt, no guilt, and no need for conscience as moral law or as the name for a cycle of indebtedness. The scene of phallic nomination sexualizes conscience by treating it as a regulatory function within sexual desire, as a moment in a larger scene of exappropriation.

The pun is, of course, Shakespeare's own in sonnet 151, where he writes that "conscience is born of love" and concludes with an erotic image that concretizes his realization that the essence of willing, which has drawn him and his friend to the dark lady, is inseparable from the sexual energy that causes his "nobler part" to rise "at thy name":

> No want of conscience hold it that I call
> Her love for whose dear love I rise and fall.

Con-science names the rising of the phallic Will before the enigmatic object of desire, which is not simply the *con* but the (w)hole mystery of human finitude.[47] The final three sonnets trace this continuum between naming and willing back to the "dateless lively heat" of the burning brand that heats Diana's bath (153, 154). Shakespeare's fascination with the cinders of this fire will be our theme in Chapter 5. No wonder the sonnets were not published until 1609, when the Puritan danger appeared to have subsided (though of course it had only begun a long incubation). This parody of conscience, so closely linked to *The Merchant of Venice,* and yet so much more challenging to the Puritans and their powerful political allies, could not, given Shakespeare's "surety of the peace," have dared show its head circa 1598–1600.

---

47. Sonnet 151 echoes both the pornographic and the poetological motifs characteristic of several of the eighty Latin epigrams knows as the *Priapea;* epigrams 37 and 79 (see W. H. Parker, ed., *Priapea: Poems for a Phallic God,* 127, 195) indicate Shakespeare's debt. That Shakespeare concludes the sonnet sequence with a recovery of phallic strength is thus also an affirmation of poetry. In the interim, however, poetry itself has been transformed by the event of Shakespeare's signature and the force of a linguistic will. The essence of this transformation inheres in the displacement of phallic will from natural law into the order of language, which is irreducible to either natural or positive law. The knowledge of the *con* in conscience thus continues to pose the question of conscience (as the "nothing" which has nothing negative about it) without positing its substance in either natural or human will. Note also Shakespeare's use of poem 34 in the *Priapea,* which speaks of women who offer "willow pricks" (*verpas . . . salignas*) as signs of their sexual exploits. The "fantastic garlands" of *will*ow leaves that Ophelia makes in *Hamlet* (4.7.165–70) and Desdemona's insistence that "a green *will*ow must be my garland" (*Othello* 4.3.48; emphasis added) reinscribe this priapic motif in a uniquely Shakespearean idiom that entails something other than the phenomenality of human willing.

By way of a coda to the preceding discussion, we might note the close connection of these issues to *Much Ado about Nothing* (1600), where the "worm of conscience" (5.2.77) takes on an ambiguously phallic character that is at once corporeal and linguistic, and where Benedick himself appears as the allegorical *carduus benedictus,* the "holy thistle," or what we might simply call the "blessed prick (of conscience)." Beatrice asks Margaret, the servant who prescribes the thistle to her as a way of calming her agitated manner, whether there is "some moral in this *benedictus*" (3.4.73). Shakespeare's point is that we cannot begin to speak of the moral law before we acknowledge the reality of desire and of the silent call that draws us toward the treasure that is the "nothing" of the ring's irresistible nonknowledge.

As Benedick remarks, "man is a giddy thing" (5.4.107), easily led by desire and egotism into a bestial, conscienceless state. After Benedick has finally responded to Beatrice's appeal to his conscience, he has an interesting exchange with the callow Claudio, who is savoring the prospect of his imminent marriage to Beatrice, above all because it will give him the opportunity in effect to cuckold Benedick by playing "lusty Jove," "the noble beast in love," with Europa/Beatrice. Benedick, who knows that Claudio will soon finally receive a dressing-down for his unconscionable treatment of Hero, responds by simply pointing out to him that his bestiality has nothing godly about it (see 5.4.41–51). The play's deftly managed allegory of the loss of "the gifts that God gives" (3.5.41) transpires in the secret Eden within Leonato's arbor at Messina, where a new relation to language must be recovered in a fallen world in which "men are only turned into tongue" (4.1.318). It is to the one character in the play who can never understand the significance of his own utterance that Shakespeare gives the privilege of speaking the line that could well serve as the legend for *Much Ado About Nothing.* That, of course, is Dogberry, and the line, of course, is "God save the foundation" (5.1.312).

3 The Searing Thing: *Hamlet*'s Countersignature

What is the Sun? That which dominates all things and thus cannot be dominated, though it is only the millionth wheel of the carriage that waits before our door every night.

. . .

The seals are affixed on nature by the sun. Henceforth, one can neither exit nor enter. The judicial verdict is awaited [*décision de justice est attendue*]. This is where things stand now.

That is also why we cannot adore it. And so, perhaps, instead of complaining, we should thank it for having made itself visible.

—FRANCIS PONGE, "Le soleil placé en abîme"

Unheimlich is the ear: and *unheimlich* what it is—double; what it can become—large or small; what it can make or let happen (we can say "let," since the ear is the most obliging, the most open organ, as Freud points out, the only one the infant cannot close); and the way in which it can be pricked or lent.

—JACQUES DERRIDA, "All Ears"

There were eclipses of both the sun and the moon in the English skies between 1598 and 1601.[1] From Shakespeare's perspective, however, the momentous eclipse of the age occurred in early 1601

---

1. See Harold Jenkins's note to 1.1.117–23 in his edition of Shakespeare, *Hamlet*, 429. Gloucester's remarks in *King Lear* may also look back to the events of these years: "These late eclipses in the sun and moon portend no good to us: though the wisdom of Nature can reason it and thus, yet Nature finds itself scourg'd by the sequent effects" (1.2.91–93).

with the execution of Essex and the imprisonment of Southampton. In addition to the demise of the patrons who had sustained and inspired his art, Shakespeare also lost his father and his son. The "disasters in the sun" (*Hamlet* 1.1.121) to which Horatio alludes perhaps look back to these events only to surmise that they themselves may be the portents of still greater cataclysms. In such dire circumstances Shakespeare could not console his audience with what John Croke, speaker of the House of Commons, could say of the queen in 1601, that she enjoyed the "comfort of conscience by true religion."[2] On the contrary, Shakespeare found less and less "comfort of conscience" with every passing year. During these years, which culminated in the writing of *Hamlet,* Shakespeare not only contributed to a general ideological resistance against what historian J. E. Neale describes as Puritan efforts to "propagandize Parliament"; he also began undermining the moral theology on which the Anglican hierarchy relied. Although Neale believes that by 1597 the threat of Puritan parliamentary influence had essentially passed and that the "temperament of a new generation" had begun to set in,[3] Shakespeare continued to be alarmed by still deeper disjunctions in his poetic understanding of the world.

The crisis of conscience and will during the last years of Elizabeth's reign is Shakespeare's great theme, the theme of the paralysis and incapacitation of the Elizabethan state as it contemplated its own finitude. The imminent eclipse of sovereign power cast its shadow over every aspect of life. Catastrophe rather than restoration seemed to loom on the horizon. Much like the Counterreformation ethos Walter Benjamin describes in seventeenth-century Germany, *Hamlet*'s ethos is that of an absolute monarchy frozen in a ghostly historical interval. Benjamin argues that *Hamlet* is less a tragedy than a play of mourning or *Trauerspiel* because, rather than dying heroically, Hamlet resolves to die by accident: "Whereas tragedy ends with a decision—however uncertain this may be—

2. Quoted in J. E. Neale, *Elizabeth I and Her Parliaments,* 2:373.
3. Ibid., 2:436, 371.

there resides in the essence of the *Trauerspiel,* and especially in the death-scene, an appeal of the kind which martyrs utter."[4] Hamlet's "readiness" to die (5.2.218) is not a tragic decision but rather a response to what Benjamin calls "the over-strained transcendental impulse."[5] What Hamlet calls "the law's delay" (3.1.72) is not something that human law can remedy, for Dasein's finitude—and its destiny—is what always "puzzles the will" (3.1.80).

"Disasters in the Sun"

In his definitive study of sixteenth-century political thought, J. W. Allen unfolds the complex relation between the theory of royal supremacy and the individual conscience on which the Elizabethan settlement relied.[6] The individual had a limited freedom of conscience—if, that is, the individual was not a Puritan or a Papist— and that freedom, such as it was, relied on the sovereign rather than on God. The paradox is that Elizabethan tolerance of individual conscience depended on ceding one's freedom of conscience to the monarch precisely in order to receive it back again. Conscience was ceded neither to the divine depths of Puritan inwardness nor to the ecclesiastical authority of Church and papacy but to the sovereign. Jonathan Goldberg nicely states the paradox: "Kings exemplify what they deny their people, the right to individual conscience."[7] The individual had a conscience through a sort of proxy that was held by the queen, and one could depend on her to exercise it properly. After their disastrous mission to Ireland, Essex and Southampton were no longer willing to cede their proxies. Why they misjudged the nature of Elizabeth's power so badly, it is difficult to

4. Walter Benjamin, *The Origin of German Tragic Drama,* 137.
5. Ibid., 66.
6. See J. W. Allen, *A History of Political Thought in the Sixteenth Century,* esp. 231–70.
7. Jonathan Goldberg, *James I and the Politics of Literature,* 118.

determine; perhaps it was because they failed to understand the willingness of subjects to cede conscience to the sovereign other and thus also failed to see the coherence of the resulting body politic. Power lay precisely in the unrepresentability of the paradox of conscience. The fears of the Essex circle concerning an immediate dissolution of the settlement once the queen was dead precipitated them into a course of action that must have horrified Shakespeare, to whom the paradoxes of conscience were no secret.

Hamlet is not like Essex in this most fundamental respect: that he achieved a readiness to wait that Essex and Southampton never attained. My reading of the situation thus differs considerably from J. Dover Wilson's influential comparison of Hamlet and Essex.[8] I believe, on the contrary, that Shakespeare must have regarded Essex as a kind of Laertes who foolishly stormed into a situation that he had failed to understand. Hamlet is a kind of Essex at the outset, but later, when he becomes really interesting, he is more like Southampton, who, dressed all in black and imprisoned in the Tower, accompanied only by the faithful cat who had climbed down the chimney to be with his master, had simply to wait—perhaps for death, perhaps, as it so happened, for liberation: he was one of the first to be freed from the Tower when James I arrived in London in 1603.[9] "The cat will new, and dog will have his day," cries Hamlet (5.1.288) in what has always appeared a cryptic and even mad utterance but may well be a reference to Southampton and his cat, ready and waiting in the Tower. Hamlet's generally claustrophobic experience of life at Elsinore may have been linked for Shakespeare with the earl's dilemma.

Of course Hamlet is finally and most singularly himself alone, and what is most interesting about reading him is the task of under-

8. See J. Dover Wilson, *The Essential Shakespeare: A Biographical Adventure*, esp. 100–107.

9. Akrigg offers an account of this episode and reproduces the portrait that was painted of Southampton and his cat during their captivity (*Shakespeare and the Earl of Southampton*, 132–33); he makes no connection between the earl's imprisonment and *Hamlet*, however.

standing how Shakespeare forged, from within the historical context, something that is irreducible to it. Whatever the facts behind Shakespeare's relation to the Essex circle, and however they informed Shakespeare's creation of this curious thing that Hamlet calls "readiness," what is central to my remarks on *Hamlet* is the way the culminating notion of "readiness" in Act 5 is carefully displaced from the choice to commit revenge or not to commit revenge and is instead reinvented as a "readiness" to accept the singularity of one's fate and the inevitability of death. Rather than providing a solution to the question of conscience, "readiness" becomes Shakespeare's name for the affirmation of this question's irresolvable paradoxicality.

There are four avengers in *Hamlet:* the prince himself, Laertes, Fortinbras, and Pyrrhus, whose violent vengeance against Priam stands at the center of the Player's speech. If we were to order them from the most hesitant to the most bloodthirsty, we would have Hamlet as the most reluctant; next, Fortinbras, about whom we know very little but who seems to be methodically going about the business of avenging his father and recapturing lost territories; then Laertes as a more passionate avenger, and rather parodically so, but easily enough brought to heel by Claudius; and finally Pyrrhus, the very incarnation of conscienceless revenge. Fortinbras is only sketchily presented, and Laertes' short-lived determination to revenge Polonius is, like Hamlet's own fleeting bouts of blood lust, no more than an ironic glance at the outmoded conventions of revenge drama. As Hamlet works through the stages leading from paralyzing doubt to the stilling of the voice of conscience (which is not, however, its exhaustion or erasure), he passes through the ground zero of the Player's speech. We too must pass through the winnowing fires of conscience in the Player's depiction of Pyrrhus's revenge during the fall of Troy in order to reach the daemonic world that is the "readiness" of Hamlet's new conscience.

Once again I find encouragement for my reading in some remarks by Joel Fineman, who suggests that Shakespeare's fascination with the ear may function like "an instrument of delay and deferral" that somehow inserts a kind of spacing and timing, a certain "dilation," within the essentially visual apparatuses underlying the ideology of Elizabethan power.[10] Neither endorsing nor opposing the absolutism of the Elizabethan state, Shakespeare's auricular figurations would attenuate and even intensify the visual erotics of power and language, but in so doing they would also call it into question, explore its ground, and perhaps enable readers and theatergoers to pause to examine the nature of conscience, freedom, and the will, albeit within an essentially eroticized aesthetic practice that relies on the terms of the dominant ideology even as it works changes upon them. The ear might thus function as the figure for the suspensive "languageness of language" in the way it orients all our sensations, visual and otherwise, in advance, even as it allows us to intensify those sensations and bring them to a heightened self-presence. "I believe this helps to explain," writes Fineman, "why for Shakespeare the ear is so often a figure of momentous suspense, as in *Hamlet*, when the fall of Ilium 'takes prisoner Pyrrhus' ear,' and I believe also that this Shakespearean ear eventually determines Derrida's account of the reader's, any reader's, relation to a text, any text." The ear as Shakespeare's daemonic figure of *différance*, and as the figure that informs all those texts of literary and philosophical modernity that try to respond to the call of language, finds perhaps its most powerful and influential expression in the extraordinary allegory of conscience that lies at the silent center of the Player's speech in *Hamlet*.

The arrival of the players at Elsinore, the Player's speech, and Hamlet's soliloquy that brings Act 2, scene 2, to a close together constitute an event in the history of conscience. As the players enter, Hamlet greets them with characteristic wit and, among other things, asks one of the boy actors who plays female roles, and whom Hamlet has not seen for some time, whether "your voice,

10. Joel Fineman, "Shakespeare's Ear," 230.

like a piece of uncurrent gold, be not cracked within the ring"
(2.2.423–24). A voice can crack in the sense of losing its pitch or
timbre as a result of age or overuse, and this could cost a boy actor
his livelihood. In Hamlet's metaphor of the gold coin, the cracking
of the voice is compared to breaking the ring of the coin and thus
rendering it valueless. There is also the sexual pun on the ring as a
figure for the hymen. Hamlet's relation to Ophelia is obviously
behind this witticism, but more important, it anticipates the silent
break or caesura that occurs within Pyrrhus's ear. But the ring is at
once the hymen and that in which it breaks; the deferrals are endless, the crack within the crack, the break within the break. The
voice is itself a figure for the impossible literality of language and
the ring that joins us to it. In the flurry of Hamlet's excitement at
the players' arrival, which must have recalled for Shakespeare the
private productions he helped to stage at the country residences of
both Southampton and Essex, we are already in the midst of an
analysis of human finitude.

Hamlet asks the first Player to recite a speech from a play that
met with little popular success but was admired by those of dis-
criminating judgment for its unaffected "honest method, as whole-
some as sweet, and by very much more handsome than fine"
(2.2.441–42). Hamlet's interest is in a narrative rather than a dramatic sequence within the unnamed play, and he asks specifically
for "Aeneas' tale to Dido—and thereabout of it especially when he
speaks of Priam's slaughter." Hamlet himself recites the first dozen
lines, which recount how Pyrrhus, all in black, emerged from the
Trojan horse and how, covered in blood from the carnage he
wrought, he continues his path of destruction. There are, as we
shall see, two sources for the Player's speech. The first and most
obvious is Virgil's *Aeneid,* where Shakespeare found in Pyrrhus a
son determined to avenge a murdered father. In mourning for his
father, Achilles, who was killed by Paris, son of Priam, Pyrrhus will
revenge himself upon the father of his father's murderer. Virgil's
Aeneas recounts the story to Dido. What has not been recognized,

however, is that the details of Shakespeare's account of Pyrrhus's murder of Priam are not drawn from Virgil. From Virgil, Shakespeare retains only the emphasis on the hypnotic look of madness that Aeneas saw in Pyrrhus's burning gaze as they looked momentarily in each other's eyes (*Aeneid* 2.459). We will turn to a previously unrecognized source in a moment.

First, however, another passage in *Hamlet,* whose debt to the *Aeneid* has not been sufficiently noted, reveals that Virgil's text was important to Shakespeare's understanding of the identification between Pyrrhus and Hamlet. When Virgil's Pyrrhus emerges from the Trojan horse, he is described as being "like a serpent who after having spent the winter underground, swollen by a diet of poisonous plants, now emerges into the light, fresh and renewed, and shedding its old skin" (2.471–73).[11] In one of the most widely quoted phrases in the play, Hamlet speaks of what might await the soul after death once it has "shuffled off its mortal coil" (3.1.67).[12] But the identification between Virgil's Pyrrhus and Hamlet may be even more pervasive and extend to Hamlet's general metaphoric identity as an underground man who is alternately digging, burying, unburying, crawling, and prostrating himself in a variety of situations.

The Player takes up the narrative with Pyrrhus's search for Priam:

> Anon he finds him,
> Striking too short at Greeks. His antique sword,
> Rebellious to his arm, lies where it falls,

11. Virgil, *The Aeneid* (translation slightly modified).

12. Arthur Schopenhauer remarked in the 1850s that he regarded the "mortal coil" as one of the most obscure and mysterious phrases in all of Shakespeare (*Parerga and Paralipomena*, 2:445). I first presented this account of Shakespeare's reading of Virgil (and other facets of my reading of *Hamlet*) in Lukacher, "L'oreille de Pyrrhus: La césure de l'identification dans *Hamlet*," a paper prepared for a symposium on the work of Jacques Derrida (Cerisy la Salle, Normandy, France, July 14, 1992) and published in the proceedings of the conference. I have since read Robert Miola's *Shakespeare and Classical Tragedy*, which is also alert to the Virgilian source of "the mortal coil" (67).

> Repugnant to command. Unequal match'd,
> Pyrrhus at Priam drives, in rage strikes wide;
> But with the whiff and wind of his fell sword
> Th'unnerved father falls. Then senseless Ilium,
> Seeming to feel this blow, with flaming top
> Stoops to his base, and with a hideous crash
> Takes prisoner Pyrrhus' ear. For lo, his sword,
> Which was declining on the milky head
> Of reverend Priam, seem'd i'th'air to stick;
> So, as a painted tyrant, Pyrrhus stood,
> And like a neutral to his will and matter,
> Did nothing.
>
> (2.2.463–78)

The identification between Hamlet and Pyrrhus works on several levels. Like Hamlet, even the fiery Pyrrhus hesitates. The "hideous crash" of the citadel functions as a metaphor for the call of conscience that "takes prisoner Pyrrhus' ear." But there is something else at work in this passage beyond the psychological allegory of the *tableau vivant*.[13] While we watch the conflagration and its sequel, we also listen for the sounds of the deafening fall of the phallic tower, the marker of power and authority whose collapse seems to bring life itself to a halt. And yet within the figurations and within the music of the passage, we have still not accounted for the silent play of the letter that can be neither heard nor conceived as an idea or representation. Somewhere between reading and listening to this passage there emerges the intermittent sound of Shakespeare's name as though it had strewn itself like an acrostic through the sounds and letters that tell of Ilium's decline:

> and with a hideous cra*sh*
> T*akes* prisoner *P*yrrhus' *ear*.

13. I am indebted to Andrzej Warminski for helping me to decipher Shakespeare's countersignature in this passage.

Sh . . . akes . . . Pyr . . . ear: we are taken prisoner by this sig-
naturelike effect. It is like a secret signature that the author could
use to prove, in an emergency, that this was his work. And at the
same time Shakespeare seems to be making fun of the unpleasant
noise, the "hideous crash," of his name. This is a strangely divided
scene: at once a moment of encrypted self-authorization and a
scene of complete destruction and decline. If this thing resembling a
signature is the allegory of a self-relation, then the self in question is
in a state of dissolution. Nothing can be heard in the silence created
by the din of the falling citadel, nothing except the muted sound of
the letters in Shakespeare's name. In the stillness that signals the
trembling of an epoch and the end of a dynasty, Shakespeare gathers the strewn remnants of his own name. In this scene of self-
reflection the poet appears to discover the resources of his own
name within an epic scene of the suspended will and the struggle of
conscience. The poet seems to recognize that his signature draws
endlessly on the authority and legitimacy held in reserve by "Shakespyrrhus' ear." If we could imagine Shakespeare's work as an immense credit card, then "Shakespyrrhus's ear" is like the countersignature on the back of the card that authorizes all other uses of
the signature. And is it not Shakespeare's point that the countersignature on which the poet draws all his resources is itself the site of a
daemon, the place of burning and fire? There is something in the
countersignature that remains unreadable behind the flaming letters.[14] "Shakespyrrhus' ear" is *Hamlet*'s daemonic figure of conscience because deep within the silent voice of conscience Shakespeare discerns not the moral law, not a realm of values, but the
silent play of the letter.

The daemonic, caesura-like nonrelation at the heart of the self-
revelation of the signature is present for only a moment within the

14. See Jacques Derrida's synopsis of the relation of signature and countersignature in
Peter Brunette and David Wills, "The Spatial Arts: An Interview with Jacques Derrida,"
esp. 16–19.

Player's speech. The world intrudes itself once again and the tableau dissolves; the caesura yields to the flow of events:

> But as we often see against some storm
> A silence in the heavens, the rack stand still,
> The bold winds speechless, and the orb below
> As hush as death, anon the dreadful thunder
> Doth rend the region; so after Pyrrhus' pause
> Aroused vengeance sets him new awork,
> And never did the Cyclops' hammers fall
> On Mars's armour, forg'd for proof eterne,
> With less remorse than Pyrrhus' bleeding sword
> Now falls on Priam.
>
>   (2.2.479–87)

While the crash takes Shakespeare's ear prisoner, this, we may
presume, is the moment that matters most for Hamlet, who would
like to think that his sword will soon fall remorselessly on Claudius. The Player's speech continues for another dozen or so lines in
which Priam's reversal of fortune is piteously decried and a dis-
traught Hecuba witnesses Pyrrhus's mutilation of Priam's corpse.
The Player is so moved by his own recitation that he begins to weep,
and Hamlet, at the urging of Polonius, bids him stop. Shakespeare
has not only signed his own idiom into a motif familiar to Elizabethan tragedy;[15] he has also reinvented the relation of tragic
action and language to the materiality of the letter.

Ears are, of course, everywhere in *Hamlet,* from "the porches of
the ear" through which Claudius administers the poison to the
depths of the inner ear where Pyrrhus listens to the deafening silence of the fall of Troy.[16] But "Pyrrhus' ear" is unique not only

---

15. E.g., Thomas Norton and Thomas Sackville, *Gorboduc* 3.1, where the titular
hero alludes to "Ilion's fall," the slaughter of Priam's race, and Hecuba's woe.

16. It is generally assumed that Shakespeare derived Claudius's method of murdering
his brother from a confirmed historical event: the murder of the Duke of Urbino in 1538
by Luigi, who was a kinsman of Leonara Gonzaga, the Duke's wife (see *Hamlet,* ed.

because of the intricacy of its allegory and its classical allusions but because it is the site of the event of Shakespeare's countersignature. Before broaching that question, however, let us return to Shakespeare's sources. The central fact about Shakespeare's Pyrrhus is the elaborate tableau composed by his hesitation. I have discovered what was probably Shakespeare's classical source for this hesitation: it comes not from Virgil but from Euripides' *Hecuba,* where not only the memory of Achilles is evoked but his ghost as well. It is, furthermore, the source not only of Pyrrhus's hesitation but of Shakespeare's signature event as well. Shakespeare either knew the text or deduced it from Seneca's omissions. Shakespeare's allusion makes it unmistakably clear that he was working neither from a Latin translation of Euripides nor from Seneca's adaptation of *Hecuba* in his *Troas* (which omits the relevant scene). We can sur-

---

Jenkins, 507). Hamlet himself characterizes "The Murder of Gonzago" as an "extant" story "written in very choice Italian" (3.2.256). I believe Shakespeare put the critics on a very long goose chase with that allusion. What they have missed in their concern with an Italian event from 1538 is a later scandal concerning ear-poisoning right across the Channel in France with which, it seems common sense to assume, an English poet in the Essex-Southampton circle would have been infinitely more familiar. My source is the history of Henri IV of France, written by his court historian and published just after the king's assassination in 1610. In 1560, he recounts, François II "died of an aposteme in the ear, which was believed to be the effects of poison" (Léon Valée, ed., *History of Henry IV,* 29 n. 1). During the mid-1570s Henri III, who had succeeded Charles IX to the throne, began to suspect that he too had been poisoned through the ear *by his brother:* "The King, having fallen sick, and being in great danger of death with a pain in his ear, believed himself to be poisoned, as François II had been, and accused Monsieur" (29). Though Henri III recovered from his illness and discovered that his suspicions were groundless, these events are part of a long sequence of scandal and intrigue. François II was a son of Catherine de Medici, whose dominance over the French court from 1560 to her death in 1589 was notorious all over Europe. French ear-poisoning of an Italian vintage was a commonplace of the period. Catherine was also a well-known student of the occult, and it is very likely that much of the spectral quality in both *Hamlet* and *Macbeth* was distinctly à la Medici in Shakespeare's mind, from ear-poisoning to mystical "prospective glasses" (*Macbeth* 4.1), like the one Catherine herself used in order to gaze upon the future kings of France. What haunts Hamlet is not simply a paternal ghost but an entire regime of decadent European intrigue. That "The Murder of Gonzago" is said to be set in Vienna—that is, somewhere between Urbino and Paris—suggests the continental Catholic aura that Shakespeare himself is conjuring forth through the auricular canals of *Hamlet.*

mise only that Shakespeare somehow had access to Euripides' Greek text and could make use of it, at least to the limited extent we will examine in a moment. As someone with connections to the Essex-Southampton circle, Shakespeare might have readily found his way to the relevant texts.[17] My concern, however, is with the internal textual evidence, which is significant enough to warrant at least a reconsideration of Shakespeare's sources. What the Euripidean source enables us to substantiate is that "Pyrrhus' ear" is not only an allegory of conscience, which has always been recognized to one degree or another, but also an allegory of language itself. The relevant scene in *Hecuba* is yet another element in the inscription of Shakespeare's signature. In *Hamlet* the signature will not stop signing.

In Euripides' play, Hecuba, as a prisoner of the Greeks after the fall of Troy, has a prophetic dream in which she sees "the ghost of Achilles howling on his tomb" and demanding more sacrifices from "the miserable women of Troy" (lines 93–95). The Chorus then reports that Achilles' ghost has appeared to the Greeks and has demanded a sacrifice in which his son, Pyrrhus, will execute Polyxena, a daughter of Hecuba and Priam. Euripides' play is about the transformation of Hecuba from passive mourning to active vengeance. What must have interested Shakespeare is the hesitation Pyrrhus experiences just as he is about to sacrifice Polyxena. Like Hamlet, Pyrrhus appears incapable of obeying the injunctions of the paternal ghost. For a brief moment, Euripides' Pyrrhus is at once "willing and unwilling" (*thelon, kai athelon,* line 567). But the sword falls, and Polyxena dies. While in the Player's speech Hecuba looks on helplessly in silent horror at Pyrrhus's butchery, Euripides' Hecuba turns to vengeance because all her appeals to the conscience of the Greeks have failed.

The story of Pyrrhus and Polyxena is also recounted in book 13 of Ovid's *Metamorphoses,* but it contains no allusion whatever to

17. Peter Levi conjectures that Shakespeare's learning may have relied on John Stow's vast library (*The Life and Times of William Shakespeare,* 68).

Pyrrhus's hesitation. Euripides' play is the only source in which Shakespeare could have discovered the central element in the Player's speech. That Shakespeare read it in Greek seems indisputable as well, for it is extraordinary and beyond any possible coincidence that Euripides' Greek text should hinge on, of all things, the will: *thelon, kai athelon,* willing and not willing, or more simply, "Will and no(t) Will," which in Shakespeare's ear might have sounded something like "me and not me," "mine and not mine." In Euripides' text Shakespeare found a trace of his own signature, and then he reinvented it as "Will Shakespyrrhus."

In his important reading of *Othello,* Fineman demonstrates that from the title to Desdemona's "Willow Song," all of Shakespeare's leitmotifs are spun from a meditation on the Greek *thelon.*[18] "O-thell-o" translates as "O-will-o," which is how we might translate "Pyrrhus' ear," for despite its "rugged" beauty the Player's speech, if not a song of the will, is a tale of the will's not belonging to itself, a tale of its fundamental otherness, a tale of the possibility of its belonging to language, but ultimately a tale of the irreducible enigma of the ground of the will. That is what the event of the countersignature is all about; it arises from the imposition of a singular idiom upon the unthinkable thing itself.

Derrida has made a very important elaboration of Heidegger's thought of *Ereignis* and *Enteignis,* appropriation and expropriation, in his theory and practice of the signature. When one signs, says Derrida, one "appropriate[s] the other to oneself while leaving it as it is," letting the thing "sign for itself while signing in its place, in its name."[19]

It is important to understand how this dynamic operates in the Player's speech. Shakespeare's name gives itself to be read within the conflagration at the fall of Troy. Building on the classical sources, combining them in a unique palimpsest, Shakespeare creates a density of detail, a kind of critical mass, that makes it pos-

18. Joel Fineman, "The Sound of 'O' in *Othello:* The Real of the Tragedy of Desire."
19. Jacques Derrida, *Signsponge,* 138.

sible for the thing, the nothing, in language to sign, to sign itself *as* the historical subject William Shakespeare, to sign both his names, at just the moment the tower falls and the will is suspended. "It" is signing itself in Shakespeare's name, for he has become its persona, its instance, the place where it can dwell. "Pyrrhus' ear" is literally the ear of the other. Shakespeare's poetic experience of the impasse, the aporia, the fiery caesura, of conscience disappropriates the thing from its ontotheological strictures and allows "it" to return as a ghostly, daemonic presence. "It" needs poets in order that "it" might speak and sign in their names. *Daemonic Figures* is about nothing else but the strange asymmetry of this event of the counter-signature.

This is the site of the searing heat of conscience where the thing burns the name with the brand of the letter, within "Pyrrhus' ear." Can you not hear the "s'earing" heat that consumes the name and that burns deep within the letter? Shakespeare writes in order to feel the daemonic, searing heat within the inner ear.

Pyrrhus's name alludes to his fiery nature, his fiery colored hair, and simply to the fire (*pyr*). He is the very image of fiery revolution and revolt, and yet at the same time the very image of the will suspended in the abyss of language, of the will's division and expropriation. In the Player's speech the suspension of the will is compared to a break in a storm, which soon passes and allows thunder soon again to "rend the region." But where is this region? Is it in the phenomenal world, or is it in language? Hamlet's memory would appear to have been focused on the next line: "Aroused vengeance sets him new awork." But where does Hamlet search for such arousal? Where else but in the language of the Player's speech itself? But of course it doesn't work for him, and he complains in the soliloquy that follows of his inability to be aroused by a speech that has the power to "cleave the general ear" (2.2.557). Hamlet searches everywhere for a ground for duty and responsibility. "Pyrrhus' ear" is an allegory of the question of conscience because there the search extends beyond the audible voices of thought and reason to discover deep within the inner ear an origin for the imperative force of language, for the essence of obligation.[20] But the search fails, and Hamlet remains unsatisfied, for what he needs, a palpable ground for the law, remains beyond his grasp. He is concerned not so much with catching Claudius's conscience as with finding a ground for his own.

"The Murder of Gonzago" will prove similarly ineffective in providing an answer. Hamlet has returned from Wittenberg, full of the Pauline obsession with conscience and determined, once the ghost has spoken, to see if the voice is truly reliable. In brooding so incessantly, in so melancholy a fashion, on the reliability of the voices of conscience, Hamlet obeys a still more enigmatic imperative that comes from within the silent depths of thought and language, which is to say, from within the question of conscience. Before examining the transformation in which he is finally purged of the desire to know the ground, let us consider briefly the theological context behind the fiery allegory of "Pyrrhus' ear."

The Phylactery of the Law

The Pauline Epistles refer several times to the burning and searing of conscience.[21] But while Paul speaks of the searing, burning, and branding of conscience, he never makes it entirely clear whether this is a literal or a metaphoric description of the soul's experience of the spirit or exactly how we are to understand the various components in his account. In Paul's usage, *syneidesis* relates only

20. Edgar Allan Poe reworks all these elements in his own allegory of conscience: his "Conqueror Worm," like the serpentine Virgilian Pyrrhus, is "a crawling thing," a "blood-red thing that writhes from out / The scenic solitude"; and like Shakespeare's Pyrrhus, who is "o'ersized with coagulate gore," Poe's worm of conscience is "in human gore imbued" (Poe, *The Poems*, 325–26).

21. For a list of all New Testament references to *synedeisis* and *auto syneidenai*, see Pierce, *Conscience in the New Testament*, which also discusses those passages that deal with the burning and searing of conscience (esp. 91–94).

to bad conscience; conscience is exclusively a matter of guilt. While the law is inscribed, circumcision-like, in the heart, one does not feel the pain of being brought before the law unless and until one has transgressed the law of one's nature. The images of burning describe the experience of being judged by the internal monitor of the law. The more one is brought before the law, the more seared and burned one's conscience becomes, even to the point of being obliterated. Over time the repeatedly scarred and damaged conscience can be entirely consumed by the fire of the law, and one becomes conscienceless. Though never explicitly unpacked, Paul's account assumes at least a twofold structure in which the fire of the law as inscription or mark comes into proximity or contact with an entity of uncertain nature that is susceptible of being destroyed by the indestructible flame that judges its acts. It is as though conscience were a finite mass or surface that could sustain only so much heat before there is nothing left to be scarred or defiled. Although the law presumably remains in the heart, the individual's soul can no longer come into contact with the fire of the spirit. By the same token, however, the proper relation to the law would hold in reserve the relation called *syneidesis,* since Paul regards that judgment as being exclusively a function of punishment. When he speaks, for example, in 1 Timothy 4:2 of the use of a branding iron to perform the cauterization of conscience (*kauteridion*), the idea is that of a therapeutic use of heat to cure a disfunctional conscience, which will presumably begin to heal beneath the scar.

It remained a task for the history of theology to sort out just what might be going on in Pauline *syneidesis,* and the first step was the obvious one of formulating the bifold structure of conscience implicit in Paul's thinking. There were, of course, other ideas and terms in the New Testament that played an important role in the formalization and systematization of conscience. In Matthew 3:12, for example, John the Baptist speaks of Christ's advent and of a baptism not of water but of fire: "He will baptize you with the fire of the Holy Spirit. His winnowing fork is in his hand; he will clear his threshing floor and gather the wheat into his granary. The chaff he will burn with unquenchable fire." Mark 9:46 speaks of the fires of hell in terms of a relentlessly devouring worm: "Their worm dieth not, and the fire is not quenched." Such imagery links the punishments of conscience and the fate of the body and the soul after death. The task of medieval theology was that of accommodating the language and imagery of these punishments within the formal structures of theoretical and practical judgment.

What would eventually prove to be the solution to the problem of the division between conscience and the law, soul and spirit, probably emerged by accident. In the eleventh century the term *synderesis*, or alternatively *synteresis*, was employed to describe the innate rational resistance to the desire to sin. This might have been the result of a misreading of *syneidesis* and its various grammatical forms in the Pauline epistles.[22] Failing to grasp the relation between *syneidesis* and its Latin translation as *conscientia*, the medieval Schoolmen took the habit of contrasting their imaginary term *synderesis* to *conscientia*: the former described the law as theoretical potential—that is, what we could know if we so willed—and the latter described our practical application of this theoretical knowledge to individual cases. In general, then, a distinction was made between pure practical reason and the application of pure practical reason to particular cases. Thus was born the art of casuistry, wherein the doubting conscience was led by the learned priest through the labyrinths of casuistry to the exercise of right reason. After more than a millennium, Pauline *syneidesis* had finally given birth to a formal theology and to an immense ecclesiastical institution.

The Jesuits particularly excelled in the art of ministering to the conscience-struck sinner, so much so that in 1549 Pope Paul III "authorized all Jesuits to hear confessions of all Christians without

22. For a brief history, see Timothy Potts, *Conscience in Medieval Philosophy*. See also the excellent bibliography in Lowell Gallagher, *Medusa's Gaze: Casuistry and Conscience in the Renaissance*.

specifying the necessity of obtaining episcopal licenses."[23] The task of the Protestant religion was that of providing guidelines for correlating *synderesis* and *conscientia* outside of the strict rules of Catholic casuistry. The development of what A. C. McGiffert calls "Protestant Scholasticism" was really quite inevitable.[24] "This is Christian knowledge," writes Philip Melanchthon in *Loci Communes* (1521), "to know what the law demands, where you may find power for doing the law, and grace for sin, how you may strengthen the feeble mind against the devil, the flesh, and the world, how you may console an afflicted conscience."[25] In comparison with the elaborate rules of casuistry in the Catholic Church, Protestant casuistry was rather simple and straightforward; the question of knowing the law was a matter of self-culture and self-discipline largely bereft of external authority. And while the Puritans wanted to take this simplicity even further, wanted to open knowledge of the law to one and all, the Catholics were trying to expand their authority over access to the law. Following the Council of Trent, Pope Pius IV revoked the Jesuit privilege, and Father Carlo Borromeo followed by requiring "all confessors to be examined."[26] The Catholic doctrine of probabilism was introduced in order to enhance the persuasive power of the tropes of casuistry by appealing not only to external authority but to the inherent law of *synderesis*.[27]

23. Henry Charles Lea, *A History of Auricular Confession and Indulgences in the Latin Church*, 1:302.

24. See A. C. McGiffert, *Protestant Thought before Kant*, 141–54.

25. Quoted in ibid., 73.

26. Lea, *History of Auricular Confession*, 1:303. One of the most interesting consequences of Borromeo's decrees is to be found in the later thought of Jacques Lacan. During his seminar for 1974–75, titled *R.S.I.* (Real/Symbolic/Imaginary), Lacan decided to redefine the structure of psychoanalysis in terms of what he called "Borromean knots," which described the topological configuration through which the tripartite structure would presumably be knotted together—a covert allusion to this episode in church history. Lacan's point is that psychoanalysts too must submit to "the pass," and that the structure of psychoanalytic theory and, above all, its institutional practice are not far removed from the Borromean decree and the events following the Council of Trent.

27. Lea, *History of Auricular Confession*, 2:332–34. See also Harnack's discussion of probabilism in *The History of Dogma*, 7:101–10.

Sixteenth-century theology is a continuous chiasmus in which Protestants move outward toward institutional structure and Catholics move inward toward the law of the heart. Conscience becomes the name of these infinite and irresolvable crossings. Somewhere near the middle lies the Elizabethan settlement and the compromises of Anglican theology.[28] To understand how they attempt to plot a middle course, we might turn first to one of Shakespeare's Puritan contemporaries, the prolific William Perkins, who refers incessantly to the wounded conscience that can only be healed by Christ, the seared conscience, the worm of conscience, the bond of conscience, and the gift of conscience.[29] But it is Perkins's characterization of what he calls "practicall or Case-divinitie" that is most interesting, for he accuses the formalism of casuistry of trying "to bind conscience where God looseth it, and to loose where he binds."[30] This kind of Puritan criticism of Anglican theology, accusing it of remaining too much under the sway of a Jesuitical spirit, seems to me very close to the kind of position Shakespeare is trying to take in *Hamlet,* which will determine his subsequent treatment of conscience. Shakespeare does not, of course, lapse like Perkins into the monotony of Puritan polemic, but he does try to keep conscience unfettered, much more unfettered than the Puritans could ever have tolerated. The cultural and ideological work of Elizabethan and Jacobean theater and poetry lies somewhere in the shifting ground between the binding and the loosening of conscience.[31]

Though it was written after Shakespeare's death, Jeremy Taylor's *Ductor Dubitantium* (1660) provides the most articulate account of conscience by an Anglican theologian and one that helps us most fully to grasp the complexities of the allegory of conscience in "Pyrrhus' ear." Taylor has finally sorted out the bifold structure of conscience and he unfolds it with exemplary clarity:

28. For a sketch of this history, see Elliot Rose, *Cases of Conscience.*
29. See *William Perkins, 1558–1602, English Puritanist,* esp. 7, 31, 69, 75.
30. Perkins, *A Discourse of Conscience,* in *William Perkins,* 33.
31. See Camille Wells Slights, *The Casuistical Tradition in Shakespeare, Donne, Herbert, and Milton;* and John Wilkes, *The Idea of Conscience in Renaissance Tragedy.*

1) The *synteresis* or the first act of conscience S. Hierome calls
   scintillam conscientiae, the spark or fire put into the heart of
   man.
2) The *syneidesis,* which is specifically called conscience of the
   deed done, is the bringing fuel to this fire.
3) And when they are thus laid together, they will either shine or
   burn, acquit or condemn.[32]

All the accounts of the court of conscience from Richard Hooker to
Immanuel Kant and beyond can be reduced to Taylor's fiery allegory, for the idea of bringing fuel to the fire is really the kernel in the
shell of the more well-known image of coming before the bar of the
court and pleading one's case to the judge. The court of conscience
tries to humanize the essential facelessness of the fire of the law. But
what happens here, instead of a sentence, is that the fuel either
survives the flame or is consumed by it. The fiery crash of Ilium and
the silent pause within "Pyrrhus' ear" are figures of this Pauline
allegory in which fuel is brought to the inner fire and judgment is
awaited.

Taylor adds to his allegory of conscience a fascinating Baroque
element for which I have seen no precedent. It involves the fiery
structure of *synteresis,* which is the highest and primary function of
the law and which Taylor depicts as flames burning within what he
calls "the Phylactery."[33] He acknowledges no source for this term,
but it is also used by Milton, and both writers doubtless derived it
from the New Testament, where it appears in Matthew to describe
the small Jewish prayer boxes tied around the wrist and forehead
and containing slips of paper on which are written passages from
scripture that one may rely on during prayer. Matthew adduces the
phylakterion in order to ridicule the Pharisees who wear particularly large phylacteries, even though their knowledge of the law is

32. Jeremy Taylor, *Ductor Dubitantium,* 9.14.
33. Ibid., 9.41.

in fact so small. Taylor implants the phylactery into the soul itself and depicts the divine "dictation" that it registers as the flames of *synteresis*. The phylactery is the archive, "the keeper of records," where the flames of judgment burn without consuming the law that they embody. Moreover, these fiery laws and measures of the spirit can be brought "before the eye of conscience . . . to be read and used for directions." All this might apply to Shakespeare's allegory with the significant difference that Shakespeare speaks not of the eye of conscience but its ear. From the *thumos* of the *Iliad* to Euripides' *Orestes* and Virgil's *Aeneid*, Taylor assembles a glossary of terms and images in the history of conscience. What is important in understanding Shakespeare's relation to these images and to this history is that unlike all the others, he can never bring himself to authorize and determine the ground of the legislative, binding part of conscience. Even though the bond of duty takes many forms in his writing, Shakespeare never claims for them a ground in knowledge or feeling or faith.

Reading Readiness

In his 1966 interview with *Der Spiegel*, Heidegger speaks of the need "to prepare readiness, through thinking and poetry, for the appearance of the god or for the absence of the god during the decline; so that we do not, simply put, die meaningless deaths, but that when we decline, we decline in the face of the absent god."[34] This is Heidegger's Shakespearean moment. The word "readiness" (*Bereitschaft*), as we saw in Chapter 2, plays a significant role in *Being and Time*, where it signals the resolute openness (*Entschlossenheit*) that Dasein attains once it has negotiated the crisis of Being-guilty and faced the intractability of its relation to Being. "Readiness" signals the culminating moment for Dasein as well as

---

34. "Spiegel Interview with Martin Heidegger," 57.

for Hamlet, who, of course, famously uses this word to announce the transformation that has taken place in his relation to death (5.2.218).

The translation does not catch the echoes in Heidegger's German, which speaks of "eine Bereitschaft vorzubereiten," and later, where the English reads "the preparation of readiness," Heidegger writes "die Bereitung der Bereitschaft." It is thus a question of "readying readiness," which is to say, a question of listening to the ringing within language and finding there the "face of the absent god" (*Angesicht des abwesenden Gottes*). Here again we meet with the now-familiar motif of *der Fehl Gottes,* the divine lack, the want of holy names, near which only the poet dare dwell. What is different here is that Heidegger's meditation on the need for the saving power of the poet takes place in what is an implicitly Shakespearean context. Though Shakespeare's name does not appear, the word "readiness" (*Bereitschaft*) is so redolent of its Hamletian ethos that even (perhaps especially) in its German rendering—which draws on the long-standing dialogue between Shakespeare and German philosophy—we can have no doubt that Shakespeare silently presides over the entire scene. That Heidegger should render this homage to Shakespeare, and that he does so at precisely the point where the interviewer seems to anticipate some sort of conventional cliché about philosophy and changing the world, gives this (often remarked but little understood) moment in the interview an extraordinary edge and tension.

The use of the colloquial expression *verrecken,* which appears in quotation marks in the German, is crucial to the rugged effect Heidegger is trying to create. The English translator's rendering of it as "die meaningless deaths" gets the idea but not the abruptness of, let us say, "croaking" or "kicking the bucket." I would prefer, however, something like "so that when our reckoning comes," which gives that sense of wreck and rack, of perishing and being leveled, as well as the German sound of *verrecken* and its proximity to *verrechnen,* which means "reckoning up."

Shakespeare gives some rather curious names to those strange figures who call Hamlet toward his *Untergang,* his "going under" or "decline," as though the names themselves are part of that ringing within language which calls the poet toward the site of the absent god: Y*orick/Osric.* Something like the "o-will-o" is going on here in the "o-ric-o," as though it were the sound of laughter coming from a death's head, a certain melancholy *rictus,* which is Latin for the laughter of the open mouth and here names the uncanny laughter that calls us before the "face of the absent god."

Hamlet has already reminisced with the gravedigger about Yorick, and Osric has just departed when Hamlet responds to Horatio's plea that he not accept Claudius's invitation, which they both know is a trap. Hamlet, however, is determined to make no determination: "Not a whit. We defy augury. There is special providence in the fall of a sparrow. If it be now, 'tis not to come; if it be not to come, it will be now; if it be not now, yet it will come. The readiness is all. Since no man, of aught he leaves, knows aught, what is't to leave betimes? Let be" (5.2.215–20). The "readiness of expectation [*Erwartung*]," Heidegger calls it: "this readying of the readiness for keeping oneself open for the arrival or the default of the god [*des Sich-Offen-Haltens für die Ankunft oder das Ausbleiben des Gottes*]."[35] The "fall of a sparrow," a phrase that Shakespeare found in Matthew and in John Calvin, is Hamlet's image for the fact that he is no longer falling himself. Heidegger continues: "The experience of this default is not nothing, but rather a liberation [*Befreiung*] of human beings from what I called the fallenness into entities [*die Verfallenheit an das Seiende*] in *Being and Time.*" Once again I have rendered *Ausbleiben* as "default" rather than as "absence," which nevertheless also misses Heidegger's sense of the "nonarrival" or the "remaining withheld" of something missing from the place to which it is appointed. We are perhaps *ready* to *read* Hamlet's *read*iness.

35. Ibid., 58 (translation modified); "Spiegel-Gespräch," 101.

What readies Hamlet for readiness, what enables him to abandon the project of becoming an avenger, what readies him for death, is his discovery at sea of the documents by which Claudius hoped to engineer his death and of the means necessary to neutralize his uncle's plot. Hamlet departed Denmark with Rosencrantz and Guildenstern in a mood once again affecting Pyrrhus in "total gules": "My thoughts be bloody or be nothing worth" (4.4.65). But now, returning from England and recounting his adventures to Horatio, he appears to take a new attitude: "There's a divinity that shapes our ends, / Rough-hew them how we will" (5.2.10–11). What has happened to Hamlet? Has he become a Christian? The critical debate has been misguided, I believe, in trying to decide whether Hamlet returns to Denmark a Christian or remains a pagan. Before I address the critics, let us try to determine what "divinity" means to Hamlet.

Restless at sea because "in my heart there was a kind of fighting / That would not let me sleep," Hamlet "rashly" and out of "indiscretion" discovers the document that orders his death and proceeds to substitute for it a very different set of orders. He describes his mental state: "Ere I could make a prologue to my brains, / They had begun the play" (5.2.30–31). Having with difficulty managed to write in a "fair" hand, Hamlet must now seal the forgery with the royal signet or it will be immediately discovered: "even in that was heaven ordinant. / I had my father's signet in my purse, / Which was the model of that Danish seal" (5.2.48–50). Unlike Poe's Dupin in "The Purloined Letter," who must create an instrument with which to forge the Minister D.'s seal, Hamlet has a "model" ready to hand. Harold Jenkins's note defines model as an "exact likeness"; Philip Edwards says it means a "copy."[36] It suffices, in any case. Hamlet then remarks that his conscience is unaffected by having sent his two escorts off to their death, and even adds later that the whole episode confirms that it would be in "per-

36. See Shakespeare, *Hamlet*, ed. Edwards, 227; and ed. Jenkins, 396.

fect conscience" for him to murder Claudius (5.2.67). A strange temporality has begun to unfold around Hamlet, as well as a dizzying series of identifications. Whether or not the voice of the ghost or conscience is to be believed, Hamlet now has read the proof of Claudius's guilt in this attempted murder. Hamlet has just come from his conversation with the gravedigger, who reminded the prince that he was born on the day Old Hamlet overcame Old Fortinbras. Has not Shakespeare created for Hamlet a countersignature event? Having discovered his own name anamorphically distorted in "Shakespyrrhus' ear," Shakespeare now proceeds to unfold around Hamlet a similar correlation within utterly random letters and dates and things. The groundlessness, the burning, the unreadable fire Hamlet discovered when he inquired into the law of his duty does not suddenly resolve itself into either Christian providence or pagan necessity. Hamlet returns to Denmark with a new "readiness" to wait for what will come, knowing now, as he had not known before, that what is to come may be something from very much earlier. Shakespeare endows Hamlet with the gift of the countersigning thing that liberates him into the abyss of Dasein's finitude.

First, however, let me make the difference clear between my reading and some earlier responses to this passage. I take as my point of reference the suggestive "cultural materialist" reading by Alan Sinfield, which focuses on Calvin's dilemma in the passage in the *Institutes* that discusses "a special providence in the fall of a sparrow." Sinfield reveals that Shakespeare was influenced by the instability in Calvin's account of the relation between Senecan fatalism and Christian predestination, and that "the embarrassing overlap [in Calvin's text] between protestantism and the doctrine it seeks to repudiate" spills over into *Hamlet* itself.[37] Sinfield also believes that Elizabethan audiences would have found the play as "uplifting" as "the sermons they had heard." Sinfield is right to try to

37. Alan Sinfield, *Faultlines: Cultural Materialism and the Politics of Dissident Reading*, 228.

work some refinements upon readings (such as A. C. Bradley's) that argue for a pagan Hamlet, or readings (such as Roland Frye's) that Hamlet is a Christian. The problem is that Sinfield's own solution, that *Hamlet* itself is caught in a larger cultural confusion between the two world views, does not adequately account for Shakespeare's idioms. Shakespeare is a reader of classical and Christian texts, writing in a Christian culture. But we must not assume that his particular attention to a passage in the *Institutes* about "a special providence" indicates a conservative Calvinist streak in Shakespeare's thinking.[38]

First, Calvinism is not, as Sinfield seems to imply, synonymous with Protestantism, nor is the Calvinism of the Puritans to be confused with the Calvinism of the Anglican Church. The Puritan Calvinism that Sinfield believes he detects in Hamlet's "readiness" speech would link the notion of "a special providence" to the notion of election and thus to a certain abjection of human existence before the might of God and the authority of the law. If Shakespeare's audience thought *Hamlet* had anything to do with this sort of Calvinist sermon, they were not paying very close attention. Sinfield elides the really interesting differences that Shakespeare is keen to mark between his position and the state religion. We need to take Shakespeare's radically post-Christian ethos much more seriously and to be more careful about enlisting him in the ranks of those who support the dominant ideology. Shakespeare places the terminology of Calvinism in the service of a poetic meditation on the relation of human existence to language and death which cannot be reinscribed within the Judeo-Christian tradition. Shake-

38. Max Weber's characterization of the Calvinist attitude toward the afterlife, which holds that it was "more certain than all the interests of life in this world" (*The Protestant Ethic and the Spirit of Capitalism*, 110), suggests that very few serious Calvinists would have found *Hamlet* an edifying experience. They would also have recognized, however, that the topology of death was the play's central concern. Perhaps echoing Old Hamlet's allusion to "the porches of my ears" (1.5.63), Francis Bacon begins his "History of Life and Death" by defining his work as "the inquiry concerning *the porches of death;* that is, of the things which happen to men both a little before and a little after the point of death" (142; emphasis added). "Readiness" is being on the "porches" of life/death.

speare does not proceed by the sort of philosophical-aesthetic col-
lage that would, as Sinfield suggests, place a neo-Stoic or Senecan
view of fate in the service of a Calvinist ideology. His daemonic
reinvention of conscience in *Hamlet* is relentless in its unsettling of
all the commonplaces, for Hamlet refuses to abject himself before
the myth of either an inward divine spark or the outward conscience that is divine retribution. He simply affirms the irreducibility of his own idiom before an enigma that has neither a face
nor a figure. Sinfield's historicizing reading is finally itself an instance of the conservative ideological practice it attributes to *Hamlet*.

Hamlet's "divinity" is not a confusion of Senecan fate and the
God of Calvin in the service of state power but their transforming
reinvention. There is in Hamlet, as Benjamin remarked, something
of the abandon of the language of the martyrs, but in Shakespeare's
handling its pathos is immeasurably heightened by its infinite distance from the doctrine of grace and election. Hamlet abandons
himself to the idiom and the singular experience of time to which
he now realizes he has already been abandoned. It is his vision of
the unreadable singularity to which chance and fate have delivered
him that constitutes the essence of his transformation in Act 5.
"The interim is mine," he tells Horatio. "And a man's life's no
more than to say 'one'" (5.2.74). Through a series of uncanny
coincidences, he recognizes in his own time what Kafka's man from
the country is told, at the moment of his death, by the guardian of
the law: "This gate was made only for you. I am going to shut it
now." We might also recall sonnet 136: "Among a number one is
reckoned none." To read readiness is to be ready for oneself.

"The readiness is *all*"; there is nothing else, no knowledge to be
had of what we leave behind at death but only our readiness (not
our knowledge) to pass beneath the "face of the absent god." Our
only redemption is to grasp our life in its singular configuration; it
is a rare thing, the gift of artists and thinkers, perhaps; it is the gift
Shakespeare gives Hamlet, beyond all debt and beyond both pagan

fear and Christian guilt. The not-being-there of the god, the default in Being, may come at any time; it may have already come to us at some point in our past without our fully recognizing it; and if it has not come yet, it may still arrive at any time; the lack of the god may yet make its claim upon us. Something may happen tomorrow that reveals to me that the lack had already made me its own long before I recognized it; and if it has not come, still it will come. Our readiness to read the unique idiom of our experience of the lack in Being releases us: "Let be." Is it a mere interjection—"Enough!"— or a liberation from the world of entities, the fall upward into Dasein's abyssal finitude? Hamlet, am/let, being/releasement, being/death.

Razing the Sanctuary: *Measure for Measure*

One sentence in particular in Stephen Gosson's *School of Abuse* (1579) must have long remained in Shakespeare's thoughts. It is a line, moreover, to which Philip Sidney, who was not very prescient with respect to the prospects for the English stage, failed to respond in the *Apology for Poetry*. In a sense, Shakespeare never did anything *but* respond to Gosson's idea that the theater is a place where poets seek "to wounde the conscience": "There they set abroche strange confortes of melody, to tickle the ear."[39] In *Hamlet,* just before the players arrive, the prince remarks that the clowns in the theater succeed only in making those laugh who laugh easily in any case: "The clown shall make those laugh whose lungs are tickle a' th' sere" (2.2.332). The image is that of a tickling of the lungs which causes them to burst not into flame but into laughter. For Shakespeare, as we have seen, the wounding of conscience is the provenance not so much of poetry as of Puritanism. Such wounding is also the work of the state insofar as it intrudes into the individual's conscience and imposes its will with a burning brand.

39. Stephen Gosson, *The School of Abuse,* 32.

Hamlet's "readiness" breaches political ideology as well as poetic theology and belies perhaps Shakespeare's own uncertainty about the future of Puritan influence in the strange "interim" between the execution of Essex and the death of Elizabeth. By the time of *Measure for Measure* (1604), James I had arrived, but Shakespeare's concern about the zealots who would clean the conscience of the body politic had only become greater. In making a transition from *Hamlet* to the later plays, I want to consider some aspects of *Measure for Measure* that reveal a certain shift in Shakespeare's relation to the question of conscience. My argument is that Shakespeare came to see the Puritan appropriation of the inwardness of conscience as so profound a danger that he began what I regard as a certain defense of conscience *as* poetry and, more precisely, as the primordial heat of poetic fire. The brand burning in Diana's bath at the end of the sonnets and the searing heat of conscience in *Hamlet* are slowly gathered into a new vision of the enigma of human nature that would resist Puritan incursions into the sanctuary that is the question of conscience. Having himself dismantled several of the presuppositions concerning conscience, and having done so precisely in order to resist both the dominant Anglican ideology and its Puritan challengers, Shakespeare thought it necessary to reinvest conscience with poetic capital, to endow it with a new substantiality, and to make it the site of the promise, if not the reality, of the coming of the god. If there is a tone of affirmation in the later work, it emerges from the searing heat of conscience.

In his account of conscience in *Elements of the Philosophy of Right* (1820), Hegel distinguishes between what he calls "formal conscience," which is the abstract inwardness of infinite self-certainty where the will to know itself does not yet have a specific content, and "true conscience," which is concrete duty that wills the good in practice. He continues here the radical reinterpretation of conscience of his *Phenomenology of Spirit* (1807), in which he argued, against Kant's notion of the universal content of conscience as a relation to the pure morality of law, that what is universal in the content of conscience is not its abstract *Moralität* but the sheer contingency of the circumstances of an individual's situation: one's "ethicity" or *Sittlichkeit*. The "truth" of conscience in Hegel's earlier text is thus "the caprice of the individual, and the contingency of his unconscious natural being." Hegel draws the inevitable conclusion: "The result would be that morality would be made dependent on the necessary *contingency* of *insight*" and that "consequently, what counts is not simply knowing in general, but conscience's knowing of the circumstances."[40] If Kantian morality recalls the *synteresis* of the Schoolmen, we might say that Hegel places all the emphasis on *syneidesis* as the practice of the good rather than on *synteresis* as the universal content on which all such practices are based. What is universal for Hegel is the inevitable division within the subject that experiences as universally binding what is in fact specific to its experience. Conscience thus becomes the site of a certain sublation (*Aufhebung*) of the difference between "universal essence" and "absolutely self-contained and exclusive individuality."[41] More precisely, the place of this sublated difference is the language of subjective judgments of conscience. The "language" of "actual conscience," writes Hegel, is itself the site of this dialectical event in which the subject experiences the separation between universality and actuality "within its inner being, and finds the outer existence of this inner being in the *utterance* of its judgment [*in der Rede seiner Urteils*]."[42] What is universal is the absolute contingency of conscience *and* the fact that language is the site in which this difference is actualized in the practice of willing the dictates of conscience.

When he returns to these issues in the distinction between true and formal conscience, there is a new note of caution and of respect for the residual Kantianism that remains in the abstractness of the formal conscience: "As this unity of subjective knowledge and that which has being in and for itself, conscience is a sanctuary [*Heilig-*

40. G. W. F. Hegel, *The Phenomenology of Spirit*, 390–91, 393.
41. Ibid., 409.
42. Ibid., 406.

tum] which it would be a *sacrilege* to violate. But whether the conscience of a *specific individual* is in conformity with this Idea of conscience, and whether what it *considers* or declares *to be good* is also actually good, can be recognized only from the *content* of this supposed good."[43] As a site or "sanctuary," formal conscience is necessary for the emergence of true conscience but in itself remains without content. Although Hegel does not want to appear to violate it, he wants to make clear that formal conscience as such is not yet the good or duty. As he goes on to argue, the very nature of the certainty that the subject is afforded in the sanctuary of formal conscience can and does lead to hypocrisy and all the other potential evils to which the exercise of true conscience is always liable. He singles out the theological doctrine of probabilism as an example of the most sophisticated kind of hypocrisy, since it assures one of a good conscience as long as one is able to discover "*any* good reason" for a given action.[44] This assault on Catholic casuistry is echoed a few pages later when Hegel speaks of those Protestants who have recently converted to Catholicism as having done so in an effort to find "a fixed point, a support, and an authority" for conscience that would lie outside the concrete practices and the historicity of *Sittlichkeit* or "ethical life."[45]

All these issues are remarkably relevant to reading *Measure for Measure*. What William Empson called the play's "brooding sense of what would happen if the Puritans came to power"[46] is heightened by virtue of being set in a strangely familiar Catholic Vienna where casuistry has an oddly Puritan accent.[47] The generally uncanny tone and atmosphere emerge largely from Shakespeare's determination to create the sense of a menace that is at once very

43. G. W. F. Hegel, *Elements of the Philosophy of Right*, 164 (sec. 137).
44. Ibid., 172 (sec. 140).
45. Ibid., 186 (sec. 141).
46. William Empson, *The Structure of Complex Words*, 287–88.
47. See Leah Marcus, *Puzzling Shakespeare: Local Reading and Its Discontents*, esp. 192–99, for ways in which the play deals with English anxieties about continental Catholicism in 1604.

remote and terribly nearby. In many respects this play is the culmination of Shakespeare's fears about a possible Puritan cleanup of
the city, which appears here as the sudden return to the old law:
that is, a turn to a patriarchal and fundamentalist Puritanism. The
withdrawal of the duke into his wonted "dark corners" leaves behind the messenger (*angelos*) of the old law, Angelo. The fear of the
old law is the fear that the future will bring the return of what lay at
the beginning, for the old law is the old conscience, the Pauline
syneidesis that demands retribution, rather than Matthew's "Judge
not lest ye be judged." But the difference between old and new law,
Judaic and Christian, is not so easily sustained. The slipperiest
point, as Empson noted, is the play's concern with "sense," which
means at once judgment and pleasure. The interesting point, however, lies where these differing senses of sense cross and chiastically
exchange their senses: the point, that is, where the judgment of
conscience and the higher pleasures of instinctual renunciation become one and the same (in their difference).

This is the site of the sanctuary, and it is Angelo who places it at
risk in *Measure for Measure*:

> Having waste ground enough
> Shall we desire to raze the sanctuary
> And pitch our evils there? Oh fie, fie, fie,
> What dost thou or what art thou, Angelo?
> Dost thou desire her foully for those things
> That make her *good?*
>
> (2.3.174–77)

J. W. Lever's paraphrase is helpful: "Since there are places where
putrefying matter can be deposited, why do I want to ruin the
temple and erect a privy on its site?" But what, precisely, is "the
sanctuary"? And why the strange instability in the word "raze"
(raise)? The very distinction between "raze" in the sense of "to level

to the ground" and "pitch" in the sense of "to erect in its place," is difficult to sustain, and "pitching evils" and "razing the sanctuary" begin to appear as moments in a single process. Since enough ground has apparently already been laid waste, the only possible reason for destroying the "sanctuary" would be the pleasure one might take in erecting one's "evils" on that specific ground. Razing one sanctuary is thus part and parcel of raising still another. The pleasure, in other words, is to be derived from obliterating conscience as the site of truth, the law, and so on, and then erecting in its place a bad or guilty conscience. That is the sense of Angelo's betrayal of sense. In the place of the judgments of conscience Angelo wants the pleasures of "sense," but not just any sense—only the "sense" that can be felt, only the sensations that can be experienced, within the "sanctuary" where conscience once stood. Far from being conscienceless, Angelo has a conscience too highly developed; it has, as a Freudian might say, absorbed too many object-cathexes and channeled too much destructive libido to the ego-structures. Isabella excites his desire precisely because she appears so much like him in the purity and determination of her faith. She appears to him, in other words, like the very incarnation of his ego-ideal, the possession of which triggers the unleashing of all his pent-up destructive libido. What Angelo calls "the wanton stings and motions of the sense" (1.4.50) describe the higher pleasures of instinctual renunciation on the verge of revolt as his repressed libido begins to well up within his overdeveloped ego-structures.

And in order to conceal the entire process he falls prey to a particularly cruel and heinous hypocrisy. Recognizing the aberration of his "formal conscience," he willfully perseveres in trying to foist it upon the world in the guise of a conspicuously "true" conscience, when in fact his administration of the law is a response not to the contingencies of his situation vis-à-vis his community but to the secret source of his pleasurable sense. Angelo derives intense pleasure from violating the "sanctuary" of the "formal conscience"

and hypocritically chooses that pleasure over the concrete responsibilities of "ethical life." He is, in other words, Shakespeare's consummate depiction of the hypocrisy of moral casuistry.

Angelo wants to "raze the sanctuary" of his aberrant conscience,
which has, by his own admission, already been "sear'd." He is
himself amazed by his ability to mouth empty words to Heaven
while thinking only of Isabella, and he surmises that he may have
examined his conscience too much and as a result "sear'd" it into
unrecognizability: "The state whereon I studied / Is, like a good
thing being often read, / Grown sear'd and tedious" (2.4.7–8). The
folio reads "feard," which has been corrected in most modern
editions to "sere," meaning "dried" or "faded." Even though the
difference is not great, modern editions would do well to incorpo-
rate Rowe and Hanmer's "sear'd," which, as we have seen throughout this book, is a central figure in Shakespeare's understanding of
the question of conscience.[48]

Isabella too refers to Angelo's duplicitous experience of language
and conscience:

> O perilous mouths,
> That bear in them one and the self-same tongue
> Either of condemnation or approof,
> Bidding the law make curtsey to their will,
> To follow as it draws!
>
> (2.4.171–75)

It is precisely this effort to draw the law to one's will that results in
the searing of conscience. The duke appears to believe at the play's
conclusion that Angelo's penitent soul will recover from the searing
and scarring it has endured. The duke, however, is neither an agree-
able nor a very reliable figure, and we have no need to be quite so
sanguine as he. He is above all a confessor who instructs Juliet on
how "to arraign her conscience" (2.3.21). And it is just such ar-

---

48. See the textual note in Lever's edition of Shakespeare, *Measure for Measure*, 54.

raignments of conscience that Shakespeare finds so troublesome to the state and to civil society. Needless to say, the daemonic figures of conscience always constitute an allegory of reading.

Isabella diagnoses the malaise at Vienna as a malady of self-certainty:

> But man, proud man,
> Dress'd in a little brief authority,
> Most ignorant of what he's most assur'd—
> His glassy essence—like an angry ape
> Plays such fantastic tricks before the high heaven
> As makes the angels weep.
>
> (2.2.118–23)

Shakespeare elaborates this diagnosis by adding that the disease of self-certainty also precipitates the work of death and the destructive impulses. The courtroom under Angelo's administration is as disordered as the stews under the guidance of Pompey and Mistress Overdone. The disorder and decay have set into the bones and the consciences of the denizens of Vienna/London, and are eating them alive from within.

Throughout the play it is Claudio whom Shakespeare endows with Hamletian lyric melancholy and with the paradoxes of reflection that alone capture the tone of the time:

> To sue to live, I find I seek to die,
> And seeking death, find life. Let it come on.
>
> (3.1.43–44)

4 Frustration: Heidegger, Freud, *Macbeth*

Pitch is the distinctive and distinguishing feature of self: Nothing else in nature comes near the unspeakable stress of pitch, distinctiveness, and selving, is self-being of my own . . . In that "cleave" of being which each of his creatures shews to God's eyes alone (or in its "burl" of being/uncloven) . . .

—GERARD MANLEY HOPKINS,
Sermons and Devotional Writings

Macbeth, Act V, Sc. V. Till famine cling thee. There is a North Country word *clam* or *clem,* meaning starve . . . Richard III *clammed to death* . . . the same connection between the two senses of *cling* as between *clam* and *clamor* (the words are probably distantly akin to *claudae, close, kleis,* clasp, etc. and *cleave*) . . . the notion seems to be that of closing the throat with inanition, throttling, etc.

—GERARD MANLEY HOPKINS, *Journals and Papers*

> right,
> wrong; reckon but, reck but, mind
> But thése two; wáre of a wórld where bút these twó tell,
> each off the óther; of a rack
> Where, selfwrung, selfstrung, sheath- and shelterless,
> thóughts agaínst thoughts ín groans grínd.

—GERARD MANLEY HOPKINS,
"Spelt from Sibyl's Leaves"

The ego . . . is frustration in its essence. Not frustration of a desire of the subject, but frustration by an object in which his desire is alienated and which the more it is elaborated, the more profound the alienation from his *jouissance* becomes for the subject.

—JACQUES LACAN, "The Function and Field
of Speech and Language in Psychoanalysis"

Conscience clings; worse still, it cleaves and clings to the cleft it cuts. *Macbeth* is Shakespeare's poem of the cleaving and clinging of conscience. It is also his drama of the absolute, fatal frustration brought on by the pangs of conscience. In *Macbeth* Shakespeare reinvents the sheer negativity of Pauline conscience in terms of its fatally persistent equivocations. It is his poem of the "great clatter" (5.7.21) of conscience. As this chapter's epigraphs indicate, the poet Gerard Manley Hopkins recognized the singular idiom that *cl-* words seem to constitute in Shakespeare's writing, especially in *Macbeth*. That they also inscribe the signature of the silent din of the guilty conscience would probably come as no surprise to Hopkins. In *Macbeth* Shakespeare resumes his dwelling place near the default in Being and moves still closer to the silent play of the language of the daemon. And once again, the language of the other signs through the silent play of the letter which it strews throughout the text of *Macbeth*. It gives itself to be read only in the inaudible clamor of a recurrent cluster of consonants. But now the letters no longer compose the name of a human subject, and no trace of subjectivity remains to mediate the expropriating power of Being's self-denial behind the remnant of the constrictive *cl-*.

In order to read, and thereby make audible, the clinging clatter of the cleaving call of the materiality of the daemon, and in order better to recognize the "wreck" of conscience it brings to presence, I would like first to sketch out an argument, via Derrida, Heidegger, and Freud, that presents the dilemma of conscience in terms of an intractable frustration. Like Shakespeare's *cl-* words, frustration will henceforth be our watchword for the lack of holy names.

Versagung and the Law of Stricture

The question of conscience is frustrating because it opens onto the unreadable lack in Being. In that sense, frustration belongs not to beings but to Being itself; it is the origin of the frustration it sends to beings. Frustration, like conscience, is binding; it constricts; it applies pressure; it cuts off the flow of blood in one place and causes it to flow faster elsewhere. If conscience were not frustrating, it wouldn't be conscientious; and, vice versa, if frustration were not conscientious, it wouldn't be frustrating.

Conscience names a moment in the immense differantial movement Derrida calls "a movement of *constriction:* grip, constraint, restriction; it is a question of closing up, squeezing, containing, suppressing, subjecting, compressing, repressing, subduing, reducing, forcing, subjugating, enslaving, hemming in."[1] To this impressive list we should be sure to add "frustrating," for frustration is the constriction in Being itself that sends all the stricturing closures and all the spurts of release, all the increases of pressure and their venting. The "movement of constriction" is for Derrida the general system in which the Hegelian dialectic is itself inscribed: "That it is subject to the law of what it is the law of, that is what gives to the structure of the Hegelian system a very twisted form so difficult to grasp."[2] Before spirit, matter, energy, force there is the law of stricture, the law of the gathering together of pressure at one point in order to release it at another. Constriction is thus "transcategorical," and its imperative is always "Clench tightly in order to make be."[3] From the emergence of space-time to the blossoming of a flower, from the renunciation of instinct to the erection of the thing in the name, the law of stricture compresses force through the constriction of a ring, an annulus, or an orifice, releases it, and then gathers it again at the next level. The dialectic is a figure for the nonfigure of *gl-* or *glas,* the movement of constriction and release: "what passes, more or less well, through the rhythmic strict-ure of an annulus."[4] Between and before all oppositions, Being gives the law of stricture, *différance,* the drive of the proper, the expropriating *Ereignis,* and the frustrations of conscience.

1. Jacques Derrida, *Glas,* 99a.
2. Ibid., 121a.
3. Ibid., 244a.
4. Ibid., 109b.

Conscience clings, grips, squeezes, and occasionally passes judgment. It's frustrating, this incessant movement of the absolute as the relentless constriction and release of *différance,* "the being-there of the not-there," "the beyond of pure negativity."[5] Before nature and the before the law, there is constriction, an irreducible structure of repetition without *archē* or *telos.* It gives Being, and It gives Time, as Heidegger says: giving is the relation that "holds" Time and Being "toward each other and brings them into being."[6] But the relation is already there waiting to receive the gift given by the It (*Es*) that gives; the relation (*Verhältnis*) is already ready to hold and keep (*halten*) Time and Being in relation. And since giving is the relation between Time and Being, doesn't it appear as though It is both Itself and the relation that It gives along with the gift of Time and Being? It is always double, always already on both sides at once, creating and destroying, giving and taking, perhaps in an effort to gather Itself impossibly together into a gathering that has never been; for between It and Its relation to Itself there is always already constriction. Heidegger does not call it constriction; he refers instead to the "holding back" or "denial" (*versagen*) within sending, which is what produces the epochs in the history of Being, the history of the donations It makes precisely by withholding the relation that is the gift. A giving that holds itself back in its giving is what he famously calls a "sending" (*Geschick*). The verb *versagen,* which figures prominently in "Time and Being," means that giving becomes a sending because it is frustrated, constricted in advance, divided into two and prevented from sending or giving all of itself for the simple reason that it doesn't possess all of itself—because, in a word, there is no Itself. Sending *is* frustration; *Geschick* is *Versagung* because its nature is to be refused, denied, frustrated from having, its own nature (*Versagung* means denial, refusal, or frustration). Before anything, then, there is Frustration, the spacing-timing of the frustrating, clenching grip that squeezes Time

5. Ibid., 210a, 221a.
6. Heidegger, *On Time and Being,* 5.

and Space themselves from one place to another. Constriction is Derrida's name for the frustrating refusal within the sending of the Heideggerian gift. Conscience calls from out of what we might call no longer the Big Bang but the Big Squeeze.

One of the key words in Heidegger's *Beiträge zur Philosophie* (*Vom Ereignis*), which was written in 1935–36 but not published until 1989, is *Versagung,* which names the frustration, refusal, and denial that are at the heart of the *Ereignis*'s articulation of the relation between Being and Time. The event of *Ereignis* is essentially constituted by its refusal of something that had been promised; *Ereignis* arises precisely as a holding back of something that should have been on its way. The *Ver-* in *Versagung* and *versagen* anticipates the terms that figure prominently in Heidegger's postwar thinking, terms such as *Sage* and *sagen,* which mean "legend" and "saying" but to which he gives a significance far beyond their dictionary meanings in order to indicate the cosmological force that enables Time and Being to be sent, which is to say, to be put in motion. And that never occurs except as a frustratingly irreducible denial and refusal. There is no question of a deep and abiding unity behind and beyond the *Versagung,* no utopian or subterranean promise of an absolving redemption as thinking reaches the univocal gathering before all sendings and donations. There is nothing but the cleaving cleft of the abyssal *Versagung.* In the *Beiträge,* *Versagung* is used in conjunction with such words as *Sichverbergen,* *Verbergung,* and *Verweigerung:* hiding, refusing, keeping silent.

"The abyss," writes Heidegger in the *Beiträge,* "is the hesitant *Versagung* of the ground."[7] The "essential unfolding [*Erwesung*] of Being as *Ereignis*" occurs as the frustrating denial that is *Versagung* (372). Dasein is not somehow afflicted by the cleaving fissure of Being's refusal but arises precisely as that cleft: "En-clefting is appropriating [*Erklüftung ist Ereignung*]" (311). *Ereignis* occurs as "the *deferring refusal* [*zögernde Versagung*] and thus as the matu-

7. Heidegger, *Beiträge zur Philosophie* (*Vom Ereignis*), 380 (my translation). Subsequent references in the text cite page numbers in this edition.

ration of 'time,' the greatness of the harvest and the immensity of the sending [*Verschenkung*], and in *truth* as *clearing* for the *self-concealing*" (268). The "refusal [*Verweigerung*] [is] the first and highest *sending* of Being [*Seyns*]" (241) and thus the constitutive and "innermost constriction [*die innigste Nötigung*]" of Dasein's most originary necessity (240). The clearing that is Dasein is the site of the "*Echo of refusal*" (*Der Anklang der Verweigerung*) (108). Thinking is Dasein's listening for the frustrating denial and withdrawal of the sending that echoes within it. *Versagung* cleaves and clings to Dasein, splits it open and holds the split open. The split or cleft is thus not simply a gap or default but Dasein's fundamental relation to Being. In the epoch of "the last gods" the *Versagung* of *Ereignis* finally appropriates Dasein in its most intimate nearness: "The greatest nearness of the last gods is appropriated when the *Ereignis* as the deferring self-denial [*Sichversagen*] comes to its highest realization in the refusal [*zur Steigerung in die Verweigerung kommt*]" (411). But the cleft that clings to Dasein even as it rends it brings an immensity of meaning rather than its deprivation. To recognize that we are already constricted by the turning within the cleft of *Ereignis* is, in all its imponderable richness and inexhaustibility, a harrowing and terrifying prospect for those who do not hear the silent ringing from out of the immense frustration that is the *Ereignis*.

Nothing is more frustrating on the contemporary intellectual scene than Heidegger's frustration; nothing is more unacceptable than his uncompromising insistence on the refusal and denial within Being and time and on the fact that they constitute our own irreducible self-relation. It is far easier to transform his writing into a private chapel for the initiated or to see him as a case in point of the bad conscience of the Nazi intellectual. That Heidegger is largely responsible for both these currents can never be denied. Any writer who makes such rigorous demands must accept the consequences of readings that, in effect, refuse refusal and leave readers so frustrated that they simply stop reading and start writing their own text. Perhaps even more frustrating, it may be the case that no reader, not even Heidegger himself, can satisfy the demands of reading *Versagung*.

Refusal and frustration play a significant role in "The Origin of the Work of Art" (1935), which now appears, in light of the *Beiträge*, as the text in which Heidegger found his way through the thought of *Versagung* to *Ereignis:* "Truth occurs precisely as itself in that the concealing denial, as refusal [*das verbergende Verweigern als Versagen*], provides the constant source to all clearing, and yet, as dissembling [*Verstellen*], it metes out to all clearing the undefeatable severity of error. Concealing denial is intended to denote that opposition in the nature of truth which subsists between clearing, or lighting, and concealing."[8] In the first published version of this essay (in *Holzwege, 1950*) Heidegger goes on in the next sentence to speak of this opposition as the "primal conflict [*Urstreit*]". But in his revision of the text for a 1960 reprinting, he changed *Urstreit* to *Ereignis*.[9] The *Versagen* lies not simply within the "dissembling" of beings who misrepresent themselves and are deceived by the self-misrepresentations of others but within the very relation that cleaves and constricts Dasein to Being and thus sustains and necessitates the irreducible "dissembling" in which beings are seized. There is no "outside" to "concealing denial" because it belongs to the *Ereignis* that joins Dasein to the nature of truth, which is itself constricted by the abyssal frustration within Being itself.

Freud's *Macbeth*

While Heidegger would assume that Freud's understanding of *Versagung* pertains only to the realm of *Verstellen* and *Schein,* to the "dissembling" and "semblance" in which beings are seized, my

8. Martin Heidegger, "The Origin of the Work of Art," 55.
9. Martin Heidegger, "Der Ursprung des Kunstwerkes," 42.

reading of Freud's encounter with *Macbeth* will suggest that Shakespeare's play presented Freud with an enigma he found so dark and impenetrable that he was, perhaps despite himself, led to reflect on the possibility that the nature of truth was itself constricted by an intractable nontruth. Heidegger's animadversions against psychoanalysis in general and Freud in particular occur within the general context of his assault on the self-certainty of Cartesian modernity.[10] Heidegger rehearses all his customary analyses concerning the assumptions (*Unterstellung, suppositio*) that Cartesian science makes about the nature of evidence and certainty, and, above all, about the fundamental content of Dasein's existence, which becomes reduced to a knowable, transparent subjectivity, while everything else is pushed into the essentially untheorized category of the unconscious. Heidegger's objective in his Zollikon seminars was to reinvent the direction of the *Daseinsanalyse* of Medard Boss and Ludwig Binswanger by steering it away from the Cartesian underpinnings of Freudian theory and toward a more fully articulated sense of Dasein's experience of time and space in the analytic session. Heidegger, however, never undertook a serious reading of Freud and thus succumbs to his own assumptions about the inner workings of Freudian theory.

My concern here is not with Heidegger's frustrations vis-à-vis psychoanalysis but with the conjunction in Freud's thinking between the phenomenon of *Versagung* and Shakespeare's *Macbeth*. Reading Freud on the relation between *Versagung* and *Macbeth* reveals that he is led to the very limits of his assumptions about psychoanalysis and toward the frustrating experience of a fundamental refusal or denial.

In a letter of July 17, 1914, to Sandor Ferenczi, Freud announces his interest in the play: "I have begun to study *Macbeth* which has long tormented me without my having been able to find a solution. How curious it is that I passed the theme over to [Ernest] Jones

10. See Martin Heidegger, *Zollikoner Seminare: Protokolle-Gespräche-Briefe*, esp. 136–44.

years ago, and now here I am so to speak taking it back again. There are dark forces at work in the play."[11] A year later Freud publishes an essay, "Some Character-Types Met With in Psycho-Analytic Work," consisting of three parts. The first, "Exceptions," concerns character types with illnesses linked to congenital defects who consequently regard themselves as "exceptions" whose lives have a special logic and whose literary exemplar is Shakespeare's hunchback, Richard III. The second part, "Those Wrecked by Success," contains Freud's reading of *Macbeth*—his most extensive and detailed reading of any Shakespearean work—and a discussion of Henrik Ibsen's *Rosmersholm*. The third, "Criminality from a Sense of Guilt," is a brief reflection on the oedipal dimensions of the illnesses described. There is also a related discussion of *Macbeth* in Freud's contemporaneous lectures at the University of Vienna during the fall of 1915, which were published as *Introductory Lectures on Psycho-Analysis*. In the essay "Some Character-Types" and in the lectures, *Macbeth* is adduced as an instance of a fundamental resistance: to analyzing the etiology of illness in the essay, and in connection with the inaccessibility of certain elements in the analysis of dreams in the lecture course. And the name Freud gives to this resistance is *Versagung*.

This term entered the vocabulary of psychoanalysis in his 1912 paper titled "Types of the Onset of Neurosis" ("Über neurotische Erkrankungstypen"). Frustration is the first of four ways in which a neurotic illness can be triggered: "The most obvious, the most easily discoverable and the most intelligible precipitating cause of the onset of neurotic illness lies in that external factor which may be generally described as *frustration* [*Versagung*]. The subject was healthy so long as his need for love was satisfied by a real object in the external world; he becomes neurotic as soon as this object is withdrawn from him without a substitute taking its place" (*SE* 12:231). The second way involves the patient's failure to fulfill

---

11. Quoted in Ernest Jones, *The Life and Work of Sigmund Freud*, 2:372.

"the demands of reality" and here "the accent falls on an internal change." This second type, however, ends up looking very much like the first: "Falling ill under the conditions of the second type leads directly to a special case of frustration. It is true that reality does not here frustrate *every* kind of satisfaction; but it frustrates the one kind which the subject declares is the only possible one. Nor does the frustration come immediately from the external world, but primarily from certain trends in the subject's ego" (*SE* 12:234). Patients of the third type fall ill because their development has been inhibited: "Their libido has never left its infantile fixations," and consequently they become ill "from the very fact of growing older." The fourth and most complicated type involves what Freud calls "a *relative* frustration," which is all that is needed to trigger an illness in a patient who already suffers from a "damming-up of libido" that will overwhelm the ego if it encounters the right frustration. *Versagung* plays a role in three of the four types. Freud does not want to insist on the theoretical validity of any of the four modes because the relation between internal/external and quantitative/qualitative remains so slippery that it becomes difficult to distinguish a subject who is able to "elude the frustration" from one who falls ill.

The larger theoretical project of the essay is interesting especially for the light it casts on Freud's reading of *Macbeth* and *Versagung* three years later. Freud's guiding impulse in "Types of the Onset of Neurosis" is to avoid any formal theoretical model and to limit his account only to "impressions arrived at empirically." This phrase from the essay's opening sentence is repeated in its concluding line: "Psychoanalysis has warned us that we must give up the unfruitful contrast between external and internal factors, of experience and constitution, and has taught us that we shall invariably find the cause of the onset of neurotic illness in a particular psychical situation, which can be brought about in a variety of ways" (*SE* 12:238). Freud's expectation is that an empirical account of causality involves both sides of the inside/outside opposition but within a specific economy that can never be determined in advance. Freud still has the certain expectation "that we shall invariably find the cause."

Versagung apparently names the external component in causality. But as we saw in Freud's account of the second way of falling ill the frustration does not "come immediately from the external world, but primarily from certain trends in the subject's ego"; that is, though it originates inside the ego, it appears to come from the outside at the moment the illness is triggered. The problem of causality is thus, at the outset, a problem of metaphor. Freud's self-assurance that he can empirically discern causes rests upon the metaphor of inside/outside that is itself reversible; how can an economy of quantity and quality be determined if the very difference between inside and outside remains impossible to decipher? Freud's rhetorical emphasis on the principles of certainty may be his effort to contain the "dark forces at work" here.

There is a connection in Freud's thinking between *Versagung,* the certainty of empirical causal explanation, and *Macbeth.* They all come unexpectedly together toward the end of one of his *Introductory Lectures,* "Difficulties and First Approaches," in the context of a discussion of what he calls the inaccessibility of the "essence of dreams." Here he reflects on the obscurity shrouding the origin of dreams that persists even after one has considered both the internal and external stimuli:

> Where the rest of the dream comes from remains obscure.
>
> Let us notice, however, one peculiarity of dream-life which comes to light in this study of the effects of stimuli. Dreams do not simply reproduce the stimulus; they work it over, they make allusions to it, they include it in some context, they replace it by something else. This is a side of the dreamwork which is bound to interest us since it may perhaps bring us nearer to the essence of dreams [*das Wesen des Traumes*]. When a person constructs some thing as a result of a stimulus, the stimulus need not on that

account exhaust the whole of the work. Shakespeare's *Macbeth*,
for instance, was a *pièce d'occasion* composed to celebrate the
accession of the king who first united the crowns of three king-
doms. But does this immediate historical occasion cover the content of the tragedy? Does it explain its greatness and its enigmas?
It may be that the external and internal stimuli, too, impinging
on the sleeper, are only the *instigators* of the dream and will
accordingly betray nothing to us of its essence. (*SE* 15:96)

Here there is no talk of invariably finding causes, though what is in
question is not the formation of a specific illness but the general
phenomenon of dreams. What is important about this passage is
that the question of "essence" and of the unfolding of the dream
event beyond the inside/outside opposition now stands in for what
the 1912 essay had called *Versagung*. *Wesen* now begins to name
the instability that went unacknowledged in the articulation of *Versagung* in "Types of the Onset of Neurosis." *Wesen* thus also names
a shift in Freud's certainty concerning the power of psychoanalysis
to determine causes.

The instability within the notion of *Versagung* is the focus of
much of Freud's attention in "Some Character-Types Met With in
Psycho-Analytic Work." For Freud no less than for Heidegger,
reading frustration is frustrating as *Versagung* becomes the name
of inside/outside phenomena as well as of the difference between
them. It becomes, in other words, another name for conscience
(*Gewissen*): "Analytic work has no difficulty in showing us that it
is the forces of conscience [*Gewissensmächte*] which forbid the
person to gain the long-hoped-for-advantage [*Gewinn*] from the
fortunate change in reality. It is a difficult task, however, to discover
the essence and origin of these judging and punishing tendencies,
which so often surprise us by their existence where we do not
expect to find them" (*SE* 14:318). Whereas the four types of patients fell ill because their expectations were somehow frustrated or
denied, those discussed in "Some Character-Types" fall ill precisely

because they have achieved everything they anticipated; that is why Freud calls them "Those Wrecked by Success." They experience the fulfillment of their goals the way the other four kinds of patients experienced the disappointment of theirs.

The task of the essay, then, is to explain how it is that success can function like frustration. Success becomes a frustration, people go into denial when they achieve long-sought goals, because the attainment of success triggers the memory of long-past frustrations, which, as Freud remarks, involve oedipal prohibitions and their surrogates in the voice of conscience: "Psycho-analytic work teaches that the forces of conscience [*Gewissenskräfte*] which induce illness in consequence of success, instead of, as normally, in consequence of frustration [*Versagung*], are closely connected with the Oedipus-complex, the relation to father and mother—as perhaps, indeed, is our sense of guilt in general" (*SE* 14:331). The dormant oedipal frustration within such patients was only waiting for the external stimulus of success to trigger its release. The relation of frustration to success thus involves the analyst's ability to reconstruct the temporal relations, the time line, that would reveal how and why there should be an excess of oedipal guilt that could be unleashed on the ego so unexpectedly. "Those wrecked by success" are wrecked by conscience, which is to say by a *Versagung,* a refusal, a denial of the instinctual nature that they internalized long ago. It is this time line that will obsess Freud in his search for the "essence" of *Macbeth.*

In the first edition of *The Interpretation of Dreams* (1900) Freud had noted in passing that *Macbeth* is about the contrast between the curse of childlessness and natural succession (*SE* 4:266). It is the play's historical allegory that interested Freud in the *Introductory Lectures on Psychoanalysis,* as we saw, and he begins his argument in "Those Wrecked by Success" by turning to the "remarkable analogies" between *Macbeth* and the accession of James I in 1603 as a result of the childlessness of the queen who put his mother, Mary Stuart, to death: "The 'virginal' Elizabeth, of whom it was rumored that she had never been capable of childbearing and who had once described herself as 'a barren stock,' in an anguished outcry at the news of James's birth, was obliged by this very childlessness of hers to make the Scottish king her successor. And he was the son of the Mary Stuart whose execution she, though reluctantly, had ordered, and who, in spite of the clouding of their relations by political concerns, was nevertheless of her blood and might be called her guest" (*SE* 14:320). Freud reads the play as Shakespeare's confirmation of the lesson of James's accession, demonstrating "the curse of unfruitfulness and the blessings of continuous generation." Macbeth's desire "to found a dynasty," even though the Witches have foretold that Banquo is the father of kings, is what Freud thinks is "overlooked if Shakespeare's play is regarded only as a tragedy of ambition." Freud was obviously struck by the link between Elizabeth and Lady Macbeth, even to the point of seeing Mary's execution as the paradigm for Duncan's murder.

(Later in my reading of *Macbeth* I will turn to its link to the Gunpowder Plot of November 1605 and to the trial and execution of the Jesuit Henry Garnet who was beheaded in May 1606. The play's allusions to the trial further complicate the historical dimension of its meanings but by no means lessen the significance of the issues Freud raises. Freud had no suspicion of the relation between *Macbeth* and the Gunpowder Plot. My interest will be on the way Shakespeare incorporated contemporary events into his ongoing examination of the question of conscience.)

Freud proceeds from his speculation about the historical allegory behind Macbeth's "fruitless crown" (3.1.61) to suggest that Holinshed's account also implies, though indirectly, that childlessness was a factor in the fate of the Macbeths. Though Holinshed says nothing explicit about childlessness, Freud argues that he leaves "warrant enough—both time and occasion—for this probable motivation." Holinshed's own emphasis is on Macbeth's effort to conceal his bad conscience. After remarking that Macbeth's reign was exemplary in its contribution to the "public weal of his subjects," Holinshed adds that Macbeth's ability to govern "the realm for the

space of ten years in equal justice . . . was but the counterfeit zeal
of equity showed by him, partly against his natural inclination, to
purchase thereby the favor of the people."[12] Despite his cruelty and
his duplicity in hiding it for so long, Holinshed continues, Macbeth
was nevertheless tortured by "the prick of conscience": "For the
prick of conscience (as it chanceth ever in tyrants and such as attain
to any estate by unrighteous means) caused in him ever to fear lest
he should be served of the same cup as he had ministered to his
predecessor." The moral reading was not, however, sufficient for
Freud to explain why Macbeth descends into brutality and why
Lady Macbeth goes mad. Freud's apparent misreading of Holinshed is no simple misunderstanding; his whole point is that the
moral reading, the allegory of conscience, belies a kernel of historical truth, which Freud sees in the ten-year delay between the
couple's coming to power and their decline. Freud is relentless in his
historicization of conscience, and he may well be right.

   In the *Introductory Lectures*, Freud referred to *Macbeth*'s content or *Inhalt*. In the second part of "Some Character-Types," he
refers to the chronology of the plot as its *Stoff*, its basic stuff or
materiality. The plausibility and, more exactly, the manipulation of
chronology—in Holinshed and, above all, in Shakespeare—is decisive to Freud's reading. For him, the central and decisive point in
Shakespeare's handling of the plot is his condensation of the chronology found in Holinshed, for ten years elapse in Holinshed between the murder of Duncan and the other crimes committed by
the Macbeths; in Shakespeare it is a matter of days. There would
have been plenty of time, Freud argues, for the royal couple to
confront the terrible ironies that fate had dealt them, time for the
extremity of their will to power to be agonizingly thwarted by the
affliction of childlessness. Shakespeare creates an extraordinary aesthetic effect but does so at the price of concealing what for the
psychoanalyst is the crucial element. Following Shakespeare's ma-

   12. Raphael Holinshed, *Shakespeare's Holinshed: Holinshed's Chronicle* (1587), 19–
20.

nipulation of the time line, Freud finds his way to what he regards as the crucial insight into the character of the historical Lady Macbeth, about whom Holinshed has no details whatsoever to offer. Freud's thesis is a suggestive one: that *Macbeth*, read in conjunction with Holinshed and the historical allegory of James's relation to Elizabeth, becomes a cipher to the role of childlessness in both the historical source and, of course, in Tudor-Stuart history. The implications of these deductions for reading the play itself become quite paradoxical and challenging.

Shakespeare's play, Freud maintains, is riddled by an insoluble problem: "The contradiction remains that though so many subtle interrelations in the plot [*Stückes*], and between it and its occasion, point to a common origin in the theme of childlessness, nevertheless the economy of time in the tragedy expressly precludes [*ausdrücklich ablehnt*] a development of character from any motives but those inherent in the action itself [*aus anderen als den innerlichsten Motiven*]" (*SE* 14:322). The dramatic genius of the play inheres in its focus on the terrors of conscience as the fundamental issue, while the historical and analytical reality points to the external *Versagung* of barrenness. The "economy of time" (*die zeitliche Ökonomie*) conceals the external frustration within the enigma of Lady Macbeth's psychological crisis. Freud regards this *Ablehnung*, this "omission" or "exclusion," as central to "the great poet" Shakespeare's art, which proceeds by internalizing the *Versagung* and thus deflecting a truly analytical inquiry. As Freud remarked earlier in the essay apropos of Richard III, this evasion of the spectator's power of critical reflection serves to strengthen one's identification with the hero. The concealment of the historical genealogy of Lady Macbeth's illness is precisely the element that universalizes her experience and engages our attention.

Freud concedes that his solution remains a hypothesis in the face of an insoluble problem: "What, however, these motives can have been which in so short a space of time [*so kurzer Zeit*] could turn the hesitating, ambitious man into an unbridled tyrant, and his

steely-hearted instigator into a sick woman gnawed by remorse, it
is, in my view, impossible to guess [*erraten*]." The onset of their
illness becomes the play's ultimate mystery, since it is hidden behind "a triple obscurity of the bad preservation of the text, the
unknown intention of the dramatist, and the hidden purport of the
legend [*Sage*]." And while all these obstacles "overwhelm us . . .
and paralyse our thinking [*Denken*]," analysis nevertheless tries
"to grasp this effect [*diese Wirkung . . . zu begreifen*]." The analyst
struggles against frustrations, refusals, and denials on all sides
without any promise of certainty.

     Freud is not content, however, to leave things at this impasse and
proceeds to pass a psychoanalytic judgment on Shakespeare's art-
istry in *Macbeth*. He cites J. Darmstetter's introduction to his 1887
edition of the play to the effect that the events in the plot seem "to
crowd breathlessly on one another." Almost every critic since William Hazlitt and Samuel Taylor Coleridge has made a similar comment, but Freud draws a novel thesis from this commonplace. He
feels, in the final analysis, that the play's compression is finally
unjustifiable, regardless of the dizzying aesthetic effect it produces:
"The sacrifice of common probability [is] justified [*rechtfertigen*]
only when it merely interferes with probability, and not when it
breaks the causal connection [*die kausale Verknüpfung aufhebt*]."
It is as though Freud's frustration at not being able to be certain
about the causality behind the plot takes the form of this reprisal
against what he regards as Shakespeare's chaotic aesthetic. Instead
of merely "leaving the time-duration indeterminate," Shakespeare
"expressly limit[s] it to a few days" (*SE* 14:323); he thus, Freud
insists, removes the action from "natural time" and in fact "breaks"
the link to time.

     The question of *Versagung* has been transformed into the ques-
tion of the play's "time-duration" (*der Zeitablauf*) and its relation
to "natural time" (*die natürliche Zeitfolge*). Freud poses a very
serious question concerning Shakespeare's art and its sources. After
committing a brutal murder in order to found a dynasty, would the

historical Macbeths have descended into barbarity and madness ten years later because they could contain their evil natures and endure "the prick of conscience" no longer? Freud insists there had to have been another external frustration: that is, their childlessness. Moreover, in the context of Tudor-Stuart relations the irony of childlessness is also preeminent, since the queen who murdered her rival in order to protect her own dynastic ambitions had just ceded the throne to the son of her victim. Consider what Freud is saying from an ideological point of view: why would Shakespeare at once mark all of these inconvertible historical elements *and* obscure them in so complex a fashion? Would not his internalization of conscience have been a prudent aesthetic concealment at a time of uncertainty? Might not his apparent endorsement of the moral, psychological interpretation of the Macbeths after the fashion of Holinshed be in part a ruse, an apotropaic gesture meant to ward off scrutiny by all but the wisest? Freud directly confronts the relation of time to the strategies of concealment, and his reading points to something essential in Shakespeare's art. The frustrations of the Macbeths, of Elizabeth, of Shakespeare, and of Freud himself become difficult to separate.

Before turning to *Macbeth* and the problem of situating this irresolvable reversibility of *Versagung* within Shakespeare's language, let us briefly consider the immense frustration that the question of Shakespeare's identity constituted for Freud. As we have seen, *Macbeth* was for Freud synonymous with the difficulty of establishing the certainty of psychoanalytic categories and methods. In "A Child is Being Beaten" (1919) Freud once again turns to *Macbeth* at the very moment in his argument when the certainty of his distinction between ego drives and sexual drives appears to dissolve: "As is well known, all the signs [*Kennzeichen*], on which we are accustomed to base our distinctions, tend to melt into one another as we come nearer to the source" (*SE* 17:187). Freud then proceeds to offer an analogy in which he seems to see himself in the place of Macbeth and Banquo as they hear the enigmatic promise of the Weird Sisters, who, having uttered their seeming paradoxes, vanish into the air. "The earth hath bubbles, as the water has, / And these are of them," says Banquo; to which Macbeth responds, "and what seem'd corporal, / Melted as breath into the wind" (1.3.79–82). Like the daemonic thing called conscience, the Witches are the origin of an utterance whose binding and prophetic power disrupts the expectations human beings have of natural and positive law. Here Freud calls this intangible and unreadable substance *Stoff*, the same term he used to describe the enigmatic essence of the temporality of the play's plot (Freud's context here is the troubling fantasy of beating that is the focus of the essay): "So perhaps like the promise [*Verheissung*] of the weird sisters to Banquo: not clearly sexual, not in itself sadistic, but yet the *Stoff* from which both will later come" (*SE* 17:187). Ego and sexual drives, Thanatos and Eros, *being* king and *being father* to kings—these oppositions are put into play by and constricted to a third term that is not their dialectical synthesis; this is the mysterious *Stoff* that is the promise and the haunting power of conscience. And the ungraspable, relentless movement of this undialecticizable *différance* is always linked in Freud's mind to *Macbeth* and to the enigma of Shakespeare's art.

Freud is also troubled, however, by the mystery of Shakespeare's identity. In his brief remarks on *Hamlet* (which never troubled him as *Macbeth* did), Freud adduced the death of Shakespeare's father as a possible factor in triggering the pale, sickly cast of the son's oedipal guilt and his revisitation of the scene of the incest prohibition (*SE* 5:264–66). In his reading of *Macbeth*, Shakespeare's response to the historical allegory was uppermost in Freud's consideration, though he adduces no personal biographical elements. In retrospect, however, and in light of the strange twist Freud's view of Shakespeare eventually took, this concern with the psychology of life in James's court may already belie Freud's suspicions, however vague and unformed, about "the man from Stratford."

There is no evidence that anything occurred to alter Freud's thinking about Shakespeare between the publication of his reading of *Macbeth* in 1916 and his discovery in 1926 of Thomas Looney's *Shakespeare Identified* (1920). Much to the chagrin of Freudians and Shakespeareans alike, Freud remained an Oxfordian, believing that the works of Shakespeare were composed by Edward de Vere, the seventeenth earl of Oxford (1550–1604), from 1926 until his death in 1939. In his recent essay "Freud and the Man from Stratford," Peter Gay has opined that Freud's adherence to this view was largely the result of an old man's caprice and impatience with uncertainties: "His patience grew shorter as well, particularly as he repeatedly set dates for his probable demise. This, too, is why when he was getting old he entered into the two most eccentric commitments of his life, both revisionist in the extreme—the identification of Moses as an Egyptian and of Shakespeare as the earl of Oxford."[13] Gay believes that "Freud's impatient compulsion to tackle enigmas" ultimately led him to these regrettable conclusions. I believe Gay is fundamentally correct, and I want only to add some precisions that will enable us to understand Freud's peculiar historical theories not only as the result of impatience but as efforts to resolve the deepening problem we have been considering under the heading of *Versagung*.

Moses and Shakespeare are for Freud the great figures in the history of conscience and thus his great precursors in the discovery of psychoanalysis. As we saw in Chapter 1, Freud's thesis concerning Moses and the origins of conscience and Jewish guilt was an effort to discover a historical situation in which a series of unprecedented instinctual demands were made upon the Jewish people from an external—that is, Egyptian—source. Moses the Egyptian was Freud's solution to the need for an external frustration which alone could account for the historical emergence of the unique experience of conscience in the Judeo-Christian world. Freud himself is at once heir to Jewish guilt and strangely outside it; he occupies an uncanny topology on the outside of the inside. The

13. Peter Gay, *Reading Freud,* 44.

rejection of the man from Stratford and the adoption of Looney's Oxford theory were predicated on the same need to find an external explanatory mechanism that could account for Shakespeare's unique insight into the nature of conscience and, above all, for the fact that Shakespeare broke through the idealistic moral theory of conscience and grasped the roots of guilt in the oedipal complex. The role of the historical allegory in the reading of *Macbeth* might already have been a step toward abandoning the man from Stratford. The slipperiness of the notion of *Versagung* continually impeded Freud's determination to find a historical causality for what otherwise appeared a moral phenomenon. The certainties of psychoanalytic theory and its search for the historical etiology of conscience and moral law can be purchased only at the price of suspending the question of time and by a corresponding assumption concerning what "natural time" constitutes. The earl of Oxford's authorship of the plays would explain at once the penetrating insight into Tudor-Stuart relations and provide an entire context of courtly experience at the center of Elizabethan power that could alone, so Freud surmised, explain "Shakespeare's" insights into the real bases of the experience of conscience and moral law. The Egyptian prince and the English aristocrat would thus be the great precurors and transmitters of psychoanalytic knowledge in the ancient and modern worlds.

That Oxford was not the author of the plays and that Moses was probably not an Egyptian attest to the dangers of trying to answer the question of conscience and of trying to resolve the nature of *Versagung* and the temporal enigma it entails. Freud's insistence on his own will to power and on investing himself by inventing his own precursors also attests to the rashness and perhaps the folly of assuming that the essence of willing lies in one's own will to will. Freud's work is not, however, diminished by the erroneous historical hypotheses on which he tried to found it. The greatness of *Moses and Monotheism* has little to do with Moses and much to do with Paul; the insights into Shakespeare's plays remain provocative and suggestive despite the stubborn determination to externalize the unseizable *Versagung* in the unlikely figure of Edward de Vere.

Here are some of Freud's comments on the man from Stratford in a letter to Arnold Zweig of April 2, 1937: "We will have a lot to discuss about Shakespeare. I do not know what still attracts you to the man from Stratford. He seems to have nothing at all to justify his claim, whereas Oxford has almost everything. It is quite inconceivable to me that Shakespeare should have got everything secondhand—Hamlet's neurosis, Lear's madness, Macbeth's defiance and the character of Lady Macbeth, Othello's jealousy, etc. It almost irritates me that you should support the notion."[14] Zweig had earlier offered, in an apparently conciliatory gesture, a kind of theoretical compromise where he conceded that Oxford, though not the author of the plays, nevertheless exerted "a profound influence on Sh., indeed regenerated him, as it were. . . . He is, however, not the author of Sh.'s works, but the begetter."[15] The extremity of Freud's position thus becomes unmistakable. Zweig is going out of his way to humor Freud, but Freud will have nothing of it and only becomes even more deeply entrenched. Freud's insistence that the man from Stratford has "nothing at all" to recommend his authorship and that de Vere has "almost everything" stems from his profound sense that what constitutes reliable evidence is a clear causal link within the calculability of "natural time." We must be careful not to feel superior to Freud at the moment when he argues passionately for a patently absurd thesis, for the fact is that Freud had gone up to the abyss of Dasein's finitude. That he could not bear to look over the edge and instead retreated into the banalities of the will to power and the self-certainties of modernity constitutes in itself a memorable drama in the history of conscience and *Versagung*.

14. Freud, *Letters of Sigmund Freud and Arnold Zweig*, 140.
15. Ibid., 138.

"Rubs and Botches": The Clinging of Conscience in *Macbeth*

Referring in "Some Character-Types" to an article on *Macbeth* by Ludwig Jekels, Freud suggests that Macbeth and his queen may be "like two disunited parts of a single psychical individuality, and it may be that they are both copied from a single prototype [*Nachbilder eines einzigen Vorbildes*]" (*SE* 14:324). He cites several of the many incidents in the play where something said by Macbeth becomes something experienced by Lady Macbeth: "Thus what he feared in his pangs of conscience is fulfilled in her: she is incarnate remorse after the deed, he incarnate defiance." This extremely interesting idea goes to the heart of the play's allegory of conscience. Before turning to the relevant details, however, we should reflect for a moment on what Freud might have meant by this "prototype" (*Vorbild*). Since Elizabeth figures so prominently in the historical allegory, she would in a sense lie behind the machinations of the Macbeths. Shakespeare would have incorporated the historical Macbeths and the Elizabethan background to James's accession within his own articulation of the allegory of conscience that is *Macbeth*. It is Shakespeare's own developing sense of the question of conscience that is in fact the "prototype" of the Macbeths. Their words and actions are so intimately interrelated because they are at once intertwining figures on the dramatic stage and allegorical explorations of the question of conscience. In a later essay, "Neurosis and Psychosis" (1924), Freud actually defines conscience and the superego as the "ideal prototype [*Idealvorbild*] of that state towards which all the ego's endeavours are bending" when it tries to reconcile the inner demands of the ego-structures with "the demands of reality" (*SE* 19:151). In the same essay, and for the last time in his writing, Freud employs the term *Versagung* as he tries once again to situate the frustrations that jeopardize the ego's ability to satisfy these competing demands. Such an account is

Shakespearean in the fundamental sense in which Shakespeare explores the reversibility of inside/outside in *Macbeth*.

Macbeth's hands are bloodied during the murder of Duncan, which Lady Macbeth cannot bring herself to participate in because of the inhibiting resemblance between the sleeping king and her father. Macbeth wonders whether "all great Neptune's ocean will wash this blood clean from my hand?" (2.2.59–60), but it is, of course, Lady Macbeth who famously internalizes in her mad scene what turns out to be an inexhaustible act of purification. She repeats in her trance not only the act but the word itself: "What, will these hands ne'er be *clean?*" (5.1.41; my emphasis). Conscience clings the way the blood clings to the hands of the Macbeths, not as a physical stain but as an irrepressible and incontrovertible compulsion to repeat. I emphasize the word "clean" because it is part of a long chain of words that begin with *cl-* and that cling and cleave first to the reader's eye and then, in the aggregate, to the ear. Doubling and equivocation are issues that arise at every turn in the play; our interest will be on the nature of the language in which the structures of repetition and opposition arise, which is to say, in the *différantiel* daemonic medium that precedes the various couplings and double senses and constitutes their ground.

Another notable instance in the way Shakespeare articulates the linguistic and psychological clinging together of the Macbeths can help clarify the question of childlessness. The Macbeths are at once outside and inside one another; one knows what the other has said even without hearing it. As Macbeth privately reflects on the terrible act he is about to commit, he thinks on its aftermath and adduces the image of "Pity, like a new-born babe" (1.7.21) rising up to proclaim the crime. Lady Macbeth enters a few moments later, and even though she has not heard the speech, she proceeds to reinforce her husband's waning resolve by adducing precisely the extremity of her own resolve, which extends so far as to render her capable of dashing out the brains of a child nursing at her nipple

(1.7.54–58). At this point Freud might have recognized that Shakespeare too was alert to the childlessness of the Macbeths. In response to Lady Macbeth's apparently mad speech, Macbeth says
only: "Bring forth men-children only! / For thy undaunted mettle
should compose / Nothing but males" (1.7.73–75). Might we not
simply take this at face value? On the eve of the regicide, the Macbeths are at once hopeful of founding a dynasty and yet haunted by
both the specter of a dead child and the accusing voice of an infant
conscience. The symbiosis of the Macbeths should have told Freud
that Shakespeare was alert to the motive force of childlessness. The
child of conscience is the play's phallic signifier, for in its vulnerability and its uncanny power of survival the ghost child of an
imagined past and an impossible future marks the trace of an irreducible instability in even the most obsessive will to power. Macbeth tries to conceal a delicate conscience beneath the cloak of a
"manly readiness" (2.3.131). But his "readiness" is only a deluded
effort to hide from an insurmountable nakedness behind the garment of equivocation. In his flight from the default in Being, Macbeth empties "readiness" of the meaning Hamlet gave it as the sign
of liberation from the history of the misreadings of the meaning of
Being. Nothing could be further from Hamlet than Macbeth's reduction of "readiness" to its colloquial meaning of getting dressed
or putting on armor to cover our "naked frailties" (2.3.124). Borne
by the "sightless couriers of the air" (1.7.23), the prick of the infant
conscience is a figure for the irrepressible afterlife of any act, and
for the impossibility of "trammel[ing] up" the consequences of our
actions (1.7.3–5). Through his poetic compression of historical
time, Shakespeare uses the figures of ill-fated infants to describe the
violent futility of the Macbeths' effort to master language itself.
Shakespeare read Holinshed after Freud's fashion, though Freud
failed to recall that *Macbeth* itself preserves traces of precisely such
a reading of the ten-year interval.

The Jesuit conspiracy to murder James I doubtless provided
Shakespeare with a powerful incentive to rethink once again the

enigma of conscience. James was himself interested in the question and discussed the three kinds of conscience (sound, superstitious, and seared or "leprose") in his *Basilicon Doron*.[16] The Macbeth legend provided a remarkably accommodating medium for the recent upheaval of the Gunpowder conspiracy as well as for the other historical issues we discussed earlier. The rush of events surrounding Henry Garnet's trial and the resulting uproar against Catholics and Jesuits made the question of conscience infinitely more pressing in Shakespeare's consideration than the issue of childlessness, which he nevertheless, with customary penetration, did not fail to reconstruct.[17]

The issues of doubling and equivocation arose precisely from the immediate historical context of the controversy over conscience. When Garnet invoked equivocation during his trial, he was simply revisiting the issue of probabilism, which, as we have seen, was the acme of the Jesuit bureaucratization of conscience. The trial must have brought home to Shakespeare the hubris of the Catholics in thinking they could manipulate conscience, as though it were something they could calculate, measure, and totally appropriate for their own subjective ends. As Garnet stepped onto the scaffold, the very last thing he was asked was whether he wished "to discharge his conscience." He declined the offer.[18] Garnet was acting in accor-

16. See Henry N. Paul, *The Royal Play of 'Macbeth*,' 134–35. Also see A. C. and M. K. Kistner, "*Macbeth*: A Treatise of Conscience," which suggests Shakespeare's debt to Alexander Hume's *Ane Treatise of Conscience* (1594). On learning of the arrest of the Gunpowder conspirators, James I remarked that it was evidence of "the wonderful power of God's justice upon guilty consciences" (quoted in Kevin Sharpe, "Private Conscience and Public Duty in the Writings of James VI and I," 84–85).

17. I discuss the traces of the Gunpowder Plot in *Macbeth* in Ned Lukacher, "Anamorphic Stuff: Shakespeare, Catharsis, Lacan."

18. George Borrow, ed., *Celebrated Trials and Remarkable Cases of Criminal Jurisprudence from the Earliest Records to the Year 1825*, 1:149. Also see Christopher Pye's discussion of the political spectacle that the government made of the Garnet trial and how these events are related to the theatricality of *Macbeth* (*The Regal Phantasm: Shakespeare and the Politics of Spectacle*, 142–72). It may also be worth noting that one of the Gunpowder conspirators was hidden by friends who were renting a property owned by Shakespeare near the Blackfriars Theater (E. K. Chambers, *William Shakespeare: A Study of Facts and Problems*, 2:168).

dance with the decrees of the Council of Trent when he invoked the
right of equivocation and insisted that there were limits to what he
was required to confess. Having first learned of the conspiracy from
Robert Catesby during confession and then later from other conspirators, Garnet never denied that he knew of the plot but merely
insisted that he didn't have to tell everything he knew. The fate of
the Macbeths reveals that conscience cannot be toyed with in this
fashion and that it has a logic beyond the cunning of intellectuals.
Edmund Malone relates in the notes to his edition of *Macbeth* that
during the trial Garnet, known as "Farmer" among his coconspira-
tors (which Shakespeare alludes to in the drunken Porter episode
2.3), said of the plot to murder James I, "It would have been com-
mendable, when it had been done, though not before."[19] As Macbeth struggles to find the determination to murder Duncan, he
says: "If it were done, when 'tis done, then 'twere well / It were
done quickly" (1.7.1–2). Garnet's remark is even more extraordinary than Macbeth's in this instance and reveals what is really at
stake when one believes that the language of conscience can be fully
administered by the will.

That's what the clinging, cleaving, clamoring, clattering of conscience is all about in *Macbeth:* the fact that language cannot be
manipulated by a will that can never know its own essence. The
Macbeths believe they can find their way *clear* to a *clean* conscience. But something gets stuck and clings to them, impedes their
path, and brings them down. "There's the rub," says Hamlet
(3.2.65) of our fear of what might happen after death. Macbeth
tells his hired killers that he "requires a clearness" and wants "no
rubs nor botches in the work" of killing Banquo and Fleance
(3.1.133). The *cl-* is Shakespeare's idiom for the persistence of the
rub of conscience.

The attempt to will the essence of language, to manipulate it and
mold it to one's desires causes in *Macbeth* a disruption within

19. Shakespeare, *Macbeth*, ed. Malone, n. 75.

nature itself that includes various perturbations in the natural order and, above all, the reversal of light and darkness: "What is the night? / Almost at odds with morning, which is which" (3.4.125–26). These are phenomenal manifestations for what Shakespeare regards as the more profound aberration that has occurred between language and the human being. Though language cannot see, the specific nature of human sight is inseparable from language. Language moves invisibly within the realm of the visible. It blows through nature like the wind, unseen. The Weird Sisters and the references to "sightless substances" (1.5.49) and "sightless couriers" (1.7.23) conjure up this magical power of language to see beyond physical vision and to bring a world to presence. The appropriating force of the human will is nothing in comparison with the expropriating power of language to put a world into motion. "The soundless gathering call," writes Heidegger, "by which Saying moves the world relation on its way, we call the ringing of stillness. It is the language of being."[20] *Macbeth* echoes with the still, silent ringing of this call. Amid the disruptions of the will and nature that threaten to disjoin the very frame of things (3.2.16–17), the daemonic language of the *cl-* words reveals that such reck and wrack belong to the order of things.

The drama of the call of conscience from within the barely audible margins of poetic language functions like a play-within-the-play in *Macbeth*. In this connection we might note that Shakespeare reads himself very much as Keats reads him. For example, like Claudio's "viewless winds" in *Measure for Measure* (3.1.124), which blow in the unthought realms of death, and which Keats rewrites as the "viewless wings of Poesy" ("Ode to a Nightingale," line 33), Shakespeare's own doubletake on this line in *Measure for Measure* takes the form of the "sightless couriers" of language in *Macbeth,* suggesting an uncanny, unnatural force at work in language beyond the limits of consciousness. The "viewless wings" are

20. Heidegger, "The Nature of Language," 108.

not so much "of Poesy" as they are *of* this daemonic force of language on which poetry itself depends. The "viewless winds/wings" are figures for the materiality of language beyond grammar and trope, and yet sustaining them. It is in this "viewless," "sightless" realm that the poet dwells. As Shakespeare listens to language near the default of Being, what he hears is the silent ringing of the *cl*-words, which constitute a linguistic function more primordial than grammar or aesthetic figuration. What drones beneath the poetry of *Macbeth* is the sheer materiality of language as letter, as sound and inscription prior to human intention and will, prior to the light and to vision. This is the realm of the demon who takes hold of the Macbeths, but it is also—and this is Shakespeare's greatest achievement in *Macbeth*—the site of the *daemon* who dwells beyond the language of audible speech.

Conscience calls from within this nonhuman realm. The droning clamor of the expropriating materiality of language cannot be called what Hopkins termed an "undersong" or an "underlay," because it has no aesthetic dimension and cannot break into song. Poetic dwelling depends upon this daemonic function of language, and Shakespeare's objective in *Macbeth* is to mark both its uncanny promise and a profound sense of its danger. *Macbeth* takes tragedy to its limits, for it brings us as close to the otherness of language and Being as poetic saying can go.

Macbeth is the tragic poem of the silent call of language. Moreover, the play reflects on the nature of the very call to which it responds. Speaking to the murderers whom he has summoned to slay Banquo and Fleance, Macbeth acknowledges that these cutthroats are men, if in name only:

> Ay, in the catalogue ye go for men;
> As hounds, and greyhounds, mongrels, spaniels, curs,
> Shoughs, water-rugs, and demi-wolves, are *clept*
> All by the name of dogs: the valu'd file
> Distinguishes the swift, the slow, the subtle,

> The housekeeper, the hunter, every one
> According to the gift which bounteous Nature
> Hath in him *clos'd;* whereby he does receive
> Particular addition, from the bill
> That writes them all alike; and so of men.
>   (3.1.91–100; emphasis added)

The general designation, "men" or "dogs," provides only superficial information; "the valu'd file" gives us an accounting of the particulars that define the singular idiom enclosed in each being. The basic distinction is thus between "cleping," or calling as naming and gathering, and "enclosing," which suggests a more fundamental sense of calling as the radical individuation of beings into what is properly their own. Although the subjective imposition of concepts is a false "cleping" or calling, there is a true calling that has the power to designate the particular "gift" that is "clos'd" in each being. What is properly one's own, however, is often at odds with the way one calls oneself, which is Macbeth's point, since he clearly regards these men as scarcely human. The *cl-* marks that function of language that enables beings to be gathered into what is properly their own.

The two swimmers who "cling" together and "choke their art" (1.2.8) anticipate the fate of the Macbeths. Language equivocates with us before we can equivocate with it. Banquo notes that the "new honours" bestowed upon Macbeth by the Witches appear like ill-fitting garments that "cleave not to their mould, / But with the aid of use" (1.3.15–16). But the *cl-* of "cleave" is not like a garment; it is not like anything phenomenal, nor is it like the figurations of language that we can mistake for phenomenal things. "Cleave to my consent," says Macbeth to Banquo (1.3.146), which, in view of their bloody sequel together, seems quite infernally to play on the double meanings of "cleave": both to cling and to cut. But the *cl-* is distinct from all these semantic elements. It calls on Shakespeare from another depth of language and time. Duncan is

"clear in his office" (1.7.18). The "clamour" of an obscure bird
(2.3.59) is heard during the night of Duncan's murder. The snake of
the Banquo coat of arms "close[s]" on itself (3.2.14), which is to
say, it resists the death blow Macbeth would give it. There are many
other instances. They constitute the "rub" of language itself. The
strange ringing of the *cl-* recedes behind the anamorphic "damned
spot" (5.1.33) into the infinite distance whence the call of conscience originates. They are the "clamorous harbingers" (5.6.10) of
language beyond the will and subjectivity. They cannot be cleared
or cleaned away, and they constitute for Shakespeare the marks of
something entirely other, something for which moral conscience
and the retributions of guilt are merely ciphers, signs for the "something" that remains hidden behind the droning humming traces of
the *cl*'s.

The Macbeths tried to undo the enigmatic constriction of human
existence and language to the *cl*'s; they perish, and the world that
hung in the balance is returned to its moorings. Rather than a song
or a figure, what the *cl-* creates is a "great clatter" (5.7.21), but it is
almost entirely silent and does not occur all at once; it is slowly and
inexorably distributed throughout the entire play. Neither a word
nor a concept but rather the *différantial* band between them and
from which they both arise, it is the residue of a primordial temporality; and it is distinct from all the oppositions and relations it puts
into play. "Cleanse the stuff'd bosom of that perilous stuff," says
Macbeth as he asks the doctor to purify Lady Macbeth of the guilty
conscience that is killing her (5.3.43). There is no cleansing or
catharsis of the *cl-* however. It *cl*ings like a famine in the line that
Hopkins notes (in the epigraph to this chapter); Macbeth threatens
to hang a messenger to a tree "Till famine cling thee" (5.5.40). To
cling here means to dry up and shrivel, and Kenneth Muir follows
Furness's edition of the play in offering this compelling line from the
Coventry Mystery plays: "My heart doth clynge and cleve as clay."
The Macbeths cannot reverse the clinging of their conscience. That
is what the ontotheological tradition has always been saying. "My

way of life," says Macbeth, "is fall'n into the Seare, the yellow leaf" (5.3.23). I give this line in its folio version, which is corrected in almost all modern editions as "into the sere, the yellow leaf."[21] But as we have seen again and again, the *Seare* is a fundamental element in Shakespeare's signature, which is to say the signature of the irreducible materiality of language. It is not a question simply of the dried and yellow leaf but of the seared, burned place where conscience used to be and where now there is no more than a dusty, dessicated leaf. The *cl-* is thus also the place of heat and burning. It is the place of the daemon. The only remnant it leaves behind in its comings and goings is the ash and cinder of a *cl-*. It's frustrating.

21. See the textual notes in Muir's edition of Shakespeare, *Macbeth,* 146.

5 Shakespeare's Cinders

To learn the Transport by the Pain—
As Blind Men learn the sun!
　　　　—EMILY DICKINSON

His livelie face thy brest how did it freate,
Whose Cynders yet with envye doo the eate.
　　　　—HENRY HOWARD, Earl of Surrey

Conscience has got safely entrenched behind the Letter of
the Law; sits there invulnerable, fortified with **Cases** and
Reports so strongly on all sides;—that it is not preaching
can dispossess it of its hold.
　　　　—LAURENCE STERNE, *Tristram Shandy*

There were no suns to borrow of.
　　　　—*Timon of Athens*

The "perilous stuff" in Lady Macbeth's "stuff'd bosom" refers to
the seared remains of her conscience, the burnt cinders that lie
before the desecrated altar of the law. The repetition of "stuff" and
"stuff'd" in the same line (5.3.43) does not create a very satisfying
poetic effect; but then again, *not* creating such an effect may be
Shakespeare's point. Alexander Pope corrected it to read: "Cleanse
the full bosome of that perilous stuff."[1] More recent Shakespeareans have suggested such alternatives as "perilous grief" in place of
"perilous stuff" and "fraught" or "charged" in lieu of the "stuff'd
bosom."[2] Edmund Malone may have been the last Shakespeare
editor to defend Shakespeare's somewhat unwieldy locution in this

1. Shakespeare, *Macbeth*, ed. Pope, vol. 5.
2. See Stanley Wells and Gary Taylor, *William Shakespeare: A Textual Companion*,
note to *Macbeth* 5.3.46.

much debated line; he quotes Samuel Johnson's comment apropos of Shakespeare's use of "stuff" in *Othello:* "Stuff is a word of great force in the Teutonic languages. The elements are called in Dutch *hoefd stoffen,* or 'head stuffs.'"[3] In *Othello,* Iago ironically remarks, "I hold it the very stuff o'the conscience / To do no contrived murder" (1.2.2–3).[4] Shakespeare thinks of conscience in terms of an enigmatic materiality that can be seared, singed, scarred, and finally consumed. The law is fire, and conscience either shines or burns when summoned before the flames. Macbeth's stammering repetition belies a fundamental difficulty in saying just what kind of heat and pressure accrues in the mind to language, memory, and guilt. The stuff of conscience is the stuff with which poetic saying must concern itself, but this stuff is also the very thing that poetry can never quite say. Stuff is itself the very impasse it tries to overcome.

Shakespeare's concern is as much with the catastrophic effect of the excessive demand that Lady Macbeth has placed on her conscience as it is with the inadequacy of language to find an appropriate figure for the mysterious process that underlies most of his own intellectual labor. Damaging one's conscience is like stifling the fire by trying to burn too much incombustible fuel. One might thus be said to have stuffed too much stuff in the stuff of conscience. But does speaking about it in these terms get one any closer to understanding how it all happens, or what it might mean that our most intimate relation to time, language, and Being is like a common household activity?

Cinders of the Law

"Cinders" is another of Shakespeare's keywords for what happens when conscience begins to take the heat. In 1589 Thomas

3. Shakespeare, *Macbeth,* ed. Malone and Boswell, 9:255–56.
4. See my discussion of the semantics of "stuff" in Shakespeare and some of his contemporaries in Lukacher, "Anamorphic Stuff."

Nashe advised poets to avoid such clichés as "the cinders of Troy and the shivers of broken tranchions."[5] In Shakespeare's usage, however, cinders and stuff are the most unpoetical things in the world, even though they mark the site of what would be the most poetical thing if one could only get the words out. The *cl-* words in *Macbeth* signal both the utter frustration of trying to speak the words of Being and Being's absolute refusal to give itself to language as anything other than the *cl-*. They announce at once an absolute impasse and an amazing confirmation *that* the other signs in our language. It is the poets who bring this to pass. Until the stuff of conscience has been taken out of oblivion, it cannot become the site of the daemon. The constrictive *cl-* and the loss of heat as the ashes cool are figures of the closure of the daemonic relation, of the nonrelation and denial that are the essence of that relation; they are also signs of the daemon's departure, and perhaps of the promise of its return.

The "cinders" that threaten to consume Othello from within (4.2.73) and "the cinders of [Cleopatra's] spirits" (5.2.172) are among the most evocative and elusive figures, in Shakespeare's later writing, for the dilatory interval before the heat dissipates. They are daemonic figures of what is at once an absolute caesura and an immense and inexpressible promise. They are figures of an event that is as much internal as external, as linguistic as it is psychological, as much caloric as it is moral. Before this enigmatic hearth where the daemon appears and vanishes, in this strange topology where conscience smolders and catches fire, two worlds seem to come into contact, however mysteriously or fleetingly. It is the place of a certain transference or exchange between the language of subjective appropriation and its expropriation by the language of the other. The cinders burn or cool in a hearth that divides the human subject. Perhaps the reason Heraclitus stood by a stove when receiving visitors was to suggest to them that this ordinary place was also

---

5. Thomas Nashe, "Preface to Greene's *Menaphon*," 3:332.

the site of the *daimon*.[6] We bring something to the fire, and yet at the same time the fire draws us in. The fire of conscience draws us into the language that divides us from ourselves. It burns or smolders, consumes what is brought before it or is stifled and can no longer effect the transference.

The stuff of conscience is the household stuff of the hearth, the stuff we need in order to make a fire, in order to eat, in order to live. The fire that burns in conscience is the same fire that burns in the hearth. It burns in the difference between the world of human dwelling and all the mysteries that lie beyond it; and it burns in the difference within ourselves between what we know and think and what remains inaccessible and remote. The fire is a figure for language, and language is a figure for the fire. If it were not for language, we could not represent things to ourselves and transform them into things that make up a world in which we can live. And if the fire were not already burning within, we could never turn to it in our effort to invent our world. Language is the fire in the fundamental sense that without it there is no dwelling, no world, no life. It is not sounds, letters, words, grammar, tropes, concepts; it is fire.

In his essay, "Language," Heidegger speaks of language as the dif-ference or *Unter-schied* and suggests that we learn to think of the dif-ference as "*the* dimension, insofar as it measures out, apportions, world and thing, each to its own."[7] Language as dif-ference is neither a relation nor a distinction. It does not arise from the relation of world and thing but is instead that in which this very relation arises. Language as dif-ference both allots world and thing into their separateness and appropriates/expropriates them into one another. Language as dif-ference names not one region of Being among others but "*the* dimension" from which and into which all the other regions are transferred and exchanged. As long as there is language as dif-ference, the fire burns even when there is no heat and no flame; and there is heat and flame only because there is

---

6. See Heidegger, "Letter on Humanism," 234.
7. Heidegger, "Language," 203; "Die Sprache," 25.

language. Language as fire as dif-ference burns in the household hearth and in the hearth of conscience, for they are crossover points, daemonic places where world and thing are appropriated/expropriated to one another; they are also the sites where the invisible "unifying element" (*das Einigende*) comes nearest to human existence.[8]

In the section of *Critique of Practical Reason* titled "The Incentives of Pure Practical Reason," Kant is concerned to explain how it is that what he calls "my invisible self, my personality" constitutes a relation to a realm of "universal and necessary connection." What is it, he asks, that enables me to impute my actions to a cause that is "independent of all sensibility"? The answer begins in an analysis of conscience:

> The judicial sentences of that marvelous faculty in us called conscience are in complete agreement with this. A man may dissemble as much as he will in order to paint his recollected unlawful behavior as an unintentional error, as mere oversight, which can never be entirely avoided, and consequently as something to which he was carried along by the stream of natural necessity, and in this way try to make himself out as innocent. But he finds that the advocate who speaks on his behalf cannot silence the accuser in him when he is conscious that at the same time when he committed the wrong he was in his senses, i.e., he was in possession of his freedom.[9]

The decisive element in Kant's argument, the thing that assures the wrongdoer that "he was in possession of his freedom," is "a painful feeling caused by the moral disposition, empty in a practical sense since it cannot undo that which has been done." Pain describes for Kant the context in which we become conscious of freedom in the examination of conscience. Kant is not simply referring to our

8. Heidegger, "Language," 202; "Die Sprache," 24.
9. Immanuel Kant, *Critique of Practical Reason*, 102–3. Subsequent references in the text cite page numbers in this edition.

conscience immediately following the act but at any time, no matter how removed. That the pain doesn't go away even in connection with an event long past is absolutely crucial to Kant's argument. The "transcendental" argument need not rely on any transcendent notions of repentance, since it has the irrefutable evidence of pain: "But as a pain, repentance is entirely legitimate, because reason, when it is a question of the law of our intelligible existence (the moral law), acknowledges no temporal distinction [*keinen Zeitunterscheid*] and only asks whether the event [*Begebenheit*] belongs to me as my act, and then morally connects [*verknüpft*] with it the same feeling, whether the event occurs now or is long since past" (102).

   This is the most penetrating account of conscience to be found in Kant's work and is indispensable to everything he has to say about conscience and moral law in the *Lectures on Ethics* and *The Metaphysics of Morals*. And it is the connection between pain and the temporal index that is so remarkable. The pain we experience in conscience draws upon a time outside temporal calculability. There is "no temporal distinction" when we think about something we've done wrong, no matter how long ago it was; calculable, chronological time is irrelevant to conscience, for in conscience our experience in time opens onto another temporality entirely; it links us to something within time that is no longer temporal; it links us to the incalculable in time itself. Our freedom inheres in our ability to answer this painful call of conscience, which is also the call of something altogether uncanny in time itself.

   Our experience of the moral law outside calculable temporality and sensibility is not like the "certainty" that arises from "intellectual intuitions" concerning events in time and space. Because the moral law differs from the "temporal distinction" itself, everything in our experience that relates to the moral law remains outside the causal expectations we have regarding events in space and time. Since there is still "no physical explanation" for the existence of "the subject as a thing-in-itself," no ground in space or time for the existence of subjectivity itself, there can be no expectation of a causal explanation concerning our relation to the moral law. There is only the "assurance" of the law itself: "The moral law assures us [*versichert uns*] of this difference [*Unterschied*] between the relation [*Beziehung*] of our actions as appearances to our sensuous being and the relation by which this sensuous being is itself connected [*bezogen wird*] to the intelligible substrate in us" (103). The "difference" between these two "relations" is the difference between our sensible experience within the calculable "temporal difference" and our intelligible experience within an incalculable temporality. The freedom afforded by the moral law comes to our consciousness through pain. But there can be no causal explanation for freedom and the moral law, since causality applies only to events within space and time, not to things-in-themselves: "Such is the importance of the separation [*Absonderung*] of time (as well as space) from the existence of things-in-themselves" (106). This "separation" or "sequestration" of "the existence of things-in-themselves" from space-time is necessary if we are to receive the law's assurance; it is not to say, however, that subjective existence and the pain of conscience are not somehow related to time but only that such a relation remains deeply concealed and withdrawn from Kant's thinking, which nevertheless keeps the possibility of such a relation open beneath the "difference" and behind the "separation."

Respect (*Achtung*) is Kant's word for the connection between our sensuous being and "the intelligible substrate in us." It is a connection made up of at least two discrete moments: one involves feeling; the other entails "no kind of feeling." Kant's discussion of respect appears much earlier in the same chapter in which he discusses the role of pain, and the conclusion to be drawn is, I believe, that respect is linked to pain in ways that Kant finds troubling. "Respect for the moral law," he writes, "is a feeling produced by an intellectual cause, and this feeling is the only one we can know completely a priori and the necessity of which we can discern [*einsehen können*]" (76). But what kind of seeing or discernment is respect? As the pure will of the moral law purges away our subjective pathos and brings us closer to the absolutely minimal threshold feeling of respect, Kant's account seems to anticipate his description of the sublime a few years later in the *Critique of Judgment.*

In the later text Kant speaks not of pain but of "deprivation" and "negative satisfaction." In the relation of judgment that he calls "the sublime," everything begins with a mere glance; we look at the immensity of sea and sky as poets do who are concerned only with what strikes the eye. As we then consider the relation of this sense impression to our rational understanding of life on Earth and its relation to the solar system, of the galaxy and uncounted galaxies beyond, we realize that the imagination is unable to seize the unfolding magnitude; we are unable to comprehend all that we apprehend. It is our experience of this inadequacy that triggers the essence of the sublime relation: "this involves a deprivation of something—though in the interests of inner freedom—whilst in turn it reveals in us an unfathomable depth of this supersensible faculty, the consequences of which extend beyond reach of the eye of sense [*ins Unabsehliche*]."[10] What we discern beyond "the eye of sense" is "more a feeling of respect (which disdains charm) than of love or of the heart being drawn towards it."

The blockage that we experience in the sublime leads us to the "feeling of respect," while the blockage we experience before the moral law in the *Critique of Practical Reason* leads through the "feeling of respect" to something still more austere: "[The moral law] blocks the inclinations and the propensity to make them the supreme practical condition (i.e. self-love) for all participation in supreme legislation. This effect is on the one side merely negative; but on the other, in respect to the restrictive practical ground of pure practical reason, it is positive. And to the latter, no kind of feeling, [even] under the name of practical or moral feeling, may be assumed as prior to the moral law as its basis" (77). Respect plays

10. Immanuel Kant, *Critique of Judgment*, 123.

on both sides of the great divide between sensibility and intelligibility; it constricts them together and keeps them apart. It is
literally the feeling of losing all feeling; it is thus also at the limit
between our experience of calculable time and something entirely
different. Respect is another word for pain; it names the sensation
of pain at the very point at which it passes into the supersensible
realm—an extraordinary event and a scene of sacrifice.

"Respect is a tribute we cannot refuse to pay to the deserved
[*dem Verdienste*] whether we will or not; we can outwardly with-
hold it, but we cannot help feeling it inwardly" (*Critique of Practical Reason,* 80). In the *Critique of Judgment* this becomes the
sublime scene of sacrifice or deprivation (*Aufopferung oder Ber-
aubung*). What is "the deserved" but the law itself? And it is to the
law that we offer up our inclinations and our worldly calculations.
Respect names the peculiar experience of the pain of crossing into a
supersensible realm that involves another experience of time.

The pain of respect lies at the center of the fold or crease of the
Unterschied, the difference, between our phenomenal self and our
noumenal self. It is apropos of Trakl that Heidegger is writing in
the following passage, but what he writes rewrites what was already under way in Kant: "When the dif-ference [*Unter-Schied*]
gathers world and things into the simple onefold of the pain of
intimacy, it bids the two to come into their very nature. The difference is the command [*das Geheiss*] out of which every bidding
itself is first called, so that each may follow the command. The
command of the dif-ference has always already gathered all bidding
within itself. The calling, gathered together with itself, which gathers to itself in the calling, is the pealing as the peal [*das Läuten als
das Geläut*]."[11] We can understand more fully now the extent to
which Heidegger makes explicit the relation to time and language
that was still untheorized in Kant's account of the pain of conscience and the experience of coming before the law of a time

11. Heidegger, "Language," 207; "Die Sprache," 30.

beyond calculation. The *Einfalt* or "onefold" rings silently through time and calls things back to their being-in-the-world. Respect is the command that calls feeling and thought, that gathers thing and world, into their homecoming, into their return to that most uncanny, most daemonic, of all birthplaces.

Beyond the Maternal Relation: Conscience in *Coriolanus*

Wounds, gashes, the marks of metal cleaving through flesh, the open wounds of the dead, and the scarred wounds of the living: these are the central images of Shakespeare's Roman plays. They are the signs of pain and of the limits of what the body can endure, but they also are the signs of something in the body that is not of the body. They are Shakespeare's images for the fold or crease within nature that gathers humans into the gap of something unnatural, into the differences of the "beyond" of nature in nature itself. They are the traces of the shattering of truth and of the promise of the truth of nontruth. These gaps in nature are also terrifying marks of castration, reminders of the maternal, feminine, genital "nothing," *and* thus also reminders of what lies beyond the maternal origin itself. The wound opens onto the gash of the "nothing" of the womb which opens in its turn onto the gap in nature from which its own generativity arose. This other scene beyond opposition and beyond conflict is, of course, what Shakespeare has always experienced as the question of conscience. Not mere melancholy at the pain of conscience and not mere horror at the gap into which it calls us, the late work affirms the pain and moves beyond the realm of feeling itself.

"O perilous mouths," Isabella remarks in *Measure for Measure* (2.4.171) apropos of the villainous duplicity of Angelo's bad conscience. This is, of course, one of the most familiar medieval and early modern images for the warring voices of conscience. Some-

times there is an orderly juridical hearing before the law, and sometimes there is the chaotic clamor of discordant voices. Richard III's
dilemma comes out of the morality plays: "My conscience hath
a thousand tongues . . . crying all 'Guilty'" (5.3.194). What is
unique to Shakespeare is his disturbing synthesis or juxtaposition
of the mouth and tongue of conscience with the gash or wound in
the flesh, as though the pain of the call of conscience from within
the mind were like nothing so much as a gaping wound that speaks.

In *Julius Caesar,* which is in many respects a dress rehearsal for
Hamlet, Shakespeare is interested in exploring what he already
here calls "the interim" between Brutus's intention and the act
which, "like a phantasma, or a hideous dream," calls the afflicted
soul to suffer "an insurrection" in nature itself (2.1.64–69). The
speaking wound of conscience is a searing image from the depths of
a horrible dream, but it gathers us into the truth of the pain of the
question of conscience. Here is Antony speaking over Caesar's
corpse:

> I have neither wit, nor words, nor worth,
> To stir men's blood; I only speak right on.
> I tell you that which you yourselves do know,
> Show you sweet Caesar's wounds, poor dumb mouths,
> And bid them speak for me. But were I Brutus,
> And Brutus Antony, there were an Antony
> Would ruffle up your spirits, and put a tongue
> In every wound of Caesar that should move
> The stones of Rome to rise and mutiny.
>
> (3.2.223–32)

This most unnatural figure is, not by accident, attributed to Brutus,
who is himself the site of the break in the natural order. Antony
claims only to invent the figure of the wound as a mouth, but it is
up to Brutus to "put a tongue / In every wound of Caesar." The
rhetorical context is also important, for by endowing the wounds

of a corpse with tongues and speech, the speaker is himself endowed with the power to gather the plebeians into a collective scene
of conscience. What more effective way to move the populace and
to call them into the pain of conscience before this horrible sight!
Antony effaces his own voice and allows the open gashes to speak
for themselves and to call the mourners to account.

Putting tongues in wounds is not an image likely to pass from
memory, and Antony returns to it, but this time in the positive
sense of the consolations of good conscience: in *Antony and
Cleopatra* he bids his victorious troops to enter Alexandria and
have "your wives, your friends . . . Wash the congealments from
your wounds, and kiss / The honour'd gashes whole" (4.8.8–11).
Wounds are the focal point in *Antony and Cleopatra;* more precisely, they name the crossing from life to death and from nature to its
other. Before his suicide, Antony says "for with a wound I must be
cur'd" (4.14.77). But the miscalculations that bring the lovers to
suicide, rather than thwarting either fate or desire, strangely confirm both, for Antony and Cleopatra are themselves gaps in nature,
wounds or breaks in a human world that cannot accommodate
them. Lepidus's remark early in the play, that "we do commit /
Murther in healing wounds" (2.2.21–22), announces the impossible paradox of trying to heal or integrate the gash in nature that the
titular characters embody. They are, in effect, gashes that can never
be made whole. Enobarbus captures the strange essence of the
paradox when he says that, as all the people of Alexandria rushed
to see Cleopatra arrive on the wharf, the vacant air itself would
have rushed out of the marketplace with them, except that its doing
so would have "made a gap in nature" (2.2.216–18). It is a very
complex conceit, but it is central to Shakespeare's understanding of
the vacuum that is created by the imaginative existence of figures
like Antony and Cleopatra. In the corresponding passage that applies to Antony the strange logic Enobarbus applies to Cleopatra, it
is Cleopatra herself who reflects on Antony's existence:

> But if there be, or ever were one such,
> It's past the size of dreaming: nature wants stuff
> To vie strange forms with fancy, yet to imagine
> An Antony were nature's piece, 'gainst fancy,
> Condemning shadows quite.
>
> (5.2.95–99)

This extraordinarily difficult passage is absolutely crucial to Shakespeare's understanding in the late works of the chiasmic crossings between nature and mind. Nature does not have the "stuff" to compare with the imaginative form of Antony's existence, and it is precisely a question of existence itself as the very "stuff" or substance of human being. Only imagination (that is, existence) can imagine that existence itself might belong to nature rather than to something other than nature. And this very paradox constitutes the confirmation of the otherness and nonnaturalness of imagination, for it alone possesses the power to annul itself; it invents itself outside of nature in a pure act of mind. And this is all spoken by a woman whose existence creates a vacuum in the natural world.

The absolute asymmetry of the crossing between Dasein and nature is perhaps the most significant feature of the passage. *Antony and Cleopatra* asks us to think of existence itself as having a history, its own temporality and its own genealogy, and to wonder whether existence itself may be an entity made of some "stuff" other than the empirical "stuff" of things. In the world of this play's meditations on the elemental structure of things, the daemonic question of conscience is posed through the unlikely figure of the wound that, far from needing a cure, is itself the remedy it seeks. Everything passes through the gap that is our radical nonknowledge about the foundation of things. And so all the elementary things that make up a world seem to pass into one another. We are in the enchanted realm of what Heidegger calls "the unifying element": "even with a thought / The rack dislimns, and makes it indistinct / As water is in water. . . . I am Antony, / Yet cannot hold this visible

shape" (4.14.9–14). Cleopatra's identity is characterized by eva-
nescence, which in her case assumes the figural form of cinder and
ash: "I shall show the cinders of my spirits / Through the ashes of
my chance" (5.2.172–73). Dasein knows itself as that which disap-
pears like "water in water," or like cinders cooling to ash.

The last of his Roman plays, *Coriolanus* is the culmination of the
final stage of Shakespeare's effort to hear the question of conscience
through the unlikely orifice of the wound. Coriolanus's refusal to
reveal his wounds is a refusal to allow those wounds to become the
site of the ritual oral appropriation we saw in the two earlier Roman plays. Janet Adelman has linked the imagery of wounding in
Coriolanus to his experience of maternal deprivation. Reading the
play as though it were a psychoanalytic case history, she writes that
"the multitudinous mouth of the crowd is horrifying to Coriolanus
not only insofar as it threatens to reveal the nature of his own oral
neediness to him but also insofar as it makes the nature of his
vulnerability uncomfortably precise."[12] Coriolanus's concealment
is thus for Adelman a combination of fears of being eaten alive,
exposed, castrated, feminized, violated in every sense, and thus
deprived of his most fundamental desire, which is his effort to
substantiate his relation to the gods. Adelman reads his fateful
decision to spare Rome and thus condemn himself to death at the
hands of the Volscians as a "capitulation of his independent selfhood before his mother's onslaught."[13]

This is a provocative reading, but it has the curious effect of
reducing the play's action and language to a set of unconscious
identifications whose inexorable repetition necessitates the hero's
fatal regression to his maternal origin. In other words, Coriolanus's
crises of conscience, which begin with his refusal to display his
heroic wounds before an appreciative populace and end with his
refusal to attack the Rome that had betrayed him, appear to Adel-

12. Janet Adelman, *Suffocating Mothers: Fantasies of Maternal Origin in Shakespeare's Plays, "Hamlet" to the "Tempest,"* 153.
13. Ibid., 158.

man as expressions of the hero's hopeless effort to escape an unconscious maternal relation. Placing Adelman's psychoanalytic reading
of the play in conjunction with the earlier allegory of the wound of
conscience raises a fundamental question: is conscience in *Coriolanus* synonymous with an irrepressible maternal imperative, or is
the repressive maternal relation itself the place where something
else arises, some alternative to the ferocity of the maternal relation?
Might it not be the case that Coriolanus's final act of conscience is
not so much a "failure" because of its regression to the maternal
(which is Adelman's thesis) as it is, on the contrary, a tragic success
insofar as this very regression enables him to go beyond the internalized imperative and to hear a far more enigmatic voice of duty
and responsibility, though only at the price of his own life?

I am suggesting that Coriolanus does, in fact, become a self-
obligating being and succeed in inventing himself. The destructive
maternal imperative becomes the path to the categorical imperative. The strength of Adelman's reading is finally also its weakness,
since the maternal relation it so brilliantly foregrounds makes it
difficult for Adelman to see that Coriolanus really succeeds in his
self-invention. Adelman writes of Volumnia's last confrontation
with her son that it "is so appallingly effective because she invali-
dates his defenses by threatening to enact his most central defensive
fantasies, thereby making their consequences inescapable to
him."[14] By kneeling to her son she disarms him of his unconscious
fantasy of overpowering her and finally asserting himself. This is
why, for Adelman, Coriolanus's "fantasy of self-authorship" becomes a "failure." We must listen more closely to the language of
the play in order to hear the echoes in it of the question of conscience that here passes through and beyond the maternal relation.

Let us consider closely the famous scene where Volumnia kneels.
Her kneeling is itself a defensive measure meant to counteract her
son's turning away. It is a decisive point:

14. Ibid., 159.

> Say my request's unjust,
> And spurn me back; but if it be not so,
> Thou art not honest, and the gods will plague thee
> That thou restrain'st from me the duty which
> To a mother's part belongs. *He turns away.*
> Down ladies: let us shame him with our knees.
>   (5.3.164–69; emphasis added)

He protests that the gods themselves "look down, and this unnatural scene / They laugh at" (5.3.184–85). It is then that he relents and tells his mother she has won a victory for Rome. But in doing so, he does not choose death or failure. Adelman reads the following passage as though Coriolanus has chosen death by submitting to the mother and that the two are synonymous. On the contrary, he still has every expectation that he can work an effective peace. Listen to his language, which echoes that of Hamlet and Claudio:

> O, believe it,
> Most dangerously you have with him prevail'd,
> If not most mortal to him. *But let it come.*
> Aufidius, though I cannot make true wars,
> I'll frame convenient peace.
>   (5.3.187–91; emphasis added)

Coriolanus knows what is at stake and that he may perish. But it is *his* decision; it is *his* turn away from Volumnia that signals the turn away from the maternal imperative and toward the categorical imperative. He has succeeded in inventing himself.

We read the entire scene upside down by assuming that Coriolanus's death reveals the failure of what is a quintessentially Shakespearean response to the call of conscience. As we saw in *Hamlet,* Shakespeare's habit of thought does not follow the classical prescription in which the hero chooses death; in Shakespeare the hero listens to the call of language and conscience and time. That he perishes finally, one way or another, is beside the point. Listen also to the Volscian Aufidius in his most significant aside:

> I am glad thou has set thy mercy and thy honour
> At difference in thee. Out of that I'll work
> Myself a former fortune.
>
> (5.3.200–202)

It is Shakespeare's entire and total point in this play that Coriolanus should be painfully drawn into the fold of this "difference," and as Aufidius sees, Coriolanus has turned toward the gathering call of the difference not out of some unconscious compulsion but out of his inner freedom ("thou has set . . . "). Between this setting of himself in the difference and his fortuitous death at the hands of the cowardly Volscians, the interim belongs to Coriolanus, who has responded to the call that comes through the cinders that burn within him and which are irreducible to any natural relation, even this particularly arduous maternal relation. He is called before the enigma of the law precisely because he chooses freely to relent in his vengeance against Rome and the maternal relation that Rome embodied for him. His turn away from Volumnia is a turn away from his phenomenal self and toward the moral law. *Coriolanus* is an allegory of respect.

At the moment of his death, which comes to him as a surprise just as he brings the Volscians the peace he has forged with Rome, Coriolanus is like the Hamlet who cries "It is I, Hamlet the Dane." Coriolanus's last words are full of the bravado and self-assurance of someone who has become a self-obligating being, ready to "pass beneath the face of the absent god." Just as the Volscians are about to set upon him, he taunts them with the memory of their earlier defeat at his hands: "like an eagle in a dove-cote, I / Flutter'd your Volscians in Corioles. / Alone I did it" (5.6.114–16). Without the context of Shakespeare's larger inquiry into the nature of conscience and moral law, such moments in his writing become very difficult to read. Our contemporary interests and values notwith-standing, there is something else going on in Shakespeare than the repetition of unconscious libidinal compulsions.

Coriolanus is able to bear up under incredible pain and suffering, and he attributes this gift to the gods and is therefore contemptuous of the social custom that would, in effect, allow the plebeians to put their tongues in his wounds. It sickens him. He is too proud, too austere, too covetous of the fire that burns within him. There are numerous references in the play to the incendiary force burning within Coriolanus (cf. 4.3.25; 4.6.79; 4.6.138). But that fiery force also holds the promise of respect for the law. Cominius remarks that Coriolanus led the Volscians "like a thing / Made by some other deity than nature, / That shapes man better" (4.6.91–92). The coals burning within him could erupt into a conflagration that would consume Rome. But that would be the vengeance of the natural man striking back against an ungrateful country and a dominating mother. Coriolanus decides upon an entirely different sort of homecoming.

Reading Another Will:
Gérôme and Shakespeare

"Before" and "Since" sketch in time or space an order that
doesn't belong to them; isn't that too obvious?
                    —JACQUES DERRIDA, *Mémoires d'aveugle*

She is alive!
Behold her eyelids
Begin to part their fringes of bright gold.
                              —*Pericles*

Do you see this? Look on her, look, her lips,
Look there, look there!
                    —*King Lear*

Look at her eyelids. They are moving. And look at the anamorphic
shadow around her mouth. She is reading. The drawing is doubly
anamorphic; the eyelids flutter, and the mouth seems to be caught
in the instant of silent reading. Light and shadow in motion around
the eyes and mouth of a woman reading. The light is in front of her,
making it difficult for her to read, and so she holds the letter up to
shield her from the brightness, but also to conceal her act of reading. The anamorphic smudge or blur or stain is a dark clearing
where something extraordinary comes to light. This strange little
drawing by Jean-Léon Gérôme is almost as interesting as Holbein's
well-known *French Ambassadors* with its anamorphic skull. Here
are anamorphic eyes and a mouth reading. What Gérôme captures
is Dasein reading. In her modesty and coyness, in her subtle revelation of her need to be concealed, Chloé is conscience in the truth of

all its enigmatic nontruth. The eyelid flutters, and for an instant we think we can see an expression, but then the eyes close, and we withdraw before its withdrawal into itself. And then it all starts all over again.

It was probably an accident, this visionary sketch of conscience. It may even have begun as a mistake, an unintentional smear. But then, yes, why not draw just the shadow of an iris behind the eyelashes and improve on that shadowy smudge around the mouth. Perhaps it was then that Gérôme tore the corner off the drawing to suggest the place of the letter. It may not even have been Gérôme himself who transformed what was originally a sketch for a painting inspired by Longus's *Daphnis and Chloé* into a strange optical machine with a portion missing. Paul-Louis Courier's 1811 translation of Longus's pastoral romance had already inspired several artists. In *Idylle,* which Gérôme exhibited in 1853, Chloé is standing with Daphnis by the side of a fountain; both of them are nude, but this time Chloé's eyes are entirely closed.[1] The sketch, however, captures something entirely different in its literalization of the movement of the face in the act of reading. The result is something closer to DaVinci than a mid-nineteenth-century salon artist.

Étude de Chloé literally presents the purloined letter of conscience, for, not content simply to indicate the place of the letter with a line, Gérôme (or one of his students) actually tore off the corner of the drawing. *Étude de Chloé* depicts not the face of conscience but the relation of a human face to the phallic signifier of an absence. Daemonic figures of conscience play upon the face like shadows cast by a missing letter, anamorphic shadows streaming from an invisible light.

Chloé dwells near the default in Being, near an uninternalizable gap that gives itself to be read as the unreadable itself. She reads in the afterglow of the cinders of the absent element, illuminated by

1. See Jean-Léon Gérôme, *Idylle,* in *Jean-Léon Gérôme, 1824–1904, peintre, sculpteur, et graveur,* 105.

an extrasolar light, backlit by what Falstaff calls "cinders of the element" (*Henry IV, Part 2,* 4.1.401). The daemonic shadows cast by the absent element seem to brighten the human face and reveal its secret recesses. Chloé reads so closely, perhaps even amorously, enigmatically, tenderly, in any case. Her face appears vulnerable as it tenders itself toward the opening onto the "unifying element."

As Shakespeare's Henry VIII remarks, conscience is indeed "a tender place" (2.2.142). Suffolk's insight into the workings of Henry's conscience unveils the sexual basis of the king's apparent moral struggle over his divorce from Katherine in his desire for Anne Boleyn: "his conscience / Has crept too near another lady" (2.2.17–18). But this reading of conscience in no way mitigates for Shakespeare the delicate role conscience plays in the historical process. *Henry VIII* sexualizes conscience only in order to reveal what a truly enigmatic historical force it constitutes. The sexual basis of moral categories is no secret to a poet who thinks in terms of Anne's "soft chevrill conscience" (2.2.32), tender and delicate like a fine kidskin glove, but pliable and accommodating. If conscience names only a moment in the sexual relation, this in no way diminishes how decisive *la chose génitale* appeared to Shakespeare in his final composition, which culminates in the christening of the infant princess Elizabeth.

Gérôme's study of Chloé's face likewise recognizes that all of this is true.

WORKS CITED

Adelman, Janet. *Suffocating Mothers: Fantasies of Maternal Origin in Shakespeare's Plays, "Hamlet" to the "Tempest."* New York: Routledge, 1992.

Akrigg, G. P. V. *Shakespeare and the Earl of Southampton.* Cambridge, Mass.: Harvard University Press, 1968.

Allen, J. W. *A History of Political Thought in the Sixteenth Century.* London: Methuen, 1960.

Arnold, Matthew. *Culture and Anarchy.* Indianapolis: Bobbs-Merrill, 1970.

Bacon, Francis, "History of Life and Death." In *Works,* ed. Spedding, Ellis, and Heath, vol. 10. Boston: Taggard & Thompson, 1864.

Benjamin, Walter. *The Origin of German Tragic Drama.* Trans. John Osborne. London: NLB, 1977.

Bentley, Gerald Eades. *The Profession of Player in Shakespeare's Time, 1590–1642.* Princeton: Princeton University Press, 1984.

Bernasconi, Robert. "'The Poet of Poets, Poet of the Germans': Hölderlin and the Dialogue between Poets and Thinkers." In *Heidegger in Question: The Art of Existing,* 135–49. Atlantic Highlands, N.J.: Humanities Press, 1993.

Blanchot, Maurice. *Le pas au-delà.* Paris: Gallimard, 1973.

Borch-Jacobsen, Mikkel. *The Emotional Tie: Psychoanalysis, Mimesis, and Affect.* Stanford, Calif.: Stanford University Press, 1993.

Borrow, George, ed. *Celebrated Trials and Remarkable Cases of Criminal Jurisprudence from the Earliest Records to the Year 1825.* 2 vols. New York: Payson & Clarke, 1928.

Brownlow, F. W. *Shakespeare, Harsnett, and the Devils of Denham.* Newark: University of Delaware Press, 1993.

Brunette, Peter, and David Wills. "The Spatial Arts: An Interview with Jacques

Derrida." In *Deconstruction and the Visual Arts: Art, Media, Architecture,* ed. Peter Brunette and David Wills, 1–32. Cambridge: Cambridge University Press, 1993.

Bruns, Gerald L. *Heidegger's Estrangements: Language, Truth, and Poetry.* New Haven: Yale University Press, 1989.

Celan, Paul. "Ash-Glory." Trans. Joachim Neugroschel. In *Speech-Grille and Selected Poems.* New York: Dutton, 1971.

Chambers, E. K. *William Shakespeare: A Study of Facts and Problems.* 2 vols. Oxford: Clarendon Press, 1930.

Clark, Eva Turner. *Hidden Allusions in Shakespeare's Plays: A Study of the Oxford Theory Based on the Records of Early Revels and Personalities of the Times.* New York: William Farquar Payson, 1931.

Cohen, Derek. "Shylock and the Idea of the Jew." In *Shylock,* ed. Harold Bloom, 305–16. New York: Chelsea House, 1991.

Cripps, A. C. "Shakespeare and Will Hughes." *Times Literary Supplement,* May 28, 1938.

Cuddy, Neil. "The Conflicting Loyalties of a 'Vulgar Counselor': The Third Earl of Southampton, 1597–1624." In *Public Duty and Private Conscience in Seventeenth-Century England: Essays Presented to G. E. Aylmer,* ed. John Morrill, Paul Slack, and Daniel Woolf, 121–50. Oxford: Clarendon Press, 1993.

de Man, Paul. *Allegories of Reading: Figural Language in Rousseau, Nietzsche, Rilke, and Proust.* New Haven: Yale University Press, 1979.

Derrida, Jacques. "All Ears: Nietzsche's Otobiography." Trans. Barbara Johnson. *Yale French Studies* 63 (1982): 245–50.

——. *Aporias.* Trans. Thomas Dutoit. Stanford, Calif.: Stanford University Press, 1993.

——. "Before the Law." Trans. Avital Ronell and Christine Roulston. In *Acts of Literature,* ed. Derek Attridge, 183–220. New York: Routledge, 1992.

——. *Cinders.* Trans. Ned Lukacher. Lincoln: University of Nebraska Press, 1991.

——. "Différance." Trans. Alan Bass. In *Margins of Philosophy,* 1–28. Chicago: University of Chicago Press, 1982.

——. "Force of Law: The 'Mystical Foundation of Authority.'" Trans. Mary Quaintance. In *Deconstruction and the Possibility of Justice,* ed. Drucilla Cornell, Michel Rosenfeld, and David Gray Carlson, 3–67. New York: Routledge, 1992.

——. *Glas.* Trans. John P. Leavey, Jr., and Richard Rand. Lincoln: University of Nebraska Press, 1986.

——. "Heidegger's Ear: Philopolemology (*Geschlecht* IV)." Trans. John P.

Leavey, Jr. In *Reading Heidegger: Commemorations,* ed. John Sallis, 163–218. Bloomington: Indiana University Press, 1993.

——. *Limited Inc.* Trans. Samuel Weber. Evanston, Ill.: Northwestern University Press, 1988.

——. *Mémoires: For Paul de Man.* Trans. Cecile Lindsay, Jonathan Culler, and Eduardo Cadava. New York: Columbia University Press, 1986.

——. *Mémoires d'aveugle: L'autoportrait et autres ruines.* Paris: Réunion des Musées Nationaux, 1990.

——. *Of Spirit: Heidegger and the Question.* Trans. Geoffrey Bennington and Rachel Bowlby. Chicago: University of Chicago Press, 1989.

——. "Passions." Trans. David Wood. In *Derrida: A Critical Reader,* ed. David Wood, 5–35. Cambridge: Blackwell, 1992.

——. "Plato's Pharmacy." Trans. Barbara Johnson. In *Dissemination,* 61–172. Chicago: University of Chicago Press, 1982.

——. *The Postcard.* Trans. Alan Bass. Chicago: University of Chicago Press, 1987.

——. "Privilège." In *Du droit à la philosophie,* 9–108. Paris: Galilée, 1990.

——. *Signsponge.* Trans. Richard Rand. New York: Columbia University Press, 1984.

——. *Spectres de Marx: L'État de la dette, le travail du deuil et la nouvelle Internationale.* Paris: Galilée, 1993.

——. "White Mythology." Trans. Alan Bass. In *Margins of Philosophy,* 207–72. Chicago: University of Chicago Press, 1982.

Diogenes Laertius. *Lives of the Philosophers.* Text and translation, ed. R. D. Hicks. Loeb Classical Library. Cambridge, Mass.: Harvard University Press, 1960.

Douglas, Lord Alfred. "Shakespeare and Will Hughes." *Times Literary Supplement,* May 28, 1938.

Empson, William. *Structure of Complex Words.* Ann Arbor: University of Michigan Press, 1967.

Euripides. *Hecuba.* Trans. William Arrowsmith. In *Complete Greek Tragedies,* ed. David Grene and Richard Lattimore. Chicago: University of Chicago Press, 1960.

——. *Hecuba.* Text and translation, ed. A. S. Way. Loeb Classical Library. Cambridge, Mass.: Harvard University Press, 1953.

Fineman, Joel. "Shakespeare's Ear." In *The Subjectivity Effect in Western Literary Tradition: Toward the Release of Shakespeare's Will,* 222–31. Cambridge, Mass.: MIT Press, 1991.

——. *Shakespeare's Perjured Eye: The Invention of Poetic Subjectivity in the Sonnets.* Berkeley: University of California Press, 1986.

——. "The Sound of 'O' in *Othello:* The Real of the Tragedy of Desire." In *The Subjectivity Effect in Western Literary Tradition: Toward the Release of Shakespeare's Will,* 143–164. Cambridge, Mass.: MIT Press, 1991.

Fóti, Véronique M. *Heidegger and the Poets: Poiesis, Sophia, Techne.* Atlantic Highlands, N.J.: Humanities Press, 1992.

Foucault, Michel. *The Care of the Self.* Trans. Robert Hurley. New York: Pantheon, 1986.

——. "The Eye of Power." In *Power/Knowledge,* ed. Colin Gordon, 146–65. New York: Pantheon, 1980.

Fraser, Russell. *Shakespeare: The Later Years.* New York: Columbia University Press, 1992.

Freud, Sigmund. *Beyond the Pleasure Principle.* In *The Standard Edition of the Complete Psychological Works,* 24 vols., ed. James Strachey et al., 18:7–64. London: Hogarth Press, 1974.

——. "A Child is Being Beaten." In *The Standard Edition,* 17:175–204.

——. *Civilization and Its Discontents.* In *The Standard Edition,* 21:57–145.

——. *The Ego and the Id.* In *The Standard Edition,* 19:3–66.

——. *Gesammelte Werke.* Ed. Anna Freud et al. 19 vols. Frankfurt a/M: S. Fischer Verlag, 1987.

——. *The Interpretation of Dreams.* In *The Standard Edition,* vols. 4–5.

——. *Introductory Lectures on Psychoanalysis,* In *The Standard Edition,* vols. 15–16.

——. *Letters of Sigmund Freud and Arnold Zweig.* Ed. Ernest L. Freud, trans. Elaine and William Robson-Scott. New York: Harcourt Brace Jovanovich, 1970.

——. *Moses and Monotheism.* In *The Standard Edition,* 23:7–137.

——. "Neurosis and Psychosis." In *The Standard Edition,* 19:149–56.

——. "On Narcissism: An Introduction." In *The Standard Edition,* 14:73–102.

——. "Some Character-Types Met With in Psychoanalytic Work." In *The Standard Edition,* 14:309–33.

——. "The Theme of the Three Caskets." In *The Standard Edition,* 12:289–301.

——. "Thoughts for the Times on War and Death." In *The Standard Edition,* 14:273–300.

——. *Totem and Taboo.* In *The Standard Edition,* 13:1–162.

——. "Types of the Onset of Neurosis." In *The Standard Edition,* 12:331–38.

——. "The Uncanny." In *The Standard Edition,* 17:217–56.

Gallagher, Lowell. *Medusa's Gaze: Casuistry and Conscience in the Renaissance.* Stanford, Calif.: Stanford University Press, 1991.

Gay, Peter. *Reading Freud*. New Haven: Yale University Press, 1990.

Gérome, Jean-Léon. *Jean-Léon Gérôme, 1824–1904, peintre, sculpteur, et graveur: Ses oeuvres conservées dans les collections françaises publiques et privées*. Ed. Ville de Vesoul. 1981.

Goldberg, Jonathan. *James I and the Politics of Literature*. Stanford, Calif.: Stanford University Press, 1989.

Gosson, Stephen. *The School of Abuse*. Ed. Edward Arber. London: Constable, 1906.

Greenblatt, Stephen. "Shakespeare and the Exorcists." In *Shakespearean Negotiations: The Circulation of Social Energy in Renaissance England*, 94–128. Berkeley: University of California Press, 1988.

Gross, John. *Shylock*. New York: Simon & Schuster, 1993.

Haigh, A. E. and A. W. Pickard-Cambridge. *The Attic Theatre*. 3d ed. Oxford: Clarendon Press, 1907.

Harnack, Adolf. *The History of Dogma*. 7 vols. Trans. Neil Buchanan. New York: Dover Books, 1961.

Harsnett, Samuel. *A Declaration of Egregious Popish Impostures*. In *Shakespeare, Harsnett, and the Devils of Denham*, by F. W. Brownlow, 193–335. Newark: University of Delaware Press, 1993.

Hegel, G. W. F. *Elements of the Philosophy of Right*. Ed. Allen Wood, trans. H. B. Nisbet. Cambridge: Cambridge University Press, 1991.

——. *Grundlinien der Philosophie des Rechts*. In *Werke*, ed. Eva Moldenhauer and Karl Markus Michel, vol. 7. Frankfurt a/M: Suhrkamp, 1971.

——. *Phänomenologie des Geistes*. Ed. Hans-Friedrich Wessels and Heinrich Clairmont. Hamburg: Felix Meiner Verlag, 1988.

——. *The Phenomenology of Spirit*. Trans. A. V. Miller. Oxford: Oxford University Press, 1977.

Heidegger, Martin. "The Anaximander Fragment." Trans. David Farrell Krell and Frank A. Capuzzi. In *Early Greek Thinking*, 13–58. New York: Harper & Row, 1975.

——. *Being and Time*. Trans. John Macquarrie and Edward Robinson. New York: Harper & Row, 1962.

——. *Beiträge zur Philosophie (Vom Ereignis)*. Ed. Friedrich-Wilhelm von Hermann. In *Gesamtausgabe*, vol. 65. Frankfurt a/M: Vittorio Klostermann, 1989.

——. "Das Ding." In *Vorträge und Aufsätze*, 157–80. Pfullingen: Neske, 1954.

——. *Erläuterungen zu Hölderlins Dichtung*. Ed. Friedrich-Wilhelm von Hermann. In *Gesamtausgabe*, vol. 4. Frankfurt a/M: Vittorio Klostermann, 1981.

——. "Der Fehl heiliger Namen." In *Aus der Erfahrung des Denkens: 1910–1976,* ed. Hermann Heidegger, *Gesamtausgabe,* 13:231–36. Frankfurt a/M: Vittorio Klostermann, 1983.

——. "Hebel—der Hausfreund." In *Aus der Erfahrung des Denkens,* ed. Hermann Heidegger, *Gesamtausgabe,* 13:133–50. Frankfurt a/M: Vittorio Klostermann, 1983.

——. "Hölderlins Himmel und Erde." In *Erläuterungen zu Hölderlins Dichtung,* ed. Friedrich-Wilhelm von Hermann, *Gesamtausgabe,* 4:152–81. Frankfurt a/M: Vittorio Klostermann, 1981.

——. *Holzwege.* Ed. Friedrich-Wilhelm von Hermann. In *Gesamtausgabe,* vol. 5. Frankfurt a/M: Vittorio Klostermann, 1977.

——. *Identity and Difference.* Trans. Joan Stambaugh. New York: Harper & Row, 1974.

——. *An Introduction to Metaphysics.* Trans. Ralph Manheim. New Haven: Yale University Press, 1959.

——. "Language." Trans. Albert Hofstadter. In *Poetry, Language, Thought,* 189–210. New York: Harper & Row, 1971.

——. "Language in the Poem." Trans. Peter Hertz. In *On the Way to Language,* 159–98. New York: Harper & Row, 1971.

——. "Letter on Humanism." In *Basic Writings,* ed. David Farrell Krell, 189–244. New York: Harper & Row, 1977.

——. "Metaphysics as History of Being." Trans. Joan Stambaugh. In *The End of Philosophy,* 1–54. New York: Harper & Row, 1973.

——. "The Nature of Language." Trans. Peter Hertz. In *On the Way to Language,* 57–110. New York: Harper & Row, 1971.

——. *Nietzsche,* vol. 3, *The Will to Power as Knowledge and as Metaphysics.* Trans. Joan Stambaugh, David Farrell Krell, and Frank A. Capuzzi. San Francisco: Harper & Row, 1987.

——. *Nietzsche,* vol. 4, *Nihilism.* Trans. Frank A. Capuzzi. San Francisco: Harper & Row, 1982.

——. *On Time and Being.* Trans. Joan Stambaugh. New York: Harper & Row, 1972.

——. "The Origin of the Work of Art." Trans. Albert Hofstadter. In *Poetry, Language, Thought,* 15–88. New York: Harper & Row, 1971.

——. "Overcoming Metaphysics." Trans. Joan Stambaugh. In *The End of Philosophy,* 84–110. New York: Harper & Row, 1971.

——. *Parmenides.* Trans. André Schuwer and Richard Rojcewicz. Bloomington: Indiana University Press, 1992.

——. "Plato's Doctrine of Truth." Trans. John Barlow. In *Philosophy in the Twentieth Century,* ed. William Barrett and Henry D. Aiken, 3:251–69. New York: Random House, 1962.

———. "Remembrance of the Poet." In *Existence and Being,* ed. Werner Brock, 233–69. Chicago: Henry Regnery, 1949.

———. *Sein und Zeit.* Tübingen: Max Niemayer, 1979.

———. "Spiegel-Gespräch." In *Antwort: Martin Heidegger im Gespräch,* ed. Günther Neske und Emil Kettering, 81–114. Pfullingen: Neske, 1988.

———. "Spiegel Interview with Martin Heidegger." Trans. Lisa Harries. In *Martin Heidegger and National Socialism: Questions and Answers,* ed. Günther Neske and Emil Kettering, 41–66. New York: Paragon House, 1990.

———. "Die Sprache." In *Unterwegs zur Sprache,* 9–34. Pfullingen: Neske, 1982.

———. "Die Sprache im Gedicht." In *Unterwegs zur Sprache,* 35–82. Pfullingen: Neske, 1982.

———. "The Thing." Trans. Albert Hofstadter. In *Poetry, Language, Thought,* 163–87. New York: Harper & Row, 1977.

———. "Der Ursprung des Kunstwerkes." In *Holzwege,* ed. Friedrich-Wilhelm von Hermann, *Gesamtausgabe,* 5:1–74. Frankfurt a/M: Vittorio Klostermann, 1977.

———. "The Want of Holy Names." Trans. Bernhard Radloff. *Man and World* 18 (1985): 261–67.

———. "What Are Poets For?" Trans. Albert Hofstadter. In *Poetry, Language, Thought,* 89–142. New York: Harper & Row, 1971.

———. *What Is Philosophy?* Trans. Jean T. Wilde and William Kluback. New Haven: College & University Press, n.d.

———. "Wozu Dichter?" In *Holzwege,* ed. Friedrich-Wilhelm von Hermann, *Gesamtausgabe,* 5:269–320. Frankfurt a/M: Vittorio Klostermann, 1977.

———. *Zollikoner Seminare: Protokolle-Gespräche-Briefe.* Ed. Medard Boss. Frankfurt a/M: Vittorio Klostermann, 1987.

Hoffmann, E. T. A. "The Sandman." In *Tales of E. T. A. Hoffmann,* ed. and trans. Leonard J. Kent and Elizabeth C. Knight, 93–125. Chicago: University of Chicago Press, 1972.

Holinshed, Raphael. *Shakespeare's Holinshed: Holinshed's Chronicle (1587).* Ed. Richard Hosley. New York: Capricorn, 1968.

Hopkins, Gerard Manley. *Journals and Papers.* Ed. Humphrey House and Graham Storey. London: Oxford University Press, 1959.

———. *The Poems.* Ed. W. H. Gardner and N. H. Mackenzie. London: Oxford University Press, 1967.

———. *Sermons and Devotional Writings.* Ed. Christopher Devlin. London: Oxford University Press, 1959.

Hotson, Leslie. *Shakespeare versus Shallow.* London: Nonesuch Press, 1931.

Howard, Henry, Earl of Surrey. "In the Rude Age When Science Was Not So

Rife." In *English Sixteenth-Century Verse: An Anthology,* ed. Richard S. Sylvester, 187–88. New York: Norton, 1974.

Ingram, William. *A London Life in the Brazen Age: Francis Langley, 1548–1602.* Cambridge, Mass.: Harvard University Press, 1978.

Jones, Ernest. *The Life and Work of Sigmund Freud.* 3 vols. New York: Basic Books, 1953–57.

Jordan, W. K. *The Development of Religious Toleration in England: From the Beginning of the English Reformation to the Death of Queen Elizabeth.* New York: George Allen & Unwin, 1932.

Kant, Immanuel. *Critique of Judgment.* Trans. James Creed Meredith. Oxford: Oxford University Press, 1957.

———. *Critique of Practical Reason.* Trans. Lewis White Beck. Indianapolis: Bobbs-Merrill, 1956.

———. *Kritik der praktischen Vernunft.* Ed. Karl Vorländer. Hamburg: Felix Meiner Verlag, 1985.

———. *Kritik der Urteilskraft.* Ed. Karl Vorländer. Hamburg: Felix Meiner Verlag, 1974.

———. *Lectures on Ethics.* Trans. Louis Infield. New York: Harper & Row, 1963.

———. *The Metaphysics of Morals.* Trans. Mary Gregor. Cambridge: Cambridge University Press, 1991.

Kay, Dennis. *Shakespeare: His Life, Work, and Era.* New York: William Morrow, 1992.

Keats, John. *Complete Poems.* Ed. John Barnard. 3d ed. New York: Viking/Penguin, 1988.

Kistner, A. C., and M. K. Kistner. "*Macbeth:* A Treatise of Conscience." *Thoth* 13 (1973): 27–43.

Krell, David Farrell. *Daimon Life: Heidegger and Life-Philosophy.* Bloomington: Indiana University Press, 1992.

Lacan, Jacques. "The Function and Field of Speech and Language in Psychoanalysis." In *Ecrits: A Selection,* trans. Alan Sheridan, 30–113. London: Tavistock, 1977.

———. "Science and Truth." Trans. Bruce Fink. *Newsletter of the Freudian Field* 3 (Spring–Fall 1989): 4–29.

———. *Le Séminaire, Livre XXII: R.S.I.* (1974–75). Text established by Jacques-Alain Miller. *Ornicar?* 2 (1975): 87–105; 3 (1975): 95–110; 4 (1975): 91–106; 5 (1975): 15–66.

Lea, Henry Charles. *A History of Auricular Confession and Indulgences in the Latin Church.* 3 vols. Philadelphia: Lea Brothers, 1896.

Levi, Peter. *The Life and Times of William Shakespeare.* London: Macmillan, 1988.

Lucretius. *The Nature of Things*. Trans. Frank O. Copley. New York: Norton, 1977.

Lukacher, Ned. "Anamorphic Stuff: Shakespeare, Catharsis, Lacan." *South Atlantic Quarterly* 88 (1989): 863–98.

———. "Mourning Becomes Telepathy." Introduction to Jacques Derrida, *Cinders*, 1–18. Lincoln: University of Nebraska Press, 1991.

———. "L'oreille de Pyrrhus: La césure de l'identification dans *Hamlet*." In *Le Passage des frontières: Autour du travail de Jacques Derrida*, ed. Marie-Louise Mallet, 187–92. Paris: Galilée, 1994.

———. "The Ring of Being: Nietzsche, Freud, and the History of Conscience." In *Intersections: Nineteenth-Century Philosophy and Contemporary Theory*, ed. Tilottama Rajan and David Clark. Albany: State University of New York Press, 1994.

Lupton, Julia Reinhard, and Kenneth Reinhard. *After Oedipus: Shakespeare in Psychoanalysis*. Ithaca: Cornell University Press, 1993.

Lyotard, Jean-François. *Heidegger and the "jews."* Trans. Andreas Michael and Mark Roberts. Minneapolis: University of Minnesota Press, 1990.

McGiffert, A. C. *Protestant Thought before Kant*. New York: Harper & Row, 1962.

Marcus, Leah. *Puzzling Shakespeare: Local Reading and Its Discontents*. Berkeley: University of California Press, 1988.

Miola, Robert. *Shakespeare and Classical Tragedy*. Oxford: Clarendon Press, 1992.

Montaigne, Michel de. *The Complete Essays*. Trans. M. A. Screech. New York: Penguin, 1991.

———. *Essais*. Ed. Maurice Rat. 3 vols. Paris: Garnier, 1961.

———. *Essays*. Trans. John Florio. 3 vols. London: J. M. Dent, 1966.

Müller, Max. *Lectures on the Science of Language: Second Series*. London: Longman, Green, Longman, Roberts & Green, 1864.

Nashe, Thomas. "Preface to Greene's *Menaphon*." In *Works*, ed. R. G. McKerrow, rev. F. P. Wilson, 3:311–34. Oxford: Basil Blackwell, 1966.

Neale, J. E. *Elizabeth I and Her Parliaments*. 2 vols. New York: St. Martin's Press, 1958.

Nietzsche, Friedrich. *The Birth of Tragedy*. Trans. Walter Kaufmann. New York: Vintage, 1967.

———. *Daybreak: Thoughts on the Prejudices of Morality*. Trans. R. J. Hollingdale. Cambridge: Cambridge University Press, 1982.

———. *The Gay Science*. Trans. Walter Kaufmann. New York: Vintage, 1974.

Norton, Thomas, and Sackville, Thomas. *Gorboduc*. In *Elizabethan and Stuart Plays*, ed. Charles Baskervill, Virgil Heltzel, and Arthur Nethercot. New York: Holt, Rinehart & Winston, 1962.

Parker, W. H., ed. *Priapea: Poems for a Phallic God*. London: Croom Helm, 1988.

Paul, Henry N. *The Royal Play of "Macbeth."* New York: Macmillan, 1950.

Perkins, William. *William Perkins, 1558–1602, English Puritanist*. Ed. Thomas F. Merrill. Nieuwkoop: B. DeGraaf, 1966.

Peters, F. E. *Greek Philosophical Terms: A Historical Lexicon*. New York: New York University Press, 1967.

Pierce, C. A. *Conscience in the New Testament*. London: SCM Press, 1955.

Plato. *The Republic*. Text and translation, ed. Paul Shorey. 2 vols. Loeb Classical Library. Cambridge, Mass.: Harvard University Press, 1970.

Poe, Edgar Allan. "The Black Cat." In *Great Short Works,* ed. G. R. Thompson, 390–400. New York: Harper & Row, 1971.

———. "The Conqueror Worm." In *The Poems,* ed. Thomas Olive Mabbott, 325–26. Cambridge, Mass.: Belknap Press/Harvard University Press, 1980.

Ponge, Francis. "Le soleil placé en abîme." In *Le grand recueil: Pièces,* 154–81. Paris: Gallimard, 1961.

Potts, Timothy. *Conscience in Medieval Philosophy*. Cambridge: Cambridge University Press, 1980.

Pye, Christopher. *The Regal Phantasm: Shakespeare and the Politics of Spectacle*. New York: Routledge, 1990.

The Revised English Bible. New York: Oxford University Press/Cambridge University Press, 1989.

Rose, Elliot. *Cases of Conscience*. Cambridge: Cambridge University Press, 1975.

Rousseau, Jean-Jacques. *Emile; or, On Education*. Trans. Allan Bloom. New York: Basic Books, 1979.

———. *Julie, ou La nouvelle Héloise*. In *Oeuvres complètes,* ed. Bernard Gagnebin and Marcel Raymond, vol. 3. Paris: Gallimard/Pléiade, 1964.

Schoenbaum, Samuel. *William Shakespeare: A Compact Documentary Life*. New York: Oxford University Press, 1978.

Schopenhauer, Arthur. *Parerga and Paralipomena*. 2 vols. Trans. E. F. J. Payne. Oxford: Clarendon Press, 1974.

Seneca. *Thebais*. In *His Tenne Tragedies,* ed. Thomas Newton, 97–134. Bloomington: Indiana University Press, 1964.

Shakespeare, William. *Antony and Cleopatra*. Ed. M. R. Ridley. Arden Shakespeare. London: Methuen, 1976.

———. *Coriolanus*. Ed. Philip Brockbank. Arden Shakespeare. London: Methuen, 1975.

———. *Hamlet*. Ed. Harold Jenkins. Arden Shakespeare. London: Methuen, 1982.

———. *Hamlet*. Ed. Philip Edwards. New Cambridge Shakespeare. Cambridge: Cambridge University Press, 1985.

——. *Julius Caesar*. Ed. T. S. Dorsch. Arden Shakespeare. London: Methuen, 1973.

——. *King Henry IV, Part 2*. Ed. Giorgio Melchiori. New Cambridge Shakespeare. Cambridge: Cambridge University Press, 1989.

——. *King Henry VIII*. Ed. John Margeson. New Cambridge Shakespeare. Cambridge: Cambridge University Press, 1990.

——. *King Lear*. Ed. Kenneth Muir. Arden Shakespeare. London: Methuen, 1972.

——. *The Life of King Henry the Fifth*. Ed. Alfred Harbage. In *The Complete Works*. Baltimore: Penguin, 1972.

——. *Macbeth*. Ed. Kenneth Muir. Arden Shakespeare. London: Methuen, 1982.

——. *Macbeth*. In *The Plays and Poems*, ed. Edmund Malone, rev. James Boswell, Jr. London, 1821.

——. *Macbeth*. In *The Works of Mr. William Shakespeare*, ed. Alexander Pope, vol. 5. London: Jacob Tonson, 1723.

——. *Measure for Measure*. Ed. J. W. Lever. Arden Shakespeare. London: Methuen, 1976.

——. *The Merchant of Venice*. Ed. John Russell Brown. Arden Shakespeare. London: Methuen, 1964.

——. *Much Ado about Nothing*. Ed. A. R. Humphreys. Arden Shakespeare. London: Methuen, 1981.

——. *Othello*. Ed. Norman Sanders. New Cambridge Shakespeare. Cambridge: Cambridge University Press, 1984.

——. *Richard III*. Ed. Anthony Hammond. Arden Shakespeare. London: Methuen, 1982.

——. *Romeo and Juliet*. Ed. Brian Gibbons. Arden Shakespeare. London: Methuen, 1980.

——. *Sonnets*. Ed. Stephen Booth. New Haven: Yale University Press, 1977.

——. *The Tempest*. Ed. Stephen Orgel. Oxford Shakespeare. Oxford: Oxford University Press, 1987.

——. *The Tragedy of King Lear*. Ed. Jay L. Halio. New Cambridge Shakespeare. Cambridge: Cambridge University Press, 1993.

Sharpe, Kevin. "Private Conscience and Public Duty in the Writings of James VI and I." In *Public Duty and Private Conscience in Seventeenth-Century England: Essays Presented to G. E. Aylmer*, ed. John Morrill, Paul Slack, and Daniel Woolf, 77–100. Oxford: Clarendon Press, 1993.

Shell, Marc. "The Wether and the Ewe: Verbal Usury in *The Merchant of Venice*." In *Money, Language, and Thought: Literary and Philosophic Economies from the Medieval to the Modern Era*, 47–83. Berkeley: University of California Press, 1982.

Sinfield, Alan. *Faultlines: Cultural Materialism and the Politics of Dissident Reading.* Berkeley: University of California Press, 1992.

Slights, Camille Wells. *The Casuistical Tradition in Shakespeare, Donne, Herbert, and Milton.* Princeton: Princeton University Press, 1981.

Stambaugh, Joan. *The Finitude of Being.* Albany: State University of New York Press, 1992.

Sterne, Laurence. *Tristram Shandy.* Ed. James A. Work. Indianapolis: Odyssey Press, 1940.

Taminiaux, Jacques. "The First Reading of Hölderlin." In *Heidegger and the Project of Fundamental Ontology,* 191–212. Albany: State University of New York Press, 1991.

Tawney, R. H. *Religion and the Rise of Capitalism.* New York: Penguin, 1947.

Taylor, Jeremy. *Ductor Dubitantium.* In *The Whole Works,* ed. C. P. Eden, vol. 9. London: Longmann, Green, 1883.

Thomas, Keith. "Cases of Conscience in Seventeenth-Century England." In *Public Duty and Private Conscience in Seventeenth-Century England: Essays Presented to G. E. Aylmer,* ed. John Morrill, Paul Slack, and Daniel Woolf, 29–56. Oxford: Clarendon Press, 1993.

Tillich, Paul. "The Transmoral Conscience." In *Morality and Beyond,* 65–81. New York: Harper & Row, 1963.

Urry, William. *Christopher Marlowe and Canterbury.* London: Faber & Faber, 1988.

Vallée, Léon, ed. *The History of Henry IV.* New York: Merrill & Baker, 1903.

Virgil. *The Aeneid.* Trans. W. F. Jackson Knight. New York: Penguin, 1958.

Vlastos, Gregory. "Socrates' *Daimonion.*" In *Socrates: Ironist and Moral Philosopher,* 280–87. Ithaca: Cornell University Press, 1991.

Weber, Max. *The Protestant Ethic and the Spirit of Capitalism.* Trans. Talcott Parsons. New York: Scribner, 1958.

Wells, Stanley, and Gary Taylor. *William Shakespeare: A Textual Companion.* Oxford: Clarendon Press, 1987.

Westermarck, Edward. "The Supposed Objectivity of Moral Judgments." In *Ethical Relativity,* 3–61. Paterson, N.J.: Littlefield, Adams, 1960.

Wilde, Oscar. *The Picture of Dorian Gray.* Ed. Donald Lawlor. New York: Norton, 1988.

——. "The Portrait of Mr. W. H." In *The Artist as Critic: Critical Writings,* ed. Richard Ellmann, 152–220. New York: Vintage, 1968.

Wilkes, John. *The Idea of Conscience in Renaissance Tragedy.* London: Routledge, 1991.

Wilson, J. Dover. *The Essential Shakespeare: A Biographical Adventure.* Cambridge: Cambridge University Press, 1960.

Žižek, Slavoj. *The Sublime Object of Ideology.* New York: Verso, 1989.

INDEX